By Way of Interruption

By Way of
INTERRUPTION

Levinas and the Ethics of Communication

AMIT
PINCHEVSKI

Duquesne University Press
Pittsburgh, Pennsylvania

Published in the United States of America by:
DUQUESNE UNIVERSITY PRESS
600 Forbes Avenue
Pittsburgh, Pennsylvania 15282

Library of Congress Cataloging-in-Publication Data

Pinchevski, Amit, 1971–

By way of interruption : Levinas and the ethics of communication / Amit
Pinchevski.

p. cm.

Includes bibliographical refences and index.

ISBN–13: 978–0–8207–0376–3 (pbk. : alk. paper)

1. Lévinas, Emmanuel. 2. Communication—Moral and ethical aspects. l. Title.

B2430.L484P54 2005

175—dc22

2005021246

Printed on acid-free paper.

Contents

Abbreviations

Works by Levinas

EI   *Ethics and Infinity*. Trans. R. A. Cohen. Pittsburgh: Duquesne University Press, 1985.

LP   *Collected Philosophical Papers*. Trans. A. Lingis. The Hague: Martinus Nijhoff, 1987.

OB   *Otherwise Than Being, or Beyond Essence*. Trans. A. Lingis. Pittsburgh: Duquesne University Press, 1998.

OS   *Outside the Subject*. Trans. M. B. Smith. Stanford: Stanford University Press, 1993.

PM   "The Paradox of Morality: An Interview with Emmanuel Levinas." In *The Provocation of Levinas,* edited by R. Bernasconi and D. Wood, 168–80. London: Routledge, 1988.

PN   *Proper Names*. Trans. M. B. Smith. Stanford: Stanford University Press, 1996.

TI   *Totality and Infinity*. Trans. A. Lingis. Pittsburgh: Duquesne University Press, 1969.

TO   "The Trace of the Other." In *Deconstruction in Context: Literature and Philosophy*, translated by A. Lingis, edited by M. C. Taylor, 345–59. Chicago: Chicago University Press, 1986.

Works by Derrida

AM   "At this very moment in this work here I am." In *Re-Reading Levinas,* translated by R. Berezdivin, edited by R. Bernasconi and S. Critchley, 11–48. Bloomington: Indiana University Press, 1991.

SEC   "Signature, Event, Context." In *Margins of Philosophy,* translated by A. Bass, 307–30. Chicago: University of Chicago Press, 1982.

TB   "Des Tours de Babel." In *A Derrida Reader,* translated by J. F. Graham, edited by P. Kamuf, 244–53. New York: Columbia University Press, 1991.

VM   "Violence and Metaphysics." In *Writing and Difference,* translated by A. Bass, 79–153. Chicago: University of Chicago Press, 1978.

Works by Blanchot

IC   *The Infinite Conversation.* Trans. S. Hanson. Minneapolis: University of Minnesota Press, 1993.

WD   *The Writing of the Disaster.* Trans. A. Smock. Lincoln: University of Nebraska Press, 1995.

Acknowledgments

Writing this book would not have been possible without the help and encouragement of others to whom I am grateful.

I would like to thank Sheryl Hamilton for believing in this project right from its inception; her patience and dedication have played a vital role in the formation and execution of this work. Special thanks to Chloë Taylor for her help and support throughout. Thanks also to Bilyana Martinovski for providing helpful comments at the right moments. To John Hunting I owe many hours of thought-provoking conversation. Shlomo Giora Shoham has been a source of constant encouragement and generosity. I have benefited at different stages of writing from discussions with Robert Gibbs and Geraldine Finn.

I wish to express my appreciation to my teachers at the Graduate Program in Communications at McGill University, especially to Will Straw for always being helpful and supportive, to George Szanto for teaching how to listen, and to Charles Levin for the intellectual stimulation. I am also grateful for two Faculty of Graduate Studies and Research Fellowships from McGill University and the Department of Art History and Communication Studies, which allowed me to dedicate my time to research and writing. Sincere thanks are extended to Pearl and Simon Beitner for their warm hospitality; to Yuval Eldar for his friendship and kindness; to my great aunts Frimit and Elka for the packages; to the Fortgang family for their generous help; and to my grandmothers, Chiza and Rivka for their everlasting support. To friends and classmates who made Montreal my home away from home: Andrea Smith, Ira Wagman, Jessica Wurster, Aleksandra Tomic and Dipti Gupta.

I am indebted to Dov Shinar and the Hubert Burda Center for Innovative Communication at Ben Gurion University of the Negev for a postdoctoral fellowship. To friends and colleagues who have contributed in different ways to the completion of this project: Tamar Ashuri, Daniel Dor, Lia Nirgad, Tamar Liebes, Tirzta Elnathan, Paul Frosh and Raya Morag. At Duquesne University Press, I would like to thank Susan Wadsworth-Booth and Kathy Meyer for their dedicated work and many efforts.

To my friends with whom I shared this journey: Odi and Maria Ashkenazi, Shmulik Tossman, Nir Wein, Vered Shavit and Tali Graf. Finally, I dedicate this book to my parents, Nava and Chezi.

Sections from chapters 2 and 3 appeared as "The Ethics of Interruption: Toward a Levinasian Philosophy of Communication," *Social Semiotics* 15, no. 2 (August 2005): 211–34. A short version of chapter 4 appeared as "Displacing Incommunicability: Autism as an Epistemological Boundary," *Communication and Critical/Cultural Studies* 2, no. 2 (June 2005): 163–84.

The Other Side of Communication

And I still interrupt the ultimate discourse in which all the discourses are stated, in saying it to one that listens to it, and who is situated outside the said that the discourse says, outside all it includes. That is true of the discussion I am elaborating at this very moment.
>   —Emmanuel Levinas, *Otherwise Than Being, or Beyond Essence*

William Harben's short story "In the Year Ten Thousand," which was published in 1892, tells a futuristic tale of one afternoon shared by a father and his son in a great museum. The father recounts the story of humanity starting from the Dark Ages: it is not easy to understand the past, says the father, since "it is hard to realize that man could have been so ignorant as he was eight thousand years ago" (1892, 743). The father leads the boy to a cabinet containing a few timeworn books: "You have never seen a book," says the father, "There are only a few in the leading museums of the world." The boy is perplexed: "I cannot see what people could have wanted with them." The father explains: "to make you understand this, I shall first have to explain that eight thousand years ago human beings communicated their thoughts to one another by making sounds with their mouths, and not by mind-reading, as you and I do" (ibid.). He continues: "Humanity then was divided up in various races, and each race had a separate language. As certain sounds conveyed definite ideas, so did signs and letters; and later, to facilitate the exchange of thought, writing and printing were invented" (ibid.). The father then shows his son pictures from the past, and the boy is perplexed again: "these men have awful faces . . . they are so unlike people living now. The man you call the pope looks like an animal. They all have huge mouths and frightfully heavy jaws" (ibid., 744). The father explains that human beings had borne a resemblance to animals because in those days humans' thoughts were not refined. Social life had been similarly corrupted, as during that time "human beings died of starvation and lack of attention in cities where there were people so wealthy that they could not use their fortunes" (ibid). All that changed with a discovery that transformed the face of history—thought-telegraphy. So great was the progress in that branch of knowledge that speech was eventually employed only among the lowest of the uneducated. This discovery, states the father, civilized the world: slowly it killed evil, wrongdoings were prevented, and crime was choked out of existence. The progress of mankind culminated in the year 6021 when "all countries of the world, having then a common language, and being drawn together in brotherly love by constant exchange of thought, agreed to call themselves a union without ruler or rulers" (ibid., 747).

This story joins many other narratives in turning to the future as a source of inspiration and as an anchor for human faith in modern progress. However, what makes this futuristic tale distinctive is the explicit depiction of a link between an aspired social existence and the status of communication therein, a link that seems to be causal, namely, that perfecting the work of communication would ultimately lead to the creation of a utopian society. As a view of the future from the past, the story may also reveal something about the time and place of its writing, a period that saw the rapid expansion of transportation, electricity, telegraphy and early experiments with radio transmission—but also major social, political and economic transformations that gave rise to many social ills. The trajectories sketched out in the late nineteenth century prescribe communication with a special role in social organization, which has since been a source of hope for social change. At base, it is the hope that ideal communication would lead to the ultimate cessation of all conflicts and disputes, that once all people can achieve a common experience of reality, agree on that experience, and reach greater understanding, there will be no ignorance, intolerance or cruelty. Effective communication is thus regarded as the cure for various tribulations as well as the means for constructing a harmonious social reality. Such is the dominant understanding by which the relationship between communication and ethics has traditionally been and continues to be described and theorized, an understanding that I shall attempt to unpack and question while trying to propose a radically different conception of the relation between communication and ethics.

The dream of perfect communication is hardly new. Yearning for an angelic communion of open hearts and minds drives human imagination from the myth of the tower of Babel to the age of the global village. However, as media historians such as Armand Mattelart (1996) and John Durham Peters (1999) have shown, it is only during the modern age that communication became a distinctive concern for the integrity of both individual and social life. The development of communications technology infused scholars and practitioners alike with a new perspective and vocabulary by which to engage with traditional philosophical questions as well as with contemporary social and political problems. Communication has consequently generated a concern across mental, technical and social realms, providing both a diagnostic chart of their ills and a depository of possible cures.

That communication presents a chance for a better world does not only make existing troubles more apparent but also introduces new and perhaps even more frustrating ones. What seems to be leading aspirations for human peace is the almost inviolable status of trouble-free exchange, which makes the task of perfecting communication—specifically, the successful completion of transmission circuits and the accurate interpretation and implementation of meanings—a pressing issue. As one critic writes: "True communication—the delivery of a signal, verbal or nonverbal, conveying to the recipient an approximation of the message and a measure of its intent—would seem in our time to have its best chance ever for reduction of human tensions and enhancement of human peace" (Ardrey 1974, 154). The development of human communication, argues another, is "a tremendous step in evolution; its powers for organizing thoughts, and the resulting growth of social organizations of all kinds, wars or no wars, street accidents or no street accidents, vastly increased potential for survival" (Cherry 1978, 5). Still another advocates that "The new media come to us as a real hope for the improvement of earth communication, the potential for nothing less than total community communication and the cessation of violence because awareness and understanding ultimately minimize conflict" (Schwartz 1973, 4). Standing out among the prophets is Marshal McLuhan, who predicted the formation of a collective awareness by means of sublime interactivity: "The next logical step would seem to be, not to translate, but to by-pass languages in favor of a general cosmic consciousness . . . the condition of speechlessness that could confer a perpetuity of collective harmony and peace" (1964, 80).

When taken as a means for sharing thought, communication takes place in speech, writing, telegraph, telephone, radio, television, the Internet and, of course, in the futuristic practice of thought-telegraphy. In this respect, the transition from one form of communication to the next seems to follow a linear logic whereby one rectifies the shortcomings of the previous. The progress of communication might be seen as evolving toward perfection: print resolves the lack of durability of speech, the telegraph surmounts the physical speed of couriers, radio provides signal transmission with sound, television supplements radio with picture, and so on, better sound, better picture, faster connection, more channels. If one were to draw an imaginary line extending from such a progression, it would probably culminate in a total interfacing, what Harben's story dubs as thought-telegraphy or, alternatively, as the cosmic consciousness envisioned by McLuhan—both epitomizing the ultimate coupling of technical transaction and the longing for peace and harmony.

Having such high stakes for both private and public considerations, communication constitutes an object of desire that can never be completely satisfied. It evidences itself, inter alia, in the constant endeavor to improve communication skills from the interpersonal all the way through the international, in developing better communication techniques and practices, and in upgrading communication technologies to meet such ends. But no matter how much effort one puts into overcoming problems of communication—misunderstanding, vagueness, inconsistency, loss for words, misconstruing intended meaning, impasse and breakdown—the more there seems to be ahead. Paradoxically, problems of communication appear to be growing in correlation with the expansion of communication in everyday life. Newer and more sophisticated techniques are introduced to educate one how to be a better communicator, how to market oneself effectively by "getting the message across," and how to improve one's personal relationships, work environment, career and, finally, oneself, all by means of communication. More and better communication hence becomes the ultimate good: one cannot over consume it, there is always more of it to go around, and it has no apparent side effects.

While the idea of communication has been carefully analyzed from various social, cultural and technical perspectives, I believe that the linkage between communication and ethics has not been sufficiently scrutinized. As I hope to show in the ensuing chapters, the way in which communication has regularly been linked to ethical concerns is predicated upon the belief that better communication, understood as the exchange of ideas, knowledge and information, upholds the possibility of overcoming strife, of promoting understanding and thereby of creating greater harmony. The positive operation of communication, it is argued, allows interaction and, consequently, congenial engagement with other communicators. This perception is implicit, to a greater or a lesser extent, in accounts as divergent as communication theory, modern philosophy, political thought, social psychology and psychiatry. Studying the ways key accounts join communicational issues with ethical concerns, I shall undertake to further unfurl and problematize this conceptual linkage. This is not to invalidate the conjunction between communication and ethics—to the contrary. However, my intention is to suggest a different conception of what might be implied in the combination "ethical communication."

In a time when elaborate communication networks proliferate, questions concerning the ethical implication of communication are ever more critical. Does facility of interaction imply a greater propensity for responsive and responsible relationships? Does the ethical relation stand a better chance as new and simpler ways for communicating become increasingly available? Is the setting up of viable channels of reciprocal communication, including with those previously beyond reach, a prerequisite for ethical involvement? Does it still make sense to regard the expansion of information and knowledge as going hand in hand with the pursuit of concord and peace? Alternatively, is communication failure necessarily the decline of ethical concerns? Is the risk of collapse or impasse inevitably the limit of compassion and generosity? Could it be that the success of communication in the creation of a greater union of minds might actually preclude different ethical possibilities?

The central assertion of this work is that the ethical possibilities in communication do not ultimately lie in its successful completion but rather in its interruption. The ethical stakes in communication are most critical when there is a risk of misunderstanding, lack, and refusal of communication, and it is perhaps only at this point that there is an event of communication truly worth the name. Communication understood as the ability to reproduce meanings and effects from one mind into another is in essence an assault against the integrity of another as a distinct and singular being, as an Other. Thus, what introduces a problem for perfect communication may, in fact, be an opening for ethics insofar as there exists the possibility of encountering another as an Other. In this respect, striving for transparency of exchange might entail the reduction of individual differences and hence the foreclosure of empathic contact. The intractability of gaps separating hearts and minds does not mean the end of relation but rather calls for a relation of a different kind, one that is based neither on reciprocity nor on commonality, but instead on the irreducible difference between self and Other. Interruption is an intrinsic and positive condition of communication, indeed of ethical communication, and thus marks the beginning rather than the end of generosity and compassion.

Framework

How might one conceive of communication as other than the accomplishment of interaction and beyond the reduction or transcendence of differences? What notions should be employed in order to conceptualize communication beyond its function as thought exchange and as working to produce consensual communion? An original conceptualization of ethics as well as the correlation between ethics and communication is found in the philosophy of Emmanuel Levinas. Though extending from the phenomenological tradition of Edmund Husserl and Martin Heidegger, Levinas's thought attempts to move beyond his predecessors and offers a radical critique of Western philosophy and the ways ethics has been deployed therein. In a most dramatic shift from traditional precepts of ethics, Levinas grants the relation to the Other the priority that for centuries was given to the self.[1] His critique undercuts the fundamental configuration by which social relation has been commonly described and analyzed—the limitation imposed by viewing subjectivity as originary and autonomous and intersubjectivity as secondary to the immanence of mutually independent subjects. However, it equally challenges any presupposed or prospective unity of individuals as a condition for, or as a way to conceive of, ethical relationships.

According to Levinas, ethical relation is like no other relation: it is launched neither from initial detachment nor from initial attachment. Ethics occurs prior to the ontological status of being, beneath and before existential separateness or functional coincidence of minds. Its crux lies in a nonassimilative yet nonindifferent relation between self and Other, a relation that is neither alienating nor coalescing, a strange relation, "a distance which is also proximity" (*EI*, 11). In founding ethics in the relation to the Other, Levinas calls into question some of the most fundamental assumptions in Western philosophy and modern social thought. Perhaps one of the most crucial issues introduced by his thinking is the unfounded nature of the concern for the Other. This concern, according to Levinas, cannot be located within individual schemas, within reason or logic; it may very well be rationalized as either immanent or external to human nature, but such a move would already imply submitting ethics to some kind of metaphysical construction—an endemic tendency of philosophical discourse from Plato to Heidegger. "What does the Other concern me?" is therefore a question that has meaning only if the self is understood as a cause in and of itself irrespective of any exterior and anterior ties, only if selfhood is taken as primary within any social configuration, which assumes an embedded disinterestedness in the lot of Others. That concern for the Other transcends and even defies reason does not constitute a problem for Levinas; to the contrary, it makes manifest the heteronomy of subjectivity, the nonlocalizable location of ethics, the "irrationality" of that very concern. The relation to the Other is an inaugural experience of subjectivity; being a self means being in relation—an ethical relation—to the Other.

The challenge against monadic and unitary images of subjectivity is not, of course, distinctive to Levinas; similar ideas were previously introduced by thinkers such as Martin Buber (1970), George Herbert Mead (1967) and Mikhail Bakhtin (1986). However, what is novel in Levinas's thought is the way it radicalizes the idea of the relation to the Other. By describing subjectivity in ethical terms, Levinas defines the tie with the Other as knotted in responsibility. Responsibility for the Other does not follow meditation or calculation, nor does it result from experience or social conditioning; responsibility resides at the very basis of subjectivity. The ethical relation coming to pass as responsibility is always already a social matter, a determining factor in the reality of the interhuman, "whether accepted or refused, whether knowing or not knowing how to assume it, whether able or unable to do something concrete for the Other" (*EI*, 97). Responsibility is felt most when being exposed to the Other's otherness, to his or her irreducible difference, when encountering the Other as a singular being, as a face. The face of the Other transcends its physical attributes as a portrait or as a body; in the face one finds a demand and a question, a summation to a responsible response. It is as though one is responsible almost despite oneself: something in the face pulls toward the Other, a powerless force commanding responsibility.

Such conceptualization brings Levinas to the provocative speculation that the ethical relation is asymmetrical: one is responsible for the Other before and beyond being reciprocated by an equivalent concern—responsibility is my affair, reciprocity is the Other's. Individual responsibility does not promise that every person will respond in the same way, or even respond at all. That different individuals will act differently does not disqualify the weight of responsibility but rather repersonalizes it into the intersubjective realm. The Levinasian idea of social relations is not based on the immanency of human nature, good or bad; Levinas does not submit to assumptions such as Jean-Jacques Rousseau's that humans are essentially amiable or to presumptions such as Thomas Hobbes's of an initial rivalry. What characterizes human contact is an irredeemable ambivalence with respect to another. Yet such unpredictability is precisely what constitutes the condition for ethical engagement, and undecidability as to if and how to respond is the condition for making a responsible decision. Levinas resorts to language both descriptive and prescriptive to describe the realm responsibility affects. To that effect, he employs notions such as · proximity, exposure and vulnerability, which designate the self's fundamental predisposition to alterity, to what resides outside the subject.

Most important in the context of this work is Levinas's conceptualization of communication in terms of ethics, a theme which will be further elaborated in chapter 2. At its core is the distinction between the Said (*le Dit*) and the Saying (*le Dire*). The Said consists of the contents conveyed in language—logos, information and knowledge. The Saying, on the other hand, extends to and is absorbed in the Said but is not exhausted by it. The Saying is signification of signification itself, the giving of a Said to another person; it is the offering of signs to the Other. Saying occurs through language but is not thematizable by language: it is the fundamental mode by which one signifies response-ability to the'Other. This distinction allows Levinas to take up a critical perspective with respect to the ways communication has been traditionally theorized. According to Levinas, the tendency to view communication in terms of the Said, has dominated many conventions of communication and language, a tendency that prefigures the goal of communication in establishing certainty and truth. Levinas proposes that the primary mode of communication lies in the Saying, in addressing another, and thereby in undoing thematization in the discourse of the Said, consequently constituting the possibility of interrupting the stability of the selfsame. Language upholds a manifestation of "the Other in me," signifying the anterior accessibility of the Other to the self. As such, communication is irreducible to the circulation of information. It involves an unrepresentable relation, contact or touch: "Language, contact, is the obsession of an I 'beset' by the others" (*CP,* 123). Communication is an adventure of subjectivity always involving uncertainty, and this uncertainty is precisely what gives rise to the possibility of communication. In this way, differences touch without synthesis.

Finally, Levinas occasionally refers to the relation between the Said and the Saying, as well as to ethical relation, in terms of interruption. While occupying only a secondary place in his deliberations, my reading, which is oriented toward importing relevant ideas into communication theory and analysis, suggests that the communicational aspect of his work is best encompassed by the concept of interruption. Thus, in this study I propose to promote this concept and situate it as the main correlative between communication and ethics. Stemming from the Latin *ruptus,* which means break, tear or fissure, "interruption" implies a rupture, a spacetime opening not intended as such but one that nevertheless takes place. Interruption occurs in the puncturing of the Saying in the Said, in the constant tension between the potential of language to thematize and its primary modality as a response-ability toward the Other who is addressed. Interruption is thus immanent in communication, expressing the elemental relation of the one for the Other by both separating from and drawing to the Other. Following this reading of Levinas, it is possible to view subjectivity as an elemental site of interruption—as always and already accessible and addressable by means of the Other's interruption.

This allows extending Levinas's critical perspective by putting forward interruption as what is denied in the discourse of the Said. At issue are the discursive practices promoting the Said while purging the Saying, specifically the logos produced by the apparatuses of the state, medical-scientific discourse and philosophy. According to Levinas, all three are paramount examples of the distinctively modern effort to incorporate everything into the discourse of the Said—an a priori submission to the totalizing schemas of the universal logos of knowledge and truth. The effect is such that not only can nothing truly interrupt the power of this discourse, but also that every interruption can be immediately explained away and amended by that very discourse, thus allowing it to recommence as soon as one interrupts it. What is repudiated thereby is the possibility of unsettling the coherency of impersonal speech and consequently the chance of being exposed to the Other's singular demand.

These sensitivities have contributed to the ways other thinkers have come to challenge some of the most fundamental assumptions of established forms of communication. Such concerns are evident in Jean-François Lyotard's (1984) critique of modern production and organization of knowledge, and more explicitly in his conceptualization of the *differend* (1988), which brings to the fore the political and ethical consequences implied by their operation. Levinas's thought has also been a major inspiration for Jacques Derrida, who composed some of the most influential texts on the subject (1978, 1991a, 1999a). His analysis reveals a modality of interruption through the operation of *différance,* the nonconcept that infuses the infinite deferring/differing of oppositions, announcing the alterity of a "middle voice" (Derrida, 1982, 9).[2] Maurice Blanchot (1993, 1995) also followed a similar path in drawing together literary criticism and ethical considerations. Noteworthy in this respect is his conception of interruption as "relation of the third kind" (1993, 68). Neither seeking unity over separation nor affirmation of the whole over the singular ("relation of the first kind"), nor producing coincidence or fusion of self and Other ("relation of the second kind"), relations of the third kind transpire within the difference between self and Other. Neither inclusion nor exclusion, interruption is a relation upon which ethical communication is founded. In sum, interruption allows the Other to retain his or her singularity as a face and address in Saying. Communication understood as a form of interruption (and perhaps also vice versa) upholds the very possibility of being response-able to and for the other person.

This conceptual framework may provide a starting point for developing an ethical language by means of stretching communication to its limits, toward the Other. As such, it presents a way of thinking about communication beyond essences and ontology, and more importantly, as an ethical involvement whose stakes exceed the successful completion of its operation. Although Levinas is the main inspiration for the perspective taken in this study, my intention is not to present a strictly Levinasian analysis of communication theory and practices. Rather, my purpose is to mobilize some of the concepts developed in his thought that I find most pertinent, and for which I attempt to open up a theoretical space within communication thought.[3] The main theoretical question I consequently wish to raise is whether traditional ways of understanding communication, both as the sharing of information and as an experience of commonality, compromise communication as an ethical event.

Setting

Several scholars have attempted to promote the status of ethical considerations in the study of society, communication and language while following the concerns introduced by Levinas, either directly or by extension. One of the central figures in this respect is sociologist Zygmunt Bauman (1989, 1990, 1991, 1993, 1995), whose recent writings pursue a question once raised by Levinas:

> It is extremely important to know if society in the current sense of the term is the result of a limitation of the principle that men are predators of one another, or if to the contrary it results from the limitation of the principle that men are *for* one another. Does the social, with its institutions, universal forms and laws, result from limiting the consequences of the war between men, or from limiting the infinity which opens in the ethical relationship of man to man? (*EI,* 80)

Following Levinas, Bauman regards the preontological situation of one-for-the-Other as the very condition for any form of sociality. In his view, the basic tenet of modern social thought was that morality, rather than being a natural trait in human life, is something that has to be designed and injected into human conduct. Many modern thinkers earnestly believed that the void left by the extinct or ineffective moral supervision of the church should be filled by a carefully crafted set of rationalized rules, "that *reason* can do what *belief* was doing no more" (1993, 6). The story of modernity in general and of modern ethics in particular may then be sketched as an attempt to civilize the fickle and unreliable presocial being according to rational principles of moral conduct. Morality is the task of social institutions that hold a monopoly over the right "to tell the moral from the immoral, by representing this right as a necessity arising from incurable frailty or turpitude of man" (ibid., 9). Standardized ethical codes are what separate humans from savages, society from the nature-state and justice from cruelty. As Bauman persuasively shows, modern society has effectively robbed the individual of his or her ethical sovereignty, replacing it with rules and regulations. The proclamation that social institutions are what facilitate social life by defending individuals from their own animalistic predispositions hides in effect an ulterior motive: the limitation of the infinite responsibility of one-for-the-Other.

Managing what Bauman calls "moral proximity" is the main product of social institutions. This is achieved by three meta-techniques: (1) Ensuring separation between the two poles of action—the "doing" and the "suffering"—particularly by means of "distance technology," which eliminates face-to-face contact, thereby rendering the operation morally neutral and its effects virtually invisible; (2) The development of bureaucratic organizations based on a horizontal split of action into specialized and partial functions, and vertical gradation of competence and command, whose combined effect consists in transferring responsibility from the acting subject to an anonymous organization; (3) Exempting some "others" from the class of potential objects of responsibility, of potential faces, and/or disassembling them into aggregates of functionally specific traits—and holding such traits separate (usually by means of instrumental rationality)—so that the occasion for reassembling a "face" out of disparate "items" does not arise (1990, 31; 1993, 125). These arrangements in and of themselves do not sponsor evil; they rather enable neutralizing the disruptive impact of encountering another as Other and thereby of individual responsibility.

Bauman presents a compelling account of the different techniques of managing "moral proximity" in modern society while calling for rethinking ethics in the wake of the atrocities facilitated by modern rational mindsets. Nevertheless, his focus is mostly on the institutional manifestations of society and the ways in which these are organized to suppress moral action. Missing from his schema is the place of communication and language within what he refers to as the "social management of moral proximity." Concentrating mainly on the techniques allowing for ethical separation, his analysis does not provide a substantial account of whether and how communication is involved in such social practices. Rather than criticizing Bauman's intellectual project, this study will attempt to complement some of his speculations by questioning whether modern communication theories, understanding and practices also play a role in further dissembling responsibly.

In many respects, John Durham Peters's work (1999) supplies much of the conceptual grounding needed for engaging with the ethical stakes in communication. His project is threefold: an intellectual history of the idea of communication, a critique of the prevailing conceptualization of the term, and an alternative perspective by which to rethink communication. Studying notions associated with communication from the Greek and Christian traditions, North American spiritualism and social science, and modern continental philosophy, Peters proposes that the history of thinking about human interrelations is essentially the history of conceptualizing ideal togetherness. In an especially interesting analysis, he turns to the "horizons of incommunicability" exploring attempts to communicate with animals, aliens and machines. Rather than expanding an innate human ability to communicate with others both human and inhuman, such attempts, according to Peters, signify communication's own crisis. The problem of communication, he concludes, does not consist in the capacity to double up the self into others but in developing sensitivity to those who resist such attempts. Communication is then "more basically a political and ethical problem than a semantic or psychological one" (ibid., 269).

A central theme in his critique is communication failure and breakdown. Following an elaborate discussion of the different traditions of communication, he suggests: "Today the most influential thinkers about communication are probably Jürgen Habermas and Emmanuel Levinas" (ibid., 20). Whereas the first advocates a practice that, if generalized, entails the creation of a democratic community, the latter persists that the failure to communicate is not an ethical failure, but rather "a fitting demise for a flawed project" (ibid., 21). Peters attempts to develop a middle position between the two and presents an account of communication that "erases neither the curious fact of otherness at its core nor the possibility of doing things with words" (ibid.). Such would be a version of pragmatism open both to the uncanny and the practical, a midway that brings together the Dewey-Habermas lineage and the Heidegger-Levinas-Derrida lineage. The alternative conception he consequently proposes consists in promoting the idea of dissemination while criticizing the traditional emphasis on dialogue. According to Peters, dissemination "is far friendlier to the weirdly diverse practices we signifying animals engage in and to our bumbling attempts to meet each other with some fairness and kindness" (ibid., 62). As opposed to dialogue, which is based on reciprocity and participation, dissemination is fundamentally a receiver-oriented mode of communication, which allows privileging the Other while limiting the control of the self.

Peters's contribution in this work and elsewhere (1986, 1988, 1989a, 1989b, 1994) is invaluable, and his rigorous critique of the intellectual foundation of communication theory has been a major influence on the current study in both conception and style. Nevertheless, a few problematic issues deserve further exploration and unpacking. First, it seems to me that situating Levinas within the Heidegger-Derrida lineage, although not unfounded, is nevertheless somewhat reductive, as it precludes further investigation of Levinas's thought on its own terms. A more fundamental problem, however, is revealed by the dichotomization between dialogue and dissemination. While sharing Peters's sensitivities, I believe that the line separating Other-oriented from self-oriented communication does not run between these two modes of communication but rather within each of them. It is in this sense that the idea of interruption might provide a way for conceptualizing ethical relation without specifying the nature of the interaction. Furthermore, it may assist addressing Peters's paradoxical conclusion, which, on the one hand, advances the idea of dissemination while insisting, on the other hand, on the irreducibility of touch. Peters concedes that out of all senses touch is most resistant to mediation, recording, transmission and reproduction, thus introducing a singular event in which the Other is encountered. It should be noted that Levinas frequently describes ethical relation in a most palpable language, utilizing terms like caress, wound, trauma, contact and exposedness. However, Levinas's metaphorical language allows for much more than a discussion of actual tactility, as for him touch constitutes the meta-sense or arch-sense by which the Other makes contact (compare Bauman 1993, 93; Davies 1993, 267).

Briankle G. Chang's work (1996) takes up many of the theoretical challenges raised above by outlining an alternative schema for speculating on communication. Chang's point of departure is phenomenological philosophy, concentrating mainly on Edmund Husserl and Martin Heidegger. The discussion develops into an elaborate analysis of Jacques Derrida's critique of ontology, leading up to a deconstructive approach to communication. According to Chang, communication theories have traditionally relied on "subjectivist thesis," namely, on an implicit notion of a communicating self, always already negotiating its connection with the outer world, a relation wherein the skeptical subject mediates between the known and the unknown. Chang argues that although communication theory is not associated with only one discipline, it is still very much mortgaged to a centripetal view of communication that reinstates the centrality of a unitary subject. This brings modern communication theories to valorize identity over difference, selfsame over alterity, and understanding and sharing over misunderstanding and breakdown. "Successful" communication is thus nothing but the expansion of the selfsame, its ideas, understanding and agenda. Once communication is centered around the subject, any resistance from "out there" hindering the incessant flow of messages to and from sender and receiver(s) would mean a "failure" that requires a "solution" (see Coupland, Giles and Wiemann, 1991 and Mortensen, 1997).

Chang argues that communication theories employ too readily a Cartesian understanding of communication processes in which the self remains unaffected by otherness, advocating instead for a notion of communication that does not regard impasse as an obstacle to ethical or social relation. Most significantly, he describes the condition for the possibility of communication as its impossibility, or in his words, "The impossibility of communication is the birth *to* its possibility" (ibid., 225). Communication is thus implicated by an endemic aporia, an integral miscommunication, giving rise to its occurrence. This immediately leads to viewing the traditional body of knowledge as attempting to rescue the self from its fundamental solitude and hence as seeking to establish a clear conduit between self and Other, which ultimately allows for the callous expansion of the self. Such communication starts in the self and eventually returns to the self, and any obstruction along that way would be relegated to the negative side of communication, to noncommunication, circumscribed as a predicament to be studied and solved. Chang's conclusion is of particular importance because it articulates unequivocally that the stakes of communication lie beyond its success and completion. By opening the way to the "(im)possibility of communication" (ibid., 171), his analysis effectively provides a revision of the place of the Other within the schema of communication.

There are, nevertheless, weaker points in Chang's project. First, although offering a valuable critique of traditional communication theory, he refers only in passing to concrete theories or conceptualizations to demonstrate the issues at hand. Largely remaining within the confines of a philosophical discussion, he misses an opportunity to explore the reasons, both intellectual and historical, for the continuing blindness to otherness in communication theory. Second, Chang indeed lays down a basis for an approach in which the address of the Other is irreducible to the circulation of information, but he only intimates the significant connection of this approach with ethics. This is not to say that his analysis lacks such sensitivities, as by taking a deconstructive approach he is already assuming all the ethical responsibilities implied by this approach. Starting with Husserl and Heidegger and ending with Derrida, however, Chang does not refer to the work of Levinas, which nonetheless echoes through many of the Derridian notions he thoroughly explores. What is missed thereby is a perspective that, although fairly close and empathetic to his own (and Derrida's), may offer a more pointed engagement with the ethical stakes in communication.

Finally, Robert Eaglestone (1997) attempts to establish a literary criticism based on Levinas's philosophy. According to Eaglestone, Levinas's writing on ethics represents an example of the ways the ethical signifies through language (ibid., 7). In addition to the philosophy of the Other, Levinas develops a "language of ethics," especially through the concepts of the Said and the Saying, which provides him with a way of writing about what cannot be re-presented and thematized. Such textual engagement calls for a special kind of reading, one that Eaglestone designates as "ethical criticism." Texts could be approached ethically by attending to the

ways language reveals or conceals the Other, and by situating reading as a practice involving responsibility. Thus, critical reading
might be seen as energized and provoked by ethical commitment.
Setting out to unravel this issue, Eaglestone's project bears yet another
significance: speculating on the relation between the ethical and the
aesthetic. Levinas's work often expresses a deep-seated suspicion
toward art since for him it replaces representation with encounter
and an image with the face. Eaglestone is right in not taking
Levinas's position in relation to art as the final word on that matter.
He then follows Derrida's critique (1978) to claim that the way the
ethical signifies within the ontological can be applied to art criticism
in general, and to literary theory in particular.

Eaglestone's work also proposes an intriguing employment of
the notion of interruption. Evoking Levinas's claim that philosophy
should unfold not as the love of wisdom but rather as the wisdom
of love, he proposes that the task is one of drawing attention to the
ethical Saying entwined with the Said (ibid., 150). Such a shift of
intellectual endeavor should inspire literary criticism to develop a
language that can interrupt itself, safeguarding against the reduction
of the Saying to the Said and signification to logos. The concept of
interruption leads Eaglestone to propose that criticism, or interpretation, is a form of interruption. This entails a radical approach to
literary criticism: "The said, at home, is the quiescence resulting
from the familiar, often-used critical method, interpretations of
texts that no longer threaten or interrupt" (ibid., 177). Criticism,
therefore, prescribes interpretation with continual interruption,
disturbing and puncturing the Said, opening up the Saying in the
textual.

In terms of employing Levinas's concepts, Eaglestone proposes
an apt analysis that may be further developed to other theoretical
frameworks beyond literary criticism. Eaglestone's emphasis on the
concept of interruption provides his work with a critical edge and
an interesting attempt to develop "ethical criticism." However,
while raising some important questions, I believe that his analysis

does not exhaust the subject, especially for the field of communication. While I concur with the basic motivation in employing interruption for critical reading, I think that it could be expanded to the generality of communication and perhaps even to a more general perspective of "ethical criticism."

Approach

The task, then, is to develop a way of thinking about the ethical import of communication in terms other than its function in facilitating exchange or participation and beyond its complicity in creating greater understanding, commonality or like-mindedness. The motivation behind the approach here comes from Levinas's speculation on what might be concealed by positing communication as the coincidence of minds or unity of ideas, which is perhaps encompassed most distinctively in the following:

> I wonder whether, in that whole tradition [Western philosophy of language], language as *Said* has not been privileged, to the exclusion or minimizing of its dimension as *Saying*. There is, it is true, no Saying that is not the Saying of a *Said*. But does the *Saying* signify nothing but the *Said?* Should we not bring out, setting out from the *Saying*, an intrigue of meaning that is not reducible to the thematization and exposition of a *Said*, to that correlation in which the Saying would bring about the appearing of beings and being, "putting together" nouns and verbs into sentences, synchronizing them, in order to present a structure? The *Saying* signifies otherwise than its function as an attendant! Beyond the thematization of the Said and of the content stated in the proposition, *apophansis* signifies as a modality of an approach to the other person. The proposition is proposed to the other person. (*OS,* 141–42)

The implication of this speculation is quite radical. It suggests that communicating is not only the transfer of signs but also the giving of signs to someone, a modality of approach—a realization curiously omitted from many previous and contemporary accounts. But in addition to calling attention to this discrepancy, Levinas invites shifting the emphasis from the Said—the power to thematize, designate and represent—to the signification of the Saying, from what is signified in language to what might be signified through and by language, the contact of and the approach to the Other—the interruptive force of communication.

Studying the "work" of interruption presents a special methodological challenge. It is the challenge of writing about something that resists categorization, localization and objectification, a theme that once thematized loses its significance and along with it the very reason for investigation. Circumscribing interruption as such thus runs the risk of turning it into a rigid concept, similar to the calcifying effect of Medusa's gaze. Furthermore, dealing with interruption as unlocalizable and unobjectifiable cannot even feign a Perseus-like maneuver, that is, reflect its attributes onto a neutral surface, for such a move would entail some kind of representation, capturing something of its essence by marking out the contours of a shape. Given such complexities, the approach to be undertaken in the following will only attempt to gesture toward the possibilities opened up by the "work" of interruption while allowing for the elusiveness and inherent inconsistency involved therein.

This study proposes a distinctive approach: dislocation. The term "dislocation" denotes both (1) its lexical meaning, namely, to force something out of its correct position, tampering with the normative activity, and (2) dis-locating, pointing toward that which resists incorporation, always remaining outside, displacing and out-of-place, external or denied.[4] Dislocating communication suggests a critical perspective by which to study practices and discourses that favor the Said—that is, circulation of information, knowledge, understanding, free access and participation, accuracy and clarity—over the signification of the Saying. This takes place when seeking to unsettle some of the oppositions by which the operation of communication has commonly been described, most notably completion and failure, understanding and misunderstanding, communicability and incommunicably, speech and silence. Such dichotomization does not merely prescribe a division within the conceptual field but also a hierarchical order within each opposition, a structure whose stability depends upon the excommunication of incongruous elements—the reduction of the Saying to the Said, which is, ultimately, the suppression of interruptions. It may then be said that the more seamless and abiding is the zone designated for such an operation, the more oppressive the ways by which otherness is being excommunicated from the communicational spectrum. Hence, to undertake dislocation implies scrutinizing the ways the completion of communication is sought—an investigation that has almost obsessed traditional speculations—subjecting them to ethical criticism. In actual practice, this means disrupting the integrity of the discourse of the Said in order to show that what holds it together may be, in fact, the delegitimization of the work of interruption.

This approach is clearly informed by a deconstructive strategy, and more particularly by the double movement of overturning oppositional-conflictual dualities and fissuring an interval in between, an opening of positive displacement and transgression (Derrida 1981a, 65–66). It thus implies a special kind of reading, inhabiting texts "in a certain way," feigning a double-agent stratagem, operating "from the inside, borrowing all the strategic and economic resources of subversion from old structures" (Derrida 1997, 24). Such an operation would mean reiterating what is implicit within the epistemological frameworks or in some underlying concepts while "using against the edifice the instruments or stones available in the house" (Derrida 1982, 135). As Derrida affirms, many critics have misinterpreted deconstruction as a continuous game closed up within language, insisting that as a form of critique it necessarily implies openness toward the Other, and as such, a "positive response to alterity which necessarily calls, summons or motivates it" (1995, 168). To be sure, in proposing dislocation, I do not wish to join those who disclaim the ethical significance of deconstruction. Rather, my intention is actually to reaffirm it as a step—an essential step, but still only a step—in addressing the uninterrupted conjunction between communication and ethics. It may then be said that being motivated by Levinasian sensitivities, dislocation involves an added emphasis of responsibility to and for the Other, and in this sense is perhaps at once more modest and more pointed. Thus, problematizing the characterization of failure and lack of communication as the folding of responsive and responsible involvement serves as a step toward speculating on the possibility that such instances do not mark the end or limit of concern for another but rather an opening to the very possibility of responsibility to and for the Other. What drives dislocation, then, is the urgency to respond in front of the face, to judge and decide—indeed, to act politically—which nevertheless follows and is contingent upon the interruption of alterity, and hence upon an inevitable undecidability as to how to respond.[5] It should be immediately added that the nature of such an intervention is not, nor should it be, properly methodological, at least not in the sense of an analytical construction that precedes and is external to the objects of its investigation. Rather, as an attempt to expose the relationship between communication and ethics outside and beyond the effectual aspect of communication, dislocation is inherently exposed to the work of its own procedures. By calling attention to the place (which is also the nonplace) of interruptions, not only is this approach not immune to being interrupted, but rather, in being faithful to its own undertaking, it actually invites further interruptions, primarily of itself.

The following will comprise a critical analysis of the ways several discourses of communication have engaged with the "incommunicable" signs of otherness. My presumption is that the locus where such an engagement is most likely to occur is at the perimeters of productive-constructive procedures of communication, where a conceptual line is drawn between a zone of "positive" operation and what appears to lie beyond, defy or even threaten the internal consistency and logic of that zone. The division of "inside" and "outside"—the boundary, or the breaking point, between the terra firma of sameness and the terra incognita of alterity—is thus of paramount importance for the current investigation. At issue is the epistemological limit, which is also, presumably, the epistemological hinge upon which communication is conceptualized. As such, this hinge or limit upholds, on the one hand, a highly condensed cluster of issues pertaining directly to the event of encountering alterity while unfettering, on the other hand, the possibility of catching a glimpse of instances in which the Saying stretches beyond what could be incorporated into logos, a juncture that opens up a rift between the Said and the Saying.

Plan of the Work

My objective in this work is threefold: (1) to introduce Levinas to communication studies, (2) to re-conceptualize the conjunction of ethics and communication, and (3) to point out the ethical possibilities introduced by interruptions. The work consists of two parts: introductory (chapters 1 and 2) and critical (chapters 3, 4 and 5). The first chapter presents a preparatory analysis of the ways some central theories of communication have dealt with issues of alterity and difference. Concentrating on four major conceptions of communication (as influence, as system of control, as culture, and as critical discourse), I set out to probe into the biases governing many theoretical speculations, specifically the teleological bias toward successful completion. Such biases, I argue, are inimical to otherness since the underlying motivation in many accounts is either reducing difference or transcending difference. The purpose of the second chapter is to mobilize some of the key ideas in Levinas's philosophy into a communicational framework. In addition to providing an introductory discussion, I explore an alternative perspective of communication and put forward an analysis of the ethical importance of interruption.

The remaining chapters address three limit-cases of the discourse of the Said. While moving along the concerns expressed in each, my critical explorations involve pushing the discussion against its limits, reaching the critical breaking point whereupon different ethical possibilities may lie. In chapter 3, I take up the question of misunderstanding and incomprehensibility by way of exploring the relationship between language and ethics as prescribed by the biblical story of the tower of Babel and the challenges it symbolizes. The discussion attempts to dismantle the underlying motivations for constructing a unitary language as a means of facilitating greater concord and commonality by examining two major enterprises to "undo Babel"—Esperanto and Basic English. It is argued that the experience of misunderstanding presents a significant ethical moment in both exposing one to the Other's otherness and calling for a renewed endeavor by means of translation. As a paradigm of communication, translation approximates a mode of approach in which differences touch without merging. Chapter 4 explores a phenomenon that embodies most emphatically a communicational boundary—autism. Engaging with key texts ranging from psychiatry to social psychology, I investigate the epistemological apparatuses employed to mark what is perceived as an incommunicable boundary. The latter part of the discussion further looks at the problem of the opposition between communicability and incommunicability, suggesting that rather than marking the edge of interactive potential, that boundary is internal to communication, indeed to ethical involvement with another as Other. Finally, Chapter 5 presents a critical discussion of the ethical dimension of freedom of speech as a way to engage with the ethical significance of silence. Extending ethical questions beyond the pursuit for truth, individual freedom of expression and issues of recognition, I propose to recast response-ability to and for the silent Other as a crucial ethical-political challenge. Silence as a modality of otherness presents the opportunity to bear witness to that which exceeds the economy of free speech, a summoning to bear witness to the ethical.

ONE

The Biases of
Communication

Neither snow nor rain nor heat nor gloom of night stays these couriers from
the swift completion of their appointed rounds.
> —Inscription on the post office building in New York City

Reality, argue Berger and Luckmann (1967), always appears as
a zone of lucidity behind which there is a background of darkness. Knowledge about reality has the quality of a flashlight that
projects a narrow cone of light on what lies just ahead and immediately around, while on all sides of the path there continues to be
darkness (ibid., 44–45). Darkness, so it seems, always remains
inaccessible, beyond the reach of knowledge, and yet continues to
envelop the lighted zones.

This metaphor might also be true for the theoretical conceptions
of communication. Proposing a concept of communication establishes a perspective that may then offer a certain understanding of
an elucidated area. It implies the explication of an order according
to which things within the elucidated zone appear to operate. Yet,
a conception, like a projected light, inevitably originates from a

specific point, which is in part a product of an intellectual environment and cultural, social and political settings. Conceptions have historical and intellectual contexts, and their significance, arguably, lies not only in the insights they suggest but also in the ways they invoke the contexts from which they stem.

The following is a critical examination of four of the most fundamental theoretical accounts of communication: as influence, as a system of control, as culture and as critical discourse. While these may not represent the theoretical variety of the field, what guided the selection of the four is that all situate the study of communication at the fore of an epistemological discussion on the nature of mind, society and culture. In so doing, they mobilize distinctive theoretical frameworks in order to address questions pertaining to the work of communication processes. Each in turn circumscribes a distinct epistemological sphere, or a "zone of lucidity," while attempting to tackle questions pertaining to the status of communication within wider contexts, its various manifestations, and its proper form and operation.

The reading suggested here is in no way exhaustive of the texts analyzed. Its purpose is to explore the relationship between these conceptions, the world in which they are situated, the understandings they suggest, and the relevance of the historical and intellectual context in which they appear. However, the motivation behind circumscribing these "zones of lucidity" is out of concern for the surrounding "darkness," for what resists explication and incorporation, that is, the place—or the lack thereof—that alterity occupies within these theoretical speculations. While remaining within the "zones of lucidity," the following analysis attempts to draw attention to the murky margins, to the epistemological "twilight zones" suppressed in each conception. The critical mode of reading adopted here seeks to question the rationale of each conception by using its own terms. The objective is not to disclaim what is proposed by a theoretical account but rather to unsettle it from within by reading its texts against themselves, against their grain, in order to hint toward excluded, omitted, or otherwise denied possibilities. The purpose of this critical reading is therefore to point out conceptual blindness imposed by an unwillingness or inability to acknowledge otherness within the gamut of communicational phenomena.

Conceptions of communication are much more than a mere account of the process of communication, as they are not divorced from positions taken in relation to the reality explored. The ways in which communication has come to be viewed have much more to do with ideal models of society, community and interpersonal relationships than with communication itself, and they are in this sense biased. To the communication scholar, invoking biases of communication echoes the analysis of Harold A. Innis (1973) on time- and space-biased media. Indeed, the biases pointed out here might also be understood in terms of time and space, but probably more in the ordinary sense: the time and the place, both physical and intellectual, in which theoretical conceptions develop. Biases may, then, indicate broader political, social and intellectual concerns, which are external to the phenomenon investigated yet influence the ways phenomena are approached, and, consequently, determine what remains outside, beyond the "zones of lucidity." By problematizing the biases inhering in these conceptions, I will attempt to point out some conceptual lacunas in traditional communication theory.

Communication as Influence

Historically, the conception of communication as influence was one of the earliest attempts to formulate a systematic approach toward communication. The intensive intellectual interest giving rise to this view had been, at least in part, a response to the changing reality of the late nineteenth and early twentieth centuries, a period that presented new problems foreign to former mindsets. Industrialization, urbanization, massive waves of emigration, the rationalization of society, and the introduction of new communication technologies brought about a different social reality. On the one hand, society seemed to have never been more fragmented and atomized, but on the other hand, the novel communication technologies appeared to be opening up new avenues for experiencing togetherness. In addition, World War I had introduced the systematic use of communication media in the general war effort, taking the ancient art of "manufacturing consent" to a new level. One of the period's leading commentators, Walter Lippmann, expressed his concern as early as 1922 in his influential book, *Public Opinion:* "The creation of consent is not a new art. It is a very old one which was supposed to have died out. . . . It has, in fact, improved enormously in technic, because it is now based on analysis rather than the rule of thumb" (1957, 248). The term that came to guide the discourse over the coming decades was "propaganda." Lippmann continues: "Under the impact of propaganda, not necessarily in the sinister meaning of the word alone, the old constants of our thinking have become variables" (ibid., 248).

During the 1930s, the study of propaganda became the dominant form of communication studies in the United States. Having established itself as a series of techniques during the world war, with the help of practitioners such as Edward Bernays (1936), propaganda studies were seeking a theoretical grounding. In the 1930s, propaganda seemed to be everywhere, and for a number of scholars it was also everything. As Kenneth Cmiel notes, the basic definition of propaganda was extraordinarily expansive in those years, and commonly described any message or image designed to change one's mind (1996, 89). In the wake of the war, the word "propaganda" resonated with malicious ministries hatching schemes to control the minds of the masses. However, this broad definition allowed for further relativization: propaganda could be harnessed to either good- or ill-willed ends; propaganda, as one social scientist wrote, may be "for the good life as well as for sinister purposes" (Bruce Lannes Smith, quoted in Cmiel, 90). Influence could be exerted in order to provoke one into buying a car, electing a mayor or going on a war, all depending on who ran the operation. Minds were therefore accessible and exposed to the influence of the means of communication at all times; malicious propaganda was merely the misuse of this fact. This view, which in some places is referred to as the "hypodermic needle" or the "magic bullet" model of communication, would come under harsh criticism in later years (see Schiller 1996). Yet, it is instructive to note at this point that the initial approach to communication in the early twentieth century was of disenchantment. The world, as it appeared after the discovery of communication processes within it, could not be trusted anymore. The effect, as Cmiel suggests, was the development of skeptical and cynical views of society: the public was taught to be wary of all communication, which would present in turn some serious political problems.

One of the leading figures in establishing this conception was Harold D. Lasswell, a political scientist who studied political communication in nations and societies. For Lasswell, communication is a process that influences the environment within which it operates: when an effect is registered, be it between cells, people or nations, one can say with great certainty that communication took place. Communication thus implies action, and one way to describe this action is answering the following questions: "Who? Says what? In which channel? To whom? With what effect?" (Lasswell 1948, 37). This set of questions, according to Lasswell, establishes distinct areas of investigation in communication research: control analysis, content analysis, media analysis, audience analysis and effect analysis. Yet for Lasswell, communication exists in relation to a greater social process, and such a process can be examined in two frames of references, structure and function:

> [O]ur analysis of communication will deal with the specializations that carry on certain functions, of which the following may be clearly distinguished: (1) The surveillance of the environment; (2)

the correlation of the parts of society in responding to the environment; (3) the transmission of the social heritage from one generation
to the other. (1948, 38)[1]

According to Lasswell, communication has a structure and a function before it even commences. Communication is a "feature of
life" at every level and always has a certain task: in a living organism, it maintains internal equilibrium and "harmonious action"; in
the state, communication encompasses the aggregate relations with
the political environment, both internal and external; and in human
societies, it is the correlation between action and environment
(ibid., 38–40).

Lasswell sees in communication processes powerful political
means: a "ruling element" in a society may use communication
channels to maintain its hold, its equilibrium, in both internal and
external environments. But when channels are thus organized,
"truth" is not shared and the "ruling element" prevents harmonious
adjustment to the external environment of the state. In democracy,
as opposed to a regime of "ruling elements," communication
processes are based on free exchange rather than on restriction,
which, in turn, brings the layperson closer to the leader in terms of
their worldview. Lasswell does not expect communication to supply perfect knowledge and thereby produce an entirely enlightened
public; instead, he advocates for the more modest notion of "equivalent enlightenment" that would permit both layperson and leader
"to agree on the broad outlines of reality" (ibid., 51).

For Lasswell, successful communication allows, in principle, the
transferring of messages from one communicator to another, and it
is complete only when people "understand the same sign in the
same way" (1946, 83). The main problem of communication is,
therefore, efficiency. Lasswell deems efficient communication the
cure for modern social ills, most significantly for producing a rationally organized society and an enlightened public. The task is fight-
ing what might interfere with efficient communication—at the

technical level, censorship or curtailment of travel; at the social level, the problem of ignorance. For Lasswell, ignorance means the "absence at a given point in the process of communication, of knowledge which is available elsewhere in the society" (1948, 47). In democracy, communication is of special importance because "rational choices depend on enlightenment, which in turn depends on communication" (ibid., 51). Efficient communication has therefore the potential to challenge manipulative attempts to influence or confuse people.

Lasswell's notion of communication resonates with that of the American social psychologist Carl Hovland. Hovland, purports Wilbur Schramm (1963), was one of the four "founding figures" of the field, along with Lasswell, Kurt Lewin and Paul Lazarsfeld. According to Hovland's definition, communication is "the process by which an individual (the communicator) transmits stimuli (usually verbal symbols) to modify the behavior of other individuals (communicators)" (1948, 371). Like Lasswell, Hovland believes that at its core communication is a process by which an individual affects the actions of others. Hovland's main interest was persuasion and attitude change, in which he became involved during World War II, when he was called to work at the U.S. Army research program. His subsequent work on "persuasive communication" might be described as a combination of the Aristotelian principles of rhetoric and the theoretical framework of group psychology: supplementing logos, ethos and pathos with audience variables and group conformity patterns. The focus of the work was on the conditions influencing opinion change throughout the communicational spectrum: the operation of mass media, the working relations between executives and workers, the potential for offsetting "disruptive foreign propaganda," and the possibility of counteracting "racial, ethnic, and religious prejudices interfering with the consistent operation of democratic values" (Hovland, Janis and Kelly 1953, 1).

Hovland assumes that an individual holds initial opinions (that is, beliefs, anticipations, evaluations) and attitudes (basic, "unconscious" reactions toward a person, object or symbol), and that both could be changed in response to communicational stimuli. Successful communication would occur when communication influences both levels, stimulating one's "motives so as to foster acceptance of the recommended opinion" (ibid., 12). The process of communication—indeed, of persuasive communication—is thus devoid of immanent values; it flows from a communicator who delivers "stimuli" to evoke a "recommended opinion" in the audience. Communication is deemed a priori a form of (unidirectional) influence, and as such the remaining problem, which is basically technical, is in how well it functions. In other words, the problem of communication is the resilient elements in the world, which tenaciously resist influence and persuasion. It seems that Hovland, like Lasswell, removes the process of communication from the world and disassembles it only to put it back together again to discover that the world is what hinders an effective process.

Whereas for Hovland the group was the object of externally exerted influence, for Katz and Lazarsfeld the locus of influence was within the group. In *Personal Influence* (1955), possibly one of the most cited texts in communication studies, Katz and Lazarsfeld effectively invert the hierarchy of communication influence as previously described by Lasswell and Hovland. Interpersonal communication within the group was now declared as having a significant impact on people's opinions and attitudes. According to Katz and Lazarsfeld, an individual is not simply an end unit in the process of communication; he or she has a "two-fold capacity as a communicator and as a relay point in the network of mass communication" (ibid., 1). The investigation suggests that the effect of influence is of a two-step flow: mass media first influence opinion leaders, that is, individuals who are more exposed to and knowledgeable about certain media according to their interests and education (fashion, movies, politics, and the like); these opinion leaders, in turn, pass on the influences stemming from the media to other people. Communication thus flows both vertically and horizontally, to people and between people. But more importantly, what this study shows is that mass media do not dictate what people think, but rather what they think about. This distinction is notewothy since by demonstrating that the more significant locus of influence was the interpersonal, Katz and Lazarsfeld reintroduced the community—families, friendships, work colleagues and neighbors—into the communicational map. The "rediscovery" of person-to-person communication had a definitive impact on communication studies. Katz and Lazarsfeld were able to prove empirically that the traditional model of communication influence was at least inaccurate, thereby challenging the understanding that minds are directly accessible to messages produced by propaganda machines. Yet, the impact of this study exceeded the mere understanding of communication flow.

The intellectual backdrop of the 1940s was dominated by dismal accounts of the oppressive and antidemocratic effect mass media had on postwar American society. Intellectuals such as C. Wright Mills (1956), William H. Whyte (1957) and David Riesman (1961) portrayed an unsettling picture of the late industrialized society, characterized by weak social ties, alienation, atomization and anonymity. American society in particular was seen as a mass society highly vulnerable to the influence of media technologies pushing people to conform to middle-class ideals. At a time when intellectuals and laypersons alike were concerned with the fate of American democracy, *Personal Influence,* which was begun in 1944 and published only in 1955, gave new hope. Katz and Lazarsfeld "rediscovered" the communal ties and proved, empirically, the continued primacy of face-to-face civil society in a modern industrialized society. Interpersonal communication in small communities was defined as the buffer against social cohesion, and its prevalence confirmed that the United States was not on the verge of political and cultural totalitarianism (Simonson 1996).

At first glance, Katz and Lazarsfeld seem to offer a critical account of the views identifying communication with influence.

However, when examining the epistemological underpinning of *Personal Influence,* it appears that the study that appeases concerns about the strengthening effects of communication media essentially exposes the deeper levels of human interaction to further influence. Katz and Lazarsfeld do not dispute the notion that places influence as the prime feature of communication, as shared by theorists such as Lasswell and Hovland; they merely differ in their understanding of the communication process. Studying the interpersonal was done in order to "inquire in what ways informal interpersonal communication might account for the success (or the lack of success) of an influence-attempt stemming from the mass media" (Katz and Lazarsfeld 1955, 82). Thus, by identifying the locus of influence in interpersonal communication, they effectively situate face-to-face communication as an extension to influence originating outside this realm. Katz and Lazarsfeld explicate how person-to-person communication can be manipulated, providing a schema for more sophisticated and subtler ways of influence. In this respect, *Personal Influence* may be regarded as the continuation of communication-as-influence by other means, indeed in more refined ones, and as such it contributes to a further disenchantment of the world wherein communication transpires.

In sum, this conception frames communication within the context of influence, persuasion and manipulation. Communication is understood as a means having an a priori power to influence the targeted destinations. Its archetypical mode is of exertion: favoring change and movement over stasis and passivity, communication processes progress in an arrowlike manner toward prospective targets. Yet once influence is taken as intrinsic and natural in every communication, what then merits further explication is opposition to change and the inability to influence. On this view, the standard form of communication as mobilizing attitudes and opinions requires no further explanation; what merits explanation are the ways by which enclaves of resistance ward off such attempts.

Whether the employment of communication in the pursuit of greater influence is appropriate or not is, presumably, a political and ethical question. However, within this theoretical framework the intrinsic authority of the communication initiator is not questioned—in fact, such an authority is unavoidable, it seems, for it might be working to foil much more sinister undertakings (foreign propaganda, ignorance, prejudice, and so on). The result is that the study of "who says what to whom to what effect?" essentially reifies, if not legitimizes, existing paths of influence and domination (Krippendorff 1989, 194). The communication process, although in itself described as a manifestation of power, remains beyond the political realm: it is merely a means that can be harnessed to confirmatory or insidious ends, while the inherent power-position of the communicator (in most cases a speaker and a man) and of the process itself are deemed inconsequential.

Communication as a System of Control

The concept "communication theory" is no older than the 1940s, when it first meant the mathematical model of signal processing, or Information Theory (Peters 1999, 9). Information Theory developed from a series of studies on telephony at Bell Laboratories in the 1940s, led by mathematician Claude Shannon. Shannon was working on a mathematical model of cryptography that would enable the capacity for more telephone calls on one line, allowing for greater efficiency in utilizing allotted frequencies. He recorded his findings in a confidential report, *Communication Theory of Secrecy Systems* (Mattelart 1996, 223). Research into cryptography and "secrecy systems" was in high demand during World War II in the telecommunication war waged between the Allied Forces and Germany. Scientists and mathematicians on both sides of the Atlantic such as Alan Turing, Norbert Wiener, John von Neumann, Warren Weaver, as well as Shannon, were joined by an effort to crack the German codes of the *Enigma* machine while developing their own techniques for coded messaging. The principles developed then became the basis for a new conception of communication, one based on the exchange of information.

In 1949, Shannon and Weaver published *The Mathematical Theory of Communication* in which they expounded upon the main notions of this concept.[2] The book opens with the following explication:

> The word *communication* will be used here in a very broad sense to include all of the procedures by which one mind may affect another. This, of course, involves not only written and oral speech, but also music, the pictorial arts, the theater, the ballet, and in fact all human behavior. In some connections it may be desirable to use a still broader definition of communication, namely, one which would include the procedures by means of which one mechanism (say automatic equipment to track an airplane and calculate its probable future positions) affects another mechanism (say a guided missile chasing this airplane). (Shannon and Weaver 1964, 3)

Unlike the conception that views communication as influence, in which communicators "modify" others' opinions, attitudes and behavior, this notion includes the multifarious ways "by which one mind may affect another." Shannon and Weaver allow for a much broader, in fact almost unlimited, notion of communication. But not only do they view speech, a grocery list, a rock concert, the *Mona Lisa* and the *Nutcracker* as equal "procedures" of communication, they also state that in principle all human behavior is a form of communication. Moreover, the highest level of abstraction of this notion has to do with how one (automatic) mechanism affects another mechanism (in this case, directed to eliminate the first). On the increasingly bumpier road to abstraction, Shannon and Weaver would attempt to capture a certain attribute about the ways entities (that is, both human and inhuman) are interrelated.

According to Shannon and Weaver, the broad subject of communication presents problems at three levels, serially: Level A, how accurately can the symbols of communication be transmitted? Level B, how precisely do the transmitted symbols convey the desired meaning? and finally, at Level C, how effectively does the received meaning affect conduct in the desired way? (1964, 4). The first is a technical problem, concerning the duplication of signals from one end to the other; the second is a semantic problem, having to do with the difference between the intended meaning and the interpreted one; and the third, the effectiveness problem, involves the extent to which the meaning conveyed leads to the desired outcome, that is, the span of control. Shannon and Weaver's main contention is that "the theory of Level A is, at least to a significant degree, also a theory of levels B and C" (ibid., 6). Problems of understanding and control can be reduced to the problem of doubling-up messages, of "reproducing at one point either exactly or approximately a message selected at another point" (ibid., 31). Or, according to another rendering, Information Theory is like a "very proper and discreet girl accepting your telegrams. She pays no attention to the meaning, whether it be sad, or joyous, or embarrassing. But she must be prepared to deal with all that come to her desk" (ibid., 27). This theory, which is explicitly of signals and not of significance, collapses meanings and intentions into a cipher exchange (Peters 1988, 17). For Shannon and Weaver, the problem of all communication is that of a clean conduit, and to that effect they reorder the hierarchy of communication by putting accuracy at the top. Yet rather than denying the importance of meaning, this analysis, according to Shannon and Weaver, may provide a more robust basis for further investigation, as it "has so penetratingly cleared the air, that one is now, perhaps for the first time, ready for a real theory of meaning" (Shannon and Weaver 1964, 27). Any understanding of meaning requires first a clarification of the conditions facilitating the reproduction of messages from one end to the other, hence the significance of a general model of communication.

The model proposed by Shannon and Weaver involves the flow of information through five parts: the information source selects a desired message out of a set of possibilities; the transmitter changes the message into a signal that can be sent through a channel; the receiver then inverts the signal back into a message to the destination. All these functions are constant and present in all forms of communication: in music, telephony, in written texts, pictures and telegraphy. Furthermore, they seem to inhabit both the inter- and intrapersonal: "when I talk to you, my brain is the information source, yours the destination; my vocal system is the transmitter, and your ear and the associated eighth nerve is the receiver" (ibid., 7). Shannon and Weaver effectively reverse the late-nineteenth-century canonic metaphor (and Lasswell's) in which communication technologies were the nerves of the social organism; instead, the actual nerves were now the channels imparting neural impulses to and from biological "transmitters" and "receivers."[3]

The mathematical model of communication is driven by information (Weaver's term; Shannon prefers "entropy"), and information, as above, must not be confused with meaning. Two messages, one of which is heavily loaded with meaning and the other complete nonsense, would be regarded as equivalent in terms of information. Information relates not so much to content, or what is said, but to degree of freedom, to what could be said. The more of a selection of messages one has to choose from, the greater the freedom of choice, the greater the quantity of information, and hence, the greater the uncertainty. That is, there is less likelihood that someone on the "receiver" side would be able to guess the intended message. To be sure, freedom does not refer to cognitive freedom of choice or expression, or to the uncertainty in trying to figure out the correct meaning of a message. Rather, it is a statistical variable referring to the prior state of the system since information can only refer to a subsequent state (Ritchie 1986, 286). Information has significance only when introducing something new, since when a message is already known, the amount of information is virtually zero. Thus, the basic action of information is rendering the previous state obsolete; information flowing in single-file patterns does not expand or accumulate frivolously but rather "updates" the system, practically detaching it from its history.

The unfortunate characteristic of signal transmission, Shannon and Weaver explain, is that certain things are added to the signals that were not intended by the information source—namely, noise. Paradoxically, noise appears to satisfy all the conditions above: since it was not intended as such, uncertainty increases and so does the information; noise, as the ultimate uncertainty, appears to be beneficial. Yet, Shannon and Weaver clarify that only uncertainty arising by virtue of freedom of choice on the part of the sender is desirable. Uncertainty caused by noise, errors, misunderstandings or interruptions is undesirable and is to be subtracted from the original signal. Wilbur Schramm, who ardently applied the principles of Information Theory to mass communication, went even further to identify noise as any kind of stimuli competing with what the communicator put in the channel. Noise may originate from inside—"AC hum in the radio, print visible through a thin page in a magazine, day-dreaming during a class lecture," or from outside—"competing headline cues on a newspaper page, reading a book while listening to a newscast, the buzz of conversation in the library" (1955, 138). Noise causing undesired uncertainty is something that cannot be assimilated into the system and should therefore be eliminated. A desired uncertainty, in contrast, is a domesticated uncertainty, a "certain uncertainty": it is bounded to a particular law governing the communication process, which, by definition, must precede the process.

The communication system proposed by Shannon and Weaver requires that all parts of the process be on the same wavelength, tuned and predisposed toward supporting the communication flow. Communication is already implied in all the prewired parts: the channels are set; the only task is to keep them clean. Whereas scholars like Lasswell and Hovland only assume the superiority of the sender, Shannon and Weaver propose a model that establishes this superiority scientifically. For a communication to be successful, that is, efficient and informing, it should conform to the intentions of its source; it is complete only when the sender sees him or herself on the receiving side.

Further attempts at applying Information Theory to human and social behavior were undetaken by Norbert Wiener, John von Neumann and Gregory Bateson. The basic notion of communication as inherently associated with information circulation was the cornerstone for a unitary theory of mind, body and machine—cybernetics. The term, supposedly coined by Wiener (derived from the Greek *kubernētēs* for "steersman"), denotes a theory combining information, control and communication processes. Information, as Wiener writes, "is a name for the content of what is exchanged with the outer world as we adjust to it, and make our adjustment felt upon it" (1954, 17). The process of receiving and using information is a process of adjustment to the environment, a process of homeostasis.[4] The principle according to which a thermostat responds to changes in temperature—namely, to information—is basically the one governing all organic and social phenomena. All levels of life may then be seen as organized around cybernetic circuits: "To live effectively," continues Wiener (one might add "to survive"), "is to live with adequate information" (ibid., 18). Wiener categorizes communication together with control because for him the two comprise the essence of inner, psychological and social life. Communication and control integrate commands and responses (positive and negative feedback), creating a greater system constantly seeking equilibrium. This notion of communication is at odds with the understanding of communication as influence held, among others, by Lasswell and Hovland, who viewed the communication process as based on psychological energy. Furthermore, while communication for the latter was only one feature of social and political life, for the cybernetic circle it was the essence of life. The underlying assumption is that everything is connected to everything else; the remaining problem is to formulate the rules governing these connections (Heims 1977, 141).

At the end of the war, von Neumann and Wiener were seeking new avenues to further develop the ideas they had been working on for the U.S. military. Bateson, becoming acquainted with their ideas in 1946 during the Macy Foundation conference on teleological mechanisms, incorporated ideas like "digital" and "analogical" processes, coding and decoding, servomechanisms, positive and negative feedback, information, entropy, and binary systems in much of his consequent work (Lipset 1980, 179). He also became familiar with the Russellian paradox, which would become the basis for his psychiatric double-bind theory (Bateson 1972).[5] In 1951, Bateson, together with Swiss psychiatrist Jurgen Ruesch, published *Communication: The Social Matrix of Psychiatry,* a unified theory of human behavior, in which they propose: "communication is the only scientific model which enables us to explain physical, intrapersonal, interpersonal, and cultural aspects of events within one system" (1951, 5).

According to Ruesch and Bateson, there are four basic functions in every communication system, whether neural, verbal, social, mass or intercultural: evaluating, sending, channeling and receiving. At any time, a unit (neuron, person, group, nation) carries out at least one of the four functions, and what differentiates the lower levels of communication from the upper ones is the complexity of the system (ibid., 281). This view allows them to conceptualize culture as being carried and transmitted by individuals in their everyday life in an implicit (or even subconscious) way while partaking in mundane social interaction. For Ruesch and Bateson, these units are parts-in-a-system, each having a place in the overall structure; however, these units do not only operate for themselves, they also support a transcendent order, one that precedes their operation. The system exists above and beyond its parts: "The organizational continuity of the various systems is maintained, but the constituent parts are usually subject to constant replacement," and it thus follows that "In special cases, the self-destruction of the smaller entity is instrumental to the survival of the system" (ibid., 285, 289).

Bateson's later works exhibit a looser application of cybernetic principles, and one example is his double-bind theory. Bateson argues that every message contains two levels of communication: the content message, or the "digital" level, and a higher contextual level—the "analogical" level—communicating how the message should be understood. The analogical level, or the metamessage, classifies the digital, or the informational, message it carries. When applied to human communication, this view allowed Bateson to offer a new perspective on schizophrenia. According to Bateson, schizophrenia is a disorder manifested in a failure to understand the analogical dimension of communication, as schizophrenics seem incapable of placing messages in the right context, that is, of understanding metamessages. Bateson argues that if a child is raised in an environment imbued with oscillating contradictions between messages and metamessages, he or she might be more susceptible to becoming schizophrenic (Bateson 1972, 201–6). Schizophrenia is not merely a personal disorder (still, Bateson acknowledges the influence of biological predispositions); it is primarily a pathology of the communication network in which an individual is situated.[6] Schizophrenia might thus be understood as a disorder stemming from a system imbalance.

Viewed still more metaphorically than scientifically, cybernetics became for Bateson the basis for a new paradigm—a paradigm of ecology, explicating the connection between mind and nature (1979). Contrary to Freudian epistemology, which expanded the concept of mind inwards, Bateson expanded mind outwards. Cybernetic systems (including what is perceived as consciousness) are, according to Bateson, a complex system of message passing. However, these messages do not contain pure contents, but rather a representation of difference. And difference is what constitutes information, as Bateson espouses: "I suggest to you, now, that the word 'idea,' in its most elementary sense, is synonymous with 'difference.' . . . In fact, what we mean by information—the elementary unit of information—is a *difference which makes a difference*"

(1972, 459). To Bateson, such a view of cybernetics resolves the ancient dichotomy of mind and matter: mind is in matter inasmuch as it is in the system—it is an emergent property of matter. This perspective has some parallels with Spinoza's monistic metaphysics, yet contrary to classical monism, Bateson argues that "Mind is empty," it does not contain the world in terms of time and space but contains "only ideas of time and space" (Bateson 1982, 4). Mind manifests itself in nature, and vice versa: a cell reacts when hit by an enzyme, the eye's pupil responds to differences in light intensity, the brain reacts to stimuli, the tree starts blooming when it "interprets" the difference in climate as spring, and the earth's ecological system changes as a result of the greenhouse effect—all changes driven by messages communicating differences. Communication systems possess all phenomena—mind, nature and cybernetics are a necessary unity.

In conclusion, this conception seems to denote a certain cosmological order according to which "In the beginning was the system" (and cybernetics would thereby connote deus ex machina). Systems of communication and control are immanent in mind, nature and machine; they are constituted upon basic units that have pre-given functions ultimately contributing to the maintenance of the system. Yet control is not an exclusive characteristic of one or more singular units in a communication system. Control is the ultimate property of the system itself; it is the way by which the system rouses different functions that allow it to sustain its equilibrium.

Information is the rudimentary element of communication systems: it is its currency, material and fuel, and as such, it is literally in-formation—always working according to principles preceding its operation. There is no information outside the system, only noise, either interruptive or inconsequential. What remains outside cannot be subsumed by the system, or to paraphrase on Bateson's quip, it is the difference that does not make a difference. By consuming information, the system domesticates differences and uncertainty. It views the external world in terms of its homeostasis mechanisms—ferreting out the elements that facilitate its action from those that might endanger it; within these conceptual confines any other feature is simply irrelevant. Hence, successful communication means more or better wiring, or alternatively, cleaner channels with more capacity, for the greatest task of any communication is clarity, that is, the effective imparting of the sender's intentions.

Communication as Culture

In "A Cultural Approach to Communication" (1975) James Carey outlines two alternative conceptions of communication since this term entered common discourse in the nineteenth century: the transmission view and the ritual view. The two do not constitute rigidly structured conceptual frameworks; rather, each holds a collection of theories and models that share some characteristics and a general approach to communication.

The transmission view of communication is the commonest view in Western industrial cultures and dominates contemporary lexical definitions of the term. Communication as transmission signifies "imparting, sending, transmitting, or giving information to others" and regards communication "as a process and as a technology that would . . . spread, transmit, and disseminate knowledge, ideas, information further and faster with the end of controlling space and people" (ibid., 3, 5). This view stems from the terminology of transportation, which is probably the source for notions such as flow, circulation, exchange, channel and network, originally referring to goods and people and later on to information and signals. The introduction of the telegraph, which marked, as Carey (1989) explains, the separation between message and messenger, unchained the notion of communication from the traditional transportation world. Communication was progressively becoming the exclusive quality of an etheric exchange, independent of bodily encounter, as the telegraph presented the technological capability of extending one mind to another.[7] Communication as transmission, Carey summarizes, is "a process whereby messages are transmitted and distributed in space for the control of distance and people" (1975, 3). The archetypical form of communication on this view, then, is tantamount to persuasion, influence, attitude change, socialization through the transmission of information, or behavior modification (Carey 1989, 42). Carey's criticism is that communication studies have been dominated by the transmission model, which in the present context corresponds with both conceptions of communication as influence and as a system of control, and with most of the scholars discussed above, some of whom are also mentioned in Carey's analysis (ibid., 51–53).

As an alternative, Carey proposes the ritual view of communication.[8] For Carey, the ritual view not only offers a critical evaluation of the transmission model but also, and perhaps mainly, provides a new approach, and indeed a new vocabulary, to study communication. Communication, according to the fundamental definition proposed by Carey, is "a symbolic process whereby reality is produced, maintained, repaired and transformed"; to study communication is thus "to examine the actual social process wherein significant symbolic forms are created, apprehended, and used" (ibid., 10, 17). The ritual view, Carey adds, "is not directed toward the extension of messages in space but the maintenance of society in time; not the act of imparting information but the representation of shared beliefs" (ibid., 6). Understood as ritual rather than transmission, communication would involve performance rather than movement, participation rather than consumption, meaning or beauty rather than strategy or results, evocation or calling rather than influence or effectiveness (Rothenbuhler 1998, 125). In establishing this view, Carey implies two significant points, which bear heavy epistemological weight: first, communication is an expression of commonality, a collective process of participation and sharing; second, reality is not given, it is not there to be discovered, but is socially constructed by communication processes.

With such broad claims about communication and reality, these points merit further unpacking.

The ritual view of communication upholds the homonym of the Latin *communicare,* which means to impart, to share and to make common (Peters 1999, 7). The linguistic root is *mun,* which is found in words such as "communion," "community" and "common." Thus, the word "communication" denotes an action or experience transpiring in communion or in collectivity. In situating the notion of communication on the grounds of common experience, Carey draws on several sources; among those mentioned are Max Weber, Emile Durkheim, Kenneth Burke, Hugh Duncan and Clifford Geertz. Carey's notion of communication is more specifically inspired by Raymond Williams's understanding of society as "a form of communication through which experience is described, shared, modified, and preserved" (1966, 18). Yet the greatest influence (as Carey himself acknowledges) comes from the work of American social thinkers such as Charles Horton Cooley and John Dewey, whose conceptualizations of communication seem to resonate throughout Carey's ritual view.

Charles Horton Cooley's social thought contests the separation between individual and society since the two do not "denote separable phenomena, but are simply collective and distributive aspects of the same thing" (1967, 37). For Cooley, the human mind is social, or, alternatively, society is mental, and in short, mind and society are two aspects of the same thing. As he writes, "A separate individual is an abstraction unknown to experience, and so likewise is society when regarded as something apart from individual" (ibid., 36). Cooley sees in the traditional community the morally ideal social organization. In a community, he claims, "individual minds are merged and the higher capacities of the members find total and adequate expression" (1983, 33). According to Cooley, recreating the spiritual essence of *Gemeinschaft,* of face-to-face community, was one of the most important challenges of the modern era. Cooley, along with several American thinkers such as Robert Park,

John Dewey and Josiah Royce, also known as the Progressives, was concerned with the direction American society appeared to be taking, and more specifically with the fate of American democracy. Following the large emigration waves of the late nineteenth century and the urban and industrial development that followed, it seemed that the American society had become a "lonely crowd." These transformations led Progressive thinkers to seek ways for redeeming the alienated society from what they regarded as perilous to the democratic spirit of the country.

As Peters (1989b) notes, it was the ideal of the small town that led many of the Progressives' aspirations. Unlike the Enlightenment, which rejected the benighted village for the sophisticated city, and unlike Romanticism, which condemned the decadence of the urban center while opting for the more authentic country, the Progressive movement and its adherents tried to have it both ways. Cooley, most distinctively, believed that the spirit of the country could save the city, and the element he designated as having the potential of bringing together *Gemeinschaft* and *Gesellschaft* was communication. For Cooley, communication is the element that could produce a great community, a constellation of many communities at a distance, a community of communities. In fact, Cooley presents a view of communication that incorporates both transmission and ritual views: in his writings, communication appears as both a "fellowship in thought" and a "destruction of distance" (Peters 1999, 184–85). Captivated by the expansion of communications technology, Cooley regarded them as the ultimate means for expanding the human mind, which was tantamount for him to the social mind. As he writes, "the new communication has spread like morning light over the world, awakening, enlightening, enlarging, and filling with expectation" (Cooley 1983, 88). What Cooley refers to as "the recent marvelous improvement of communicative machinery" (ibid., 54), presented him with an actual possibility of reaching a unity of mind. In sum, Cooley believes that by extending the process of communication, disorder would give way to social order, to democratic unity and, ultimately, to moral commonwealth (Simonson 1996, 330).

Like Cooley, John Dewey was also concerned with the social reality of his time. Dewey shared Cooley's hope in mass communication as a means for producing a greater unity, and like Cooley, his aim was also to transform the Great Society into a Great Community. However, in contrast to Cooley, Dewey was much less idealistic regarding the nature of communication. He did not share Cooley's spiritual view of mental unity, nor did he concur with Cooley's view of the role communication might have in producing greater unity of mind. For Dewey, communication was not about putting private minds *en rapport* with others; rather, communication was about bringing people to full participation in public life (Peters 1989a, 205). For Cooley, what was actually being communicated mattered little so long as communication was actually taking place; for Dewey, however, the contents were crucial. The unity Dewey was seeking was not of an organic nature but rather of understanding and solidarity, as he writes in *Democracy and Education:* "There is more than a verbal tie between the words common, community, and communication. Men live in a community in virtue of the things which they have in common; and communication is the way in which they come to possess things in common" (1966, 4). Communication, as he defines the notion, is the process by which people come to partake in the experience of the public: "Communication is a process of sharing experience till it becomes a common possession. It modifies the disposition of both the parties who partake in it" (ibid., 9). Dewey thus attempts to formulate social experience without idealistic cosmology. For him, the ideal community is not based on mental unity but rather on the construction of an intelligent public by means of discursive social practices (an idea that would be developed by Mead and even more by Habermas). The problem Dewey identifies is that modern complexity has presented conditions previously unknown, the most important of which is a dispersed public, which Dewey deems "so bewildered that it cannot find itself" (1954, 123). His main concern is, therefore, "discovering the means by which a scattered, mobile, and manifold public may so recognize itself as to define and express its interests" (ibid., 146). Thus, communication is precisely the means for creating the democratic ideal of a Great Society: "Till the Great Society is converted into a Great Community, the Public will remain in eclipse. Communication can alone create a great community. Our Babel is not one of the tongues but of the signs and symbols without which shared experience is impossible" (ibid., 142).

The two accounts are indeed different, but they share a common understanding of communication and its place in the world: promoting an experience of solidarity, the collective practice of communication has a social and political role in establishing (or, for Cooley, reestablishing an already embedded sense of) communal organization. Carey shares this understanding, and adds: "In our predominantly individualistic tradition, we are accustomed to think of thought as essentially private. . . . I wish to suggest, in contradistinction, that thought is predominantly public and social" (1973, 15). Following Cooley and Dewey, Carey suggests that private experience should be understood as an aspect of the public experience. Communication is about creating (or, again, according to Cooley, recreating a lost) togetherness, unity and community; it concerns the participation of individuals in building something that is beyond themselves—a sense of greater like-mindedness.

This leads to the second significant point Carey makes by which the operation of communication effectively constructs a common experience that is taken as "reality": "This is a ritual view of communication emphasizing the production of a coherent world that is then presumed for all practical purposes, to exist" (1989, 85). This conception of communication offers both a model of reality and a model for reality—communication is at once a structure and a process of structuring. To describe communication is not only to describe the circulation of ideas but also the social and cultural forms that enshrine these ideas (ibid., 86). Symbols might then be viewed as a means to revamp the world: rather than merely serving as a means of communicating with other individuals or future generations (Lasswell's definition), symbols are a means to create reality (compare Leeds-Hurwitz 1993, 34). As opposed to the transmission view, which is quite disenchanted with communication, Carey calls for the reenchantment of communication, as it is the fundamental tool of world-building. "Of all the things," he echoes Dewey, "communication is the most wonderful" (Carey 1975, 1).

However, the process of creating, transforming, sustaining and repairing reality seems to operate under a specific assumption—that this is a violent process:

> Reality is, above all, a scarce resource. Like any scarce resource it is there to be struggled over, allocated to various purposes and projects, endowed with given meanings and potentials, spent and conserved, rationalized and distributed. . . . Therefore, the site where artists paint, writers write, speakers speak, filmmakers film broadcasters broadcast is simultaneously the site of social conflict over the real. . . . It is a conflict over the simultaneous codetermination of ideas, techniques, and social relations. (1989, 87)

Since there is no objective reality, the struggle is over what could be declared as real, and the "real" is always under dispute while different forces attempt to redefine the coordinates by which the world is ordered (compare Berger and Luckmann 1967). If communication is to be understood as a process whereby reality is "produced, maintained, repaired and transformed," and if reality is "a scarce resource," it follows that the process of communication is essentially conflicting. Put together with Carey's first significant point underscoring communication as an experience of commonality, it appears that public life is pursued by means of struggle. At any given time, there is a dominant order, or cultural hegemony, which is contested, and once the contestation registers and transforms the collective definition of the "real," others take their turn to challenge the status quo. Alternately, this might mean that if one does not appear to challenge what is perceived as "real," then one is effectively reinstating willy-nilly the current cultural definitions. It remains debatable whether one can take a neutral position in this process, that is, neither perpetuating existing structures nor contesting them. Carey's analysis leaves little room for the possibility of occupying a position independent of the production of togetherness.[9]

The process described by Carey is a fight for recognition and for the definition of what Dewey called a "shared experience." Out of the perpetual struggle, a greater fellowship is formed, one that subsumes the different oppositions and produces an order yet to be contested. The distilled social phenomenon Carey seems to be describing is of conflict, and taken to the extreme it appears that conflict over what is common is a fundamental feature of commonality itself. The immanency of conflict in the ritual view has some important political implications, particularly in ascribing political significance to mundane phenomena, or more precisely, to the phenomena of the mundane. Here individual processes of meaning-making take up special significance in defining social reality and, perhaps more importantly, in challenging existing cultural and symbolic structures. This line of investigation has been followed by scholars such as John Fiske (1989) and Stuart Hall (1980), who analyze sites of semiotic resistance and speculate on the modes of decoding that are in opposition to the hegemonic viewpoint.

To recapitulate, the conception that regards communication as culture as presented by Carey's ritual view provides a reflexive understanding of reality and of the social processes by which it is constructed. Communication as ritual resonates with notions such as sharing, fellowship, association and participation. In opposition to concepts that view communication as influence or as a system of control, communication for Carey is a tool for creating a sense of shared reality. In this respect, Carey is closest to Dewey, who sees communication as a means for creating a community of like-mindedness. However, the process is, according to Carey, essentially antagonistic, as reality is defined through a dialectical struggle that serves to reconstruct a common sense of reality. There is more than a coincidental Hegelian tone here, for Carey's conception of communication is very much situated within a paradigm of power, one that views power as both instrumental to and manifested by the experience of togetherness. More than Carey cares to admit, his idea of communication appears to be a means by which individuality is transcended, violently. Although remaining in the background of his analysis, violence seems to be the driving force of the collective processes he describes. Thus, the violence exerted by influence (Lasswell, Hovland, Katz and Lazarsfeld) and the violence enforced by the system (Shannon and Weaver, Wiener, Bateson) is ultimately traded for the violence of commonality and community.

Communication as Critical Discourse

The roots of the conception of communication as critical discourse may go back as far as Plato's description of the Socratic dialogue as a method by which opposing arguments are evaluated, discussed and criticized in order to attain, eventually, the truth. As Craig (1999) notes, the tradition of critical social theory also runs from Marx through the Frankfurt school and other Marxists (and post-Marxist) theories, culminating in the work of philosopher Jürgen Habermas.

Habermas's conceptualization of communication draws from several traditions, mainly from the philosophy of Kant, Weber and Durkheim; American pragmatism, especially the work of Mead; and the critical theory of Adorno and Horkheimer. A considerable part of Habermas's vast body of work is devoted to the development of the theory of communicative action in which he places communication at the heart of both critical and constructive intellectual explorations (1984, 1987). The theory of communicative action has three main concerns: (1) to develop a concept of rationality that is no longer connected to individualistic and subjective premises of modern philosophy and social theory; (2) to develop a two-level concept of society that integrates both implicit structure of knowledge, sociocultural background (what he refers to as the life-world) and structure of coordination and self-regulatory systems in society; and(3) to sketch out, against the background of critical theory, a theory of modernity that suggests a redirection rather than an abolishment of the project of Enlightenment (McCarthy, in Habermas 1984, vi). Communicative action has relevance to all the above concerns in proposing a model that facilitates mutual understanding, coordinated action, socialization and transformation of the social world.

Habermas maintains that every communication act bears an intrinsic *telos,* which is oriented toward reaching mutual understanding. Communication is goal-oriented in the sense that every communicative engagement involves questioning, arguing and transcending presuppositions in order to transform opinions or situations judged untrue or unjust. Habermas's theory develops this aspect of communication while promoting the claim that communicative action is oriented toward understanding based on consensus among speakers:

> I shall speak of communicative action whenever the actions of the agents involved are coordinated not through egocentric calculations of success but through acts of reaching understanding. In communicative action participants are not primarily oriented to their own individual success; they pursue their individual goals under the condition that they can harmonize their plans of action on the basis of common situation definitions. (Habermas 1984, 285–86)

Reaching an agreement is not a strategic or instrumental objective of communicative action since it is not oriented toward the subordination of other views, or toward successful influence upon another rational opponent. Communicative action strives to achieve understanding *with* other people, not *upon* them; reaching understanding is a process through which active agents arrive at a non-coerced agreement, one that "cannot be merely induced through outside influence; it has to be accepted or presupposed as valid by the participants" (ibid., 287). Understanding is a process transpiring in and through communicative action, and in that respect it is a social process because it requires more than one person. Agreement, in turn, is reached by conviction, by a rational process of the validation of arguments. Since nothing can be accepted as valid unless it can be defended against all parties' objections, the process requires that all parties be both free and equal: free to express ideas and objections and equal with respect to other participants. Thus, communicative action rests upon a systematic argumentation of one's position in a way that would allow the other to alter his or her opinion based on rational calculation rather than on an emotional, nonrational response evoked by the speaker. For Habermas, the only form of communication that can support equal and free discursive engagement is rational communication, that is, a process of reflective discourse. However, it is not the conclusion of the communicative act that is most important for Habermas (for it may only produce an implicit understanding or agreement); it is the actual process of a rational discourse by which claims are scrutinized and evaluated that is emancipatory.

For Habermas, language as a means of communication already bears a built-in capacity for mutual understanding. The possibility of reaching an understanding is implicit in the linguistic structure of language—the potential for consensus inheres in human speech. Thus, the objective that leads and energizes participants to embark on a discussion is the possibility to offer an opinion, to debate and criticize other opinions and to defend one's own, all this with the intention of eventually reaching mutual understanding, however tacit it may be. Moreover, Habermas claims that using language to such an end conforms to language's basic form: "the use of language with the orientation towards reaching understanding is the *original mode* of language use" (ibid., 288). He would, therefore, regard falsification, lying, manipulation, but possibly also humor, metaphor and poetry, as either inauthentic or superfluous uses of language, for they are all "parasitical" forms of its consensus-oriented function (Levin 1989, 121). Habermas's conceptualization of communication is in stark contradiction to both conceptions of communication as influence and as a system of control, since both seem to value the success of the communication process much more than reaching egalitarian understanding among parties. In fact, communicative action would regard such conceptions of communication as distorted precisely because they give primacy to the intentions of the "sender."

Habermas stresses that the function of reaching an understanding in communicative action is based on the intersubjective nature of human speech. Language, as a manifestation of intersubjectivity, allows one to participate in a social exchange while putting oneself in the place of the other. "Only an intersubjective process of reaching understanding can produce an agreement that is reflexive in nature; only it can give the participants the knowledge that they have collectively become convinced of something" (1991, 67). Communicative action thus implies interchangeability between speakers in terms of their positions. In establishing this point, Habermas relies on George Herbert Mead's analysis of language.

In many ways, Mead's work continued that of John Dewey, who was his teacher and mentor. Like Cooley and Dewey before him, Mead challenged the separation between the individual and the social. However, what distinguishes Mead from his predecessors is his philosophical agenda. Whereas Cooley and Dewey were primarily political and social thinkers, Mead saw himself as a social behaviorist. Mead's project might be described as an attempt to explain mind, self and society in terms of communication. In this respect, he followed the explorations of Cooley and Dewey in avoiding essentialist postulations on human and social nature. In

viewing social reality as a process that gives rise to both consciousness and sociality, Mead established an approach that does
not fall into an "egocentric predicament" (Morris, in Mead 1967,
xxxii).

For Mead, communication is the active process constituting
mind, self and society; it is the element that runs across these
levels, and effectively sets them up. Mead regards minds "as phenomena which have arisen and developed out of the process of
communication and of social experience" (Mead 1967, 50). Mind
is not located in the individual, but is a product of a social process.
Mead's approach, which opposes the Cartesian meditations, sees
mental processes as bound to social existence; mind is therefore a
social function by which individuals coordinate their activities and
relationships (Lewis and Smith 1980, 142). The self is also a social
phenomenon, which is irreducible to a specific subjectivity, and
most notable in this respect is his influential distinction between "I"
and "me." Mead insists repeatedly that the self is not antecedent to
social processes—it arises simultaneously with one's ability to take
the role of the other toward oneself (ibid., 142). For Mead, the
importance of communication "lies in the fact that it provides a
form of behavior in which the organism or the individual may
become an object to himself" (Mead 1967, 138). Communication
is what enables taking the role of the other, and it is by taking on this
role that cooperative action is created. Individuals are socially predisposed toward one another and the fundamental manifestation of
this predisposition is the reality of communication. Hence, according to Mead, communication already bears an elementary social
experience of commonality; it implies "some sort of co-operation
within which the individuals are themselves actively involved as the
only possible basis for this participation in communication. You
cannot start to communicate with people in Mars and set up a society where you have no antecedent relationship" (ibid., 257).

Habermas adopts and further develops Mead's discussion of
cooperative action. Since the intersubjective is already predisposed

to understanding through the proper use of language, when adhering to the rules of communicative action, an agreement or disagreement would ultimately arise. It would then be possible to respond to a position taken by a participant in the positive or the negative: "A speaker who utters a statement *p* with a communicative intent, raises the claim that the statement *p* is true; a hearer can respond to this with a 'yes' or a 'no.' Thus with the assertoric mode of language use, communicative acts gain the power to coordinate actions via rationally motivated agreement" (Habermas 1987, 30). A communicatively achieved agreement, which stems from rational argumentation, that is, accepted by taking a "yes" or "no" position based on validity claims that can be criticized, is the basis for a coordinated and transformative action. For Habermas, the importance of coordinated action lies in the fact that it allows the transformation of the lifeworld, the hermeneutic horizon of action and interpretation, the taken-for-granted context of what is discussed (ibid., 131). According to Habermas, the lifeworld is not merely a determinant factor; rather, communicative action serves to transmit and renew cultural knowledge (ibid., 137). This allows him to propose a critical social account that has roots in the rational tradition and not—as opposed to his teachers in the Frankfurt School, Horkheimer and Adorno—in the material reality giving rise to class domination.

As Paul Ricoeur (1991) explains, for the Frankfurt School, and for the Marxist tradition in general, distorted communication is usually related to the repressive action of authority exercising techniques of censorship. An example is Herbert Marcuse's *One-Dimensional Man* (1969), which criticizes the reduction of communication spheres to modes that facilitate the progress of dominant political structures while eliminating opposition, a social reality that "justifies everything and absolves everything—except the sin against its spirit" (247). For Habermas, on the other hand, domination takes place in the sphere of communicative action itself, where the conditions for an effective execution of rational discussion are compromised and language is distorted or misused (Ricoeur 1991, 291). And yet, it is precisely here, in the sphere of communicative action, that Habermas finds potential emancipation. Still in opposition to the Marxist tradition, Habermas identifies rational discourse as the ultimate moral dimension of critique— only reason itself can liberate from coercion, domination and manipulation. In this respect, James Carey's concept of communication as culture would also fail to meet the Habermasian standards of communicative action. The communication process described by Carey, which is about reproducing social order or even producing alternative ones, falls under the categories of strategic manipulation, domination, or irrational conformity, and therefore presents forms of distorted communication. Whereas Carey prescribes togetherness based on habitual symbolic negotiation in which meaning is created and recreated but always remains relative, Habermas advocates a rationally achieved agreement, one inspired by absolute criteria.

Habermas's concern for securing a sphere in which communication could operate in accordance with principles like equality, sincerity and uprightness is indeed admirable. In this, he follows a theme central in Marxist analysis that seeks to establish spheres of interaction free from any form of domination in which individuals could come to realize their position in the political schema of power and labor. However, for Habermas, the expansion of rationality through communicative action is the ultimate liberating strategy. Rather than abandoning the project of Enlightenment, Habermas strives to excavate the constructive principles of reason and constitute around them a model of social justice. This motivation, I would argue, is the fundamental context of his work. His insistence that rationality is inherent to the linguistic structure of language is, in fact, what supports the theoretical construct; taken away, communicative action loses its most fundamental impetus. And yet, by questioning the basic notion according to which language is consensus-oriented, one would run the risk of throwing the baby out with the bathwater and missing many of Habermas's valuable contributions. So while allowing, even provisionally, this notion, one may still ask: why should this aspect of communication be the primary one? Habermas would agree that through the process of communication one comes to take the role of the other person and thus acknowledge the other, but is that not possible when meeting resistance to understanding, or better, in the event of misunderstanding? Alternatively, is it not possible that one can reasonably understand another but still not acknowledge the other? Habermas is very sensitive to problems of oppression and domination, or what he calls distorted communication, but by tying communication to reason he effectively introduces a factor that might itself be oppressive. The fact that language allows understanding does not exclusively mean that this is its ultimate purpose. And even if linguistic structures are "predisposed" toward reaching an understanding, fortifying this tendency might not necessarily lead to a more compassionate approach to others.

Habermas, much like Mead, restricts respect for others to the occurrence of understanding. According to Mead, "You cannot start to communicate with people in Mars and set up a society where you have no antecedent relationship . . . a community that lies entirely outside of your own community, that has no common interest, no co-operative activity, is one with which you could not communicate" (1967, 257–58). Imagine a community in which all members share a Habermasian passion for communicative action and in which all relationships are purely symmetrical, free, and equal. Concurrently, in another community members adhere to an "irrational" discursive principle, whatever shape it might take. Can the two communicate? Can they reach an understanding? According to Mead, communication would not be possible since it is restricted to an "antecedent relationship," to instances where there is some kind of cooperative intention. In basing communication on having something in common—however expansive and loosely understood—Mead inevitably excludes what he would regard as an act of noncoordination, thereby deeming it incommunicable. And according to Habermas, mutual understanding would be possible only when the other community follows the principles of rational communication—or in other words, when communicative action is universalized. Habermas would view what does not follow the principles of rational communication—however liberal, egalitarian and enlightened they may be—as distorted communication. I doubt, therefore, that according to the principles of communicative action a person of the "rational" community would be able to take the role of a person from the "irrational" one. Communicative action may allow taking the role of the other but not that of the Other. It would not be unfair to say that rationality might possess some oppressive features, not unlike practices Habermas has rightfully condemned. Taken to a limit, rationality, ipso facto, might also be a form of violence.

Toward a Critique of the Field

Communication theories have been penetratingly critiqued by scholars such as Natali (1986), Peters (1986, 1994, 1999), Krippendorff (1989, 1996), Ang (1994), Stewart (1995), Chang (1996), Smith (1997) and Ramsey (1998). Following some of their insights and based on the analysis above, I suggest that although different in their approach to the process of communication, the conceptions studied here share a number of important features that manifest common biases. To use the metaphor from the opening passage, though casting distinct "zones of lucidity," they all generate from parallel vicinities.

The conceptions analyzed above share, to a greater or lesser extent, a teleological notion of communication: communication has a goal, an objective, a *telos,* in the world wherein it transpires. Among the central goals are modifying the behavior of others, attaining control and system balance, creating common reality, and reaching rationally based understanding. Once established as such, communication is then expected to improve or even transform the world, and in some cases it is even regarded as the cure for fundamental social, political and moral problems. Better communication, cleaner channels, more information and greater understanding are often mentioned as ways to resolve conflicts and disputes. Thus, when communication is understood as having a preconceived goal, its failure may result in a conundrum and a quandary. Communication breakdown denotes a dreadful paralysis, for it effectively means that one failed to meet one's goals—a message failed to arrive, an intention was misunderstood or a desired impact was not achieved.

Most of the theoretical accounts studied above are, to use Natali's incisive phrase, "saturated with positivity" (1986, 24). Communication is biased to the successful completion of its tasks and ascribed with sharply dichotomized roles: good and sinister influence, information and noise, affirmation and contestation of symbolic order, understanding and misunderstanding. It follows that communication seems to have an ulterior motive insofar as it is an agent of a higher authority—democracy, stability, community, togetherness and rationality, to name but a few. Notions of communication are accordingly biased toward certainty rather than uncertainty, order rather than disorder, clarity rather than ambiguity, understanding rather than misunderstanding, efficacy rather than incapacity, function rather than dysfunction (see Ang 1994, Chang 1996). For those interested in communication, the issue has rarely been communication itself, but rather how communication processes may establish—or fail to establish—something greater. Consequently, failure of communication signifies a collapse of something other than the process itself since when the process is at the service of ideals like sharing, understanding, stability or greater certainty about togetherness, communication breakdown is basically the breakdown of such ideals. To be sure, it is possible that these ideals are worth pursuing; nevertheless, striving toward such aspirations is not without sacrifice, for the way communication has traditionally been conceptualized involves a certain bias against otherness.

Although many of the conceptualizations of communication express concern for ethical issues, they are, albeit to a varying extent, placed within a paradigm of power. As Krippendorff (1989) argues, the use of power metaphors in studying social phenomena, and in communication theories in particular, is often taken for granted and rarely questioned. Influencing, exchanging information, negotiating reality, and even reaching an understanding are all, in one way or another, manifestations of power, and notions adhering to such principles employ metaphors of violence, either directly or under the cloak of higher values and ideals. The permeation of such notions, in turn, reinforces and legitimizes existing structures of domination incorporating communication to their political arsenal, particularly that of the capitalistic social system. Furthermore, the theoretical endeavor to circumscribe the phenomenon of communication may in fact introduce yet another aspect of the power paradigm in that to varying extents the different conceptions analyzed above bear more than a coincidental tint of essentialism. In each there are certain presuppositions that determine what communication is, what might be its distillate, what it does or should contain, in short, what is communication's ontological status. The problem here is that speculating on the ontology of communication might constitute an understanding of communication that is anterior to its occurrence. As Eric Ramsey (1998) affirms, asking "what is communication?" immediately "makes communication an object and sends investigators looking for its essence" (6). When first circumscribed and only later sought out in the world, communication might already be cleansed of the messiness in which it takes place. This tendency might thereby conceal, or even compromise, the otherness inhering in communication and the Other as a possible communicator. The effect is tantamount to silencing all noises and interruptions so as to allow communication to make ends meet, so that "neither snow nor rain nor heat nor gloom of night" would prevent it from the swift completion of its appointed rounds. As Peters (1999) rightly remarks, communication, if taken as one's ability to manipulate and influence others or to reduplicate one's own mind in others, deserves to crash, and the breakdown of communication may then be "a salutary check on the hubris of the ego" (21).

The concerns expressed in traditional conceptions of communication might then be placed somewhere between visions of imparting (information, ideas, knowledge, influence) and fusion (togetherness, community, greater understanding) (see Cmiel 1996). The problems they consequently divulge, albeit important in their own context, have mostly to do with the effectiveness of communication, with accessibility and facility, or with how individuals can share their lives, coordinate their actions and understand each other better. Traditional communication theories are largely about the reduction of difference or the transcendence of difference, and consequently, the elimination of difference. As such, communication is seen as the great equalizer between places, minds and individuals in following two possible routes: either leading communicators through prepaved channels to already known destinations, or constructing bridges over what separates them as singular agents. Following this review of traditional conceptions of communication, what possibly becomes clear is the need for an alternative conception of the relation between communication and ethics. In order not to reify traditional biases, such a conception would have to go beyond visions of imparting and fusion, structure and function, *Gemeinschaft* and *Gesellschaft, telos* and power. It is perhaps time to relieve communication of its traditional duties and allow complexity, uncertainty and ambiguity, indeed otherness, to interrupt.

Two

Communication as Ethics

The encounter with otherness is an experience that puts us to a test: from it
is born the temptation to reduce difference by force, while it may equally
generate the challenge of communication, as a constantly renewed endeavor.
—Alberto Melucci, *The Playing Self*

I n this chapter, I set out to stretch the idea of communication to its
limit. By "limit" I mean the two following senses: the point of
boundary, frontier or separation, and concurrently the point at
which communication might reach an impasse, failure or possibly
breakdown. Thus, instead of approaching the subject matter from
the terra firma of a successful exchange, which, as illustrated in the
previous chapter, characterizes many of the traditional conceptions
of communication, my aim here is to explore the perimeters and
make my way in the opposite direction. I do not, however, intend
to delineate the limit as something that marks the termination or
negation of communication; rather, following Emmanuel Levinas
I propose that the limit of communication is precisely what gives
rise to communication as an ethical event. I want to further suggest

that Levinas's philosophy opens the way for a radical reconceptu-alization of the relationship between communication and ethics, and hence, for a different meaning of the combination "ethical com-munication." Its import is best encompassed in the concept of "interruption." My reading will posit interruption as bearing a spe-cial ethical significance: as a point of exposure and vulnerability upon which the relation with the Other may undergo a profound transformation. What is introduced thereby is a way of thinking about communication beyond essences and ontology, as an ethical involvement whose stakes exceed the successful completion of its operation.

The Common Foundation

In "Platonic Dialogue," Michel Serres proposes the following: "For the moment let us agree that . . . communication is only possible between two persons used to the same . . . forms, trained to code and decode a meaning by using the same key" (1982, 65). Serres's formulation is clear: in order for communication to take place there must be an antecedent background for its operation. Commu-nication is dependent upon an infrastructure constructed prior to the first exchange and the first attempt at making meaning. For Serres, the existence of a common key allows the coding and decoding of meanings. As such, this formula manifests the prototypical ele-ments of many traditional conceptions of communication as either relying on a preestablished order or involving the construction of a transcendent one.

"For the moment," Serres asks, "let us agree." Let us accept that communication is possible between two persons accustomed to the same procedures, to the same forms, exercised "to code and decode a meaning by using the same key" (Serres 1982, 65). In effect, what he asks is to agree before proceeding any further, before reading the rest of the sentence; indeed, before communi-cating. One is asked first to agree on the nature of communication—

and it is, unmistakably, an a priori commonality, accord and rapport—and only then will communication take place. Yet by the time Serres's words are read, the Platonic moment has snuck away and elimination has already been made: dialogue over polylogue, commonality over difference, and meaning over nonsense. Communication has already crystalized into a compatible form. Serres continues: "let us call *noise* the set of . . . phenomena of interference that become obstacles to communication" (ibid., 66). Already having a common goal, Serres's interlocutors now also have a common enemy—noise. Tied together by a mutual interest, they battle against interference and confusion, against something or someone with some stake in interrupting their union. United against such a "parasite," they stand on the same side of communication, on the side of the Same.[1] Serres, both as a communicator and as a formulator of communication, is thus concerned with reducing the phenomenon of communication before it actually takes place. But what if one does not agree with Serres, or for that matter with any definition of communication that forecloses the irreducible difference between self and Other?

The problem with this approach can be stated more generally: it presupposes a common foundation, one that is prior to any communication and might thereby entail disregarding otherness. Under these conditions, communication with the Other, *l'Autrui,* the always already different from the selfsame, is unconceivable. What is intimated by insisting that communication be dependent upon some type of anterior commonality is a situation of "communication before communication": the existence of a primordial connection that underpins and facilitates future exchange and that is predisposed to the occurrence of such an exchange. Such a formulation cannot include anything other than what is already implied within its form and structure. Constituted upon likeness and similitude, it runs the risk of seeing Others as variations of oneself, and at the most extreme, as one's own reflection. Communication understood in this way offers little more than a constant experience of déjà vu.

Approaching Alterity

The question of alterity unsettles all previous speculations on communication for it stretches the idea of relation to where there may be no relation. The Other, insofar as she or he is constituted by her or his fundamental difference, exceeds any commonality with the self. Collapsing the difference between self and Other into a common denominator entails compromising the Other's alterity, his or her radical difference, and ultimately forbids regarding another as an Other. It might seem that with this irreconcilable difference, any attempt at communicating would crumble into the infinite chasm of nothingness. What would then remain of the ideal concord of hearts and minds is the bitter disappointment of a promise that failed to arrive. One is left in one's own solitude, incapable of sharing it with others, an experience that is for a philosopher like Jean-Paul Sartre the essence of modern human existence: alienation, estrangement, being alone-together. Social existence is a sore experience of being with the Other, as Sartre expounds: "he is the concrete pole (though out of reach) of my flight, of the alienation of my possibilities, and of the flow of the world toward another world which is *the same* world and yet lacks all communication with it" (1969, 360). When being with Others, one is locked in an invisible room; one lives in a world populated with Others who cannot understand and share one's loneliness. In that state of affairs, society is a collection of beings surrounded by nothingness, and the rudimentary experience of a social being is of incommunicability. The way the Other unavoidably affects me is through his or her look: the Other's look is inhibiting, objectifying, making me a thing among other things. This petrifying look is what "awakens" me to myself, provoking me to conjure myself up against the Other. In such a world, Sartre states, hell is other people.

At first glance, it may appear that Sartre's position has nothing in common with that of Serres, or more generally, that the conception describing the social world as wretched by alienating otherness is in strict contrast to the one insisting that communication is indeed possible insofar as there is prior grounds of commonality. Nevertheless, what these two views do have in common, paradoxically perhaps, is their notion of communication: both posit communication as an event of synthesis, as a successful sharing and imparting of ideas, knowledge, or emotions. Only that for an existentialist like Sartre such communication can never happen and therefore one is doomed to a lonely existence encapsulated within one's own ontological boundaries, whereas according to Serres's neo-Socratic view, the wires of communication are already in place and allow, though with a constant effort, a productive exchange. For the first, ideal communication is impossible by the very nature of existence; for the latter, the ideal might be lost but is still recoverable.

The philosophy of Emmanuel Levinas, however, offers a radically different way to approach communication. It is precisely in the irreconcilable difference of alterity that Levinas founds the fundamental relationship with the Other. The relation to the Other qua Other is for Levinas the very beginning of, and the ultimate condition for, communication:

> The theme of solitude, of the basic incommunicability of the person, appears in modern thought and literature as the fundamental obstacle to universal brotherhood. The pathos of socialism crumbles against the eternal Bastille in which each of us remains his or her captive, and in which we find ourselves when the celebration is over, the torches gone out and the crowd drawn back. The despair of impossible communication . . . marks the limit of all pity, all generosity, all love. . . . But if communication thus bears the sign of failure or inauthenticity, it is because it is sought in fusion. One sets out from the idea that duality should be transformed into unity—that the social relation should end in communion. . . . The failure of communication is the failure of knowledge. One does not see that the success of knowledge would in fact destroy the nearness, the proximity of the Other. (*PN,* 103–4)

Levinas attempts to disassociate communication from essence or telos and distinguish the event of encountering the Other from any subsequent resolution of differences. By so doing, he questions the assumption that communication should end in union and that social relation should conclude in consensus. Yet he also points out that "failure" of communication is in fact failure of knowledge, and that once such communication—that is, the exchange of knowledge—is achieved, what is compromised is the nearness of the Other person, "the proximity of the Other." In other words, according to Levinas, the success of communication as a complete relaying of one mind to the Other is effectively the elimination of a fundamental relation to the Other. Its accomplishment results in the subjugation of what seems to be another relationship, one that is anterior to the moment of exchange but does not involve any a priori commonality: a relation without relation. How is that possible?

Ethics before Ontology

Levinas's thought might be prefaced as an attempt to reintroduce the Other into modern Western philosophy. According to Levinas, Western philosophy has traditionally approached phenomena from an ontological position, seeking to establish the structure of reality by the exploration of "what is." Ontological exploration, as an examination into the character of phenomena, into their nature, essence and existence, is committed first and foremost to setting up an account regarding the status of "being," delimiting the boundaries between presence and absence, being and nonbeing, between "what is" and "what is not." In Western philosophy and social thought, ontology is first philosophy. Furthermore, Levinas's critique contends that the primary site from which such explorations were launched was the self, and Western philosophy might then be described as an investigation into the self and of the world in terms of the self. By basing its explorations in the self (its existence, nature, interests, and the like) as the primary frame of reference, Western philosophy has essentially produced an elaborate theory of the selfsame, or "egology." This is not to say that the relationship between self and Other(s) was neglected or underplayed in modern social thought, rather, that such discussions followed and were fixed within a metaphysical schema determining the ontological nature of being. Hence, discussions of the characteristics of a desirable social existence came consequent to the discussions of the nature of reality. As the theories of Hobbes, Locke, Rousseau (and in different ways also those of Durkheim, Freud and Marx) show, determining the parameters of human nature as essentially good, bad, aggressive, tolerant, rational, and so on, was necessary for illustrating the problems of the social as well as for conceiving possible solutions. As a result, ethics has traditionally been an addendum to a philosophical account—the "what ought" was derived from the "what is."

Levinas's contention is radical: ethics is not a secondary level of knowledge, nor is it an outcome of a certain social structure. Levinas regards ethics as first philosophy:

> The irreducible and ultimate experience of relationship appears to me in fact to be elsewhere: not in synthesis, but in the face to face of humans, in sociality, in its moral signification. But it must be understood that morality comes not as a secondary layer . . . morality has an independent and preliminary range. First philosophy is an ethics. (*EI,* 77)

The critique of ontology brings Levinas to conceive of the relation to the Other "otherwise than being" and to found it "beyond essence." Ethics, as an involvement with that which escapes definition and incorporation but still confronts, is irreducible to ontology: it does not have an essence. Its "essence" is precisely to unsettle essences, and its "identity" is not to have an identity, to undo identities (Cohen, introduction to *EI,* 10). Concern for the Other is not a product of rational thought or calculation, nor is it a result of an agreement enforced by social institutions. Concern for the Other is the very basis of subjectivity. The involvement with an irreconcilable otherness is preontological and prior to any social contract since the experience of alterity is the most fundamental experience of subjectivity. Subjectivity is subjection to the Other inasmuch as it is an exposure and openness to otherness: "subjectivity is vulnerability, is sensibility" (*OB,* 54). In this sense, the self might be described as fissured by the Other "despite itself," always already in relation to the Other, an unthematizable relation, which comes to pass by awakening the self's sensibility.

To approach the idea differently, Levinas says that the question "Am I my brother's keeper?" has meaning only if one "has already supposed that the ego is concerned only with itself, is only a concern for itself" (*OB,* 117). Cain's complaint therefore comes out entirely from ontology—I am here, the Other is there, and I am not obligated in any way. But what is predetermined here is that the self is a self-serving, self-sufficient, unitary entity, one that is involved primarily with itself and only later with Others. The self understood in that way is identification in the strong sense: its identity as self-identity is established before entering any relationship. Conversely, Levinas, in a Copernican-like move, reverses the conception of sociality: subjectivity is ethically heteronomous; it is the locus where the Other touches and makes contact. The social is before the ontological—the relation to the Other as concern, as sociality, as ethics itself, is before and beyond ontology.

Responsibility and/as Response-ability

For Levinas, concern for the Other is expressed in responsibility for the Other. The meaning of "responsibility," however, is quite different from the way it is usually understood. It does not signify an obligation that can be accounted for ex post facto, nor liability to one's deeds or misdeeds in relation to a social or legal code. Responsibility here means exceeding rather than following social norms. Levinas sets forth responsibility as the elemental structure of subjectivity understood as vulnerability, sensitivity and sensibility. It is what marks out the contours of subjectivity, what animates the fibers of one's self by undergoing the Other: "the very node of the subjective is knotted in ethics understood as responsibility" (*EI,* 95). Responsibility does not correspond with universal rules or duties: as Zygmunt Bauman notes, duties tend to make humans alike whereas responsibility is what makes them into individuals (1993, 54). Different people might indeed respond differently in the same situations, but this is precisely what makes each individual unique—the way one responds is what distinguishes one from another. In opposition to Sartre, for whom encountering the Other entails the conjuring up of the self *against* the Other, for Levinas such conjuring up is *for* the Other.[2] Before and beneath being with-the-Other there is the ethical relation of being for-the-Other.

The responsibility Levinas speaks of is both *for* and *to* the Other: for the Other's fate, and to his or her address.[3] Responsibility is thereby repersonalized and reclaimed into the living relation between self and Other. A similar idea was expressed by Martin Buber: "The idea of responsibility is to be brought back from the province of specialized ethics, of an 'ought' that swings free in the air, into that of lived life. Genuine responsibility exists only where there is real responding" (1955, 16). However, Levinas's version of ethical relation is more radical than Buber's: while acknowledging his appreciation to Buber's philosophy of dialogue, Levinas nevertheless criticizes the reciprocity and equality of the I-Thou.[4] For Levinas, the Other comes from up high—the Other is teacher before partner. There is no symmetry in being responsible, that is, in being answerable and addressable. Since responsibility as response-ability is the very beginning of subjectivity, I am always already answerable to the Other's call, always already approachable, open, predisposed toward the Other. Such responsibility, nevertheless, has no source: it is, as Maurice Blanchot purports, an "innocent guilt" (*WD,* 22). Withdrawing me from my order—"perhaps from all orders and from order itself"—my responsibility separates me from myself, "from the 'me' that is mastery and power, from the free, speaking subject" (*WD*, 25). Responsibility as being-for-the-Other thus constitutes the primordial cradle of sociality.

Proximity of the Face

When approaching and addressing, the Other appears as a face. For Levinas, the face of the Other is more than a mere portrait or physiognomy—it is the elemental manifestation confronting and unsettling the self; it is the forefront of the Other's otherness. The face exceeds the idea of the Other in the self by putting forth a call. The Other, in coming to me as a face and addressing me, cuts all threads connecting him or her to a context or a background in which she or he may appear. As Levinas writes, "The face is signification, and signification without context . . . the Other, in the rectitude of his face, is not a character within a context" (*EI*, 86). The face transcends the representation of the Other; it signifies signification itself and expresses pure expression.[5]

The face's signature consists in "making an entry" (*TO*, 351), emerging out from the whole in which it is placed; the face's countenance is of epiphany. It escapes any grasp and defies its containment into an idea or a theme: "The face resists possession, resists my powers" (*TI*, 197). However, such resistance is not a manifestation of violence. The face is not a source of influence presenting a threat of a sanction or promising an award; it is, rather, a destitute authority—"The face is not a force. It is an authority. Authority is often without force" (*PM*, 169). The "power" of the face, so to speak, is in its powerlessness, the call the face puts forth affects me precisely because of the Other's weakness. The frailty of the face is paradoxically the source of its command: its address is what exposes my primordial responsibility toward the Other. This is why the Other, who is the one to whom I am answerable and responsible, is also the only being I can kill, or might want to kill. The face does not protect the Other from aggression, but in its nakedness it expresses: "thou shall not commit murder" (*TI*, 199).

It forbids what it cannot guarantee, thereby exposing the asymmetry in the relation between self and Other.

The face ruptures the framework in which it is placed by speaking, addressing, questioning, demanding: "Face and discourse are tied," says Levinas. "The face speaks. It speaks, it is in this that it renders possible and begins all discourse" (*EI,* 87). In contrast to the structuralist equivoque "language speaks," Levinas contends that the only thing that can speak is the face. The face questions me, causes me not to be at home with myself, evoking my preontological responsibility. Thus, one does not merely gaze at the face, one answers to the face—the response-ability to and for the Other as face is what inspires language. Yet an address might also be silent: "the beginning of language is in the face. In a certain way, in its silence, it calls you" (*PM,* 169). It is not what the face says that provokes my response—it is the very fact of its address, the moment when the Other touches by signifying, by making an impression, even if the address is silent or incomprehensible.

When walking in the street one may encounter a homeless person. One is confronted with a demand even if nothing had been said—the homeless person's face implores: he or she needs money, clothes, food. At the instant one's look meets the look of the homeless person, one feels accused, is disturbed without knowing why; one may feel for a brief moment a hostage of a person who is powerless but still has a hold. One then faces a question: what should I do now? From here on something else takes control—calculation and speculation, decision making: Should I give out money? Should I walk away? It is possible to rationalize why not to give any help, to accuse the homeless person for his or her own fate, or even to opt to look away, consciously not seeing. Yet for a fleeting moment one has already been affected, one has already lost oneself and subsequently attempts to regain one's senses. The Other has already touched, seeped in, before one can come to grips with the situation. "Consciousness," understood as self-consciousness, as selfness, "is always late for the rendezvous with the neighbor" (*LP,* 119).[6]

The commitment to the Other, evoked by his or her address, in the call that has reached me "despite myself," enacts my responsibility even if I decide not to respond, for not responding may also be a kind of response. The only way, then, to eschew this grueling weight of responsibility is by means of breaking off, disconnecting or dissociating. In order to avoid encountering the Other face-to-face, one may resort to the "art of mismeeting": crossing the street, seeing without looking, relegating to the background (Bauman 1993, 154). One works against an intangible force (or more precisely, a powerless force) that draws one out of oneself, toward the Other. Levinas calls this realm in which responsibility commands "proximity."

Proximity does not necessarily mean physical nearness. It does not refer to spatial parameters of distance, nor does it necessarily denote closeness in terms of time and space (although it may also include that). It also does not mean the annihilation of separation to the point of merger or symbiosis. The proximity of the Other, of the face, is drawing near and making near. In proximity, one is exposed, vulnerable, sensitive to the Other who appears as a face. Proximity is the realm wherein one can be affected by the Other. As Levinas writes,

> The relationship of proximity cannot be reduced to any modality of distance or geometrical contiguity, nor to the simple "representation" of a neighbor; it is already an assignation, an extremely urgent assignation—an obligation, anachronously prior to any commitment. This anteriority is "older" than the a priori. This formula expresses a way of being affected which can in no way be invested by spontaneity: the subject is affected without the source of the affection becoming a theme of representation. (*OB,* 100–101)

Proximity is not diametrically opposed to a remoteness to be diminished or overcome; rather, it consists in the extension of one's sensibility, in further exposure to the Other. Increasing knowledge, familiarity, or even understanding, cannot suppress such a "distance"—quite the contrary: this would invariably involve the replacing of the Other with a theme and the recontextualization of the face within a framework. Herein lies the paradoxical realization that the more informed one is of the Other, the less one is response-able for the Other. In every mode of knowledge, familiarity and comprehension, Levinas contends, there is the fact of making some-thing one's own: comprehension involves "the fact of taking [*pren-dre*] and of comprehending [*comprendre*], that is, the fact of englobing, of appropriating. But there is something which remains outside, and that is alterity" (*PM,* 170). Approaching the Other from the framework of knowledge, as an object of intrigue, is effec-tively opting out from the realm of proximity. The kind of proxim-ity proposed by Levinas involves the suppression of the distance opened when one steps back to reflect and evaluate, the suppression of "critical-distance": "Proximity as a suppression of distance sup-presses the distance of consciousness of . . . The neighbor excludes himself from the thought that seeks him, and this exclusion has a positive side to it: my exposure to him" (*OB,* 89). Neither co-existence nor co-presence, proximity is where the face of the Other incises through and ruptures, opening up a realm of disturbance and "restlessness" (*LP,* 121). It therefore seems that the more proximate the Other, the more unique he or she appears to be: in proximity dif-ferences touch without merging. Proximity is closeness that reifies difference.

Language and the Other

The relation to the Other as described thus far appears to be carry-ing a residue from an immemorable past. Portrayed as preontolog-ical, prior to any cognizant choice, before one's freedom to be oneself, it emanates from a past that cannot be rediscovered or accounted for, a past that was never a present: "The relationship with exteriority is 'prior' to the act that would effect it" (*OB,* 101). Yet not only am I affected "despite myself" by an immemorable past, but that past, which is prior to any a priori, comes back to haunt the present. My responsibility for the Other is not a conscious choice I made, nor is it an unconscious involvement understood in a psychoanalytic sense.[7] It is, rather, a responsibility expressing itself by interrupting self-consciousness, as if reminding me of a commitment I have never made but which is still incumbent upon me. In this respect, Levinas designates the relation to the Other as "an-archical": irreducible to knowledge and perception, to a common space or time, the difference of the Other cannot be introduced into a co-temporal relationship. Incommensurable with the here-and-now, with the present, the passing of the Other is a disturbance of the present; inassimilable in the present, "it is always 'already in the past' behind which the present delays, over and beyond the 'now' which this exteriority disturbs or obsesses" (*OB,* 100). The appearance of the Other is signified anarchically by passing through, by what cannot be carried into the present or re-presented. Thus, the Other's intrusion cannot be represented or thematized within a system of signification, within language. The Other would have to find expression otherwise.

The Said and the Saying

For Levinas, ethical language signifies through the difference between the Said (*le Dit*) and the Saying (*le Dire*). The Said is the material of language. It allows the imparting of information, knowledge and meaning from one to another by means of representation. The Said upholds the correlation between a thing and the thought of that thing—signifier, signified and referent—allowing for naming and designating of both objects and subjects in language. As Levinas writes, "Language qua said can then be conceived as a system of nouns identifying entities, and then as a system of signs doubling up the beings, designating substances, events and relations by substantives or other parts of speech derived from substantives, designating identities—in sum, *designating*" (*OB,* 40). The Said is encapsulated in the content conveyed, in the themes that are given and in the meanings assigned to them prior to and through the exchange. Language as the Said brings the world into language and language into the world by eliminating the difference between things and words—the Said reconciles lexis and universe. Its primary manifestation is in the Greek notion of logos: in a coherent discourse of reason. The Said binds language and ontology as "The birthplace of ontology is in the said" (*OB,* 42).

The work of the Said is accomplished in identification. Language as a system of nouns allows naming and identifying phenomena according to the formula: "A is B." The Said assembles words as units of identification and produces statements permitting classification: "the word identifies 'this as that,' states the identity of the same in the diverse" (*OB,* 35). Language as the Said, as words assembled in sentences in speech and writing, circumscribes a sphere of relative identity within infinite difference. Its work is in thematizing the world, in placing entities within the basic structure of "A is B," "this as that," "the assembling of terms united in a system" (*OB,* 78). This quality of collecting things into language, of synchronization, thematization and representation is not derived from the essences of things, neither from A nor from B. It is, rather, in the correlative, in the *is.* "A is B" collapses the world into ontology, rendering things present to each other, as grounds for comparison and similarity, as equally approachable and representable. The work of the sentence is in thematizing, using words as identical units, as units of identification. This is also true for this very sentence.

However, language is not reducible to the Said, to the content conveyed. Levinas points to a detail curiously omitted from many modern conventions of language and communication: that language also bears the fact of giving signs to someone, of addressing and being addressed, of *saying* the Said. The Saying expresses the relation to the one being spoken to beyond what is stated in the logos: "Beyond the thematization of the Said, and of the content stated in the proposition, [the Saying] signifies as a modality of the approach to the other person" (*OS,* 142). Levinas insists that language is essentially an expression of relation before it is a vehicle for the transmission of ideas. Language as the Saying discloses itself as a manifestation of responsibility prior to taking the form of "the *truth-that-unites*" (*OS,* 142). Language is thus for-the-Other and only later circumscribed as an independent phenomenon of sign exchange.[8] Language qua Saying is an expression of relation, of drawing close to the Other, of proposing a proposition to the Other.

Whereas the Said is characterized by representation, the Saying is characterized by signification. The Saying "touches" before it offers knowledge, it provokes before it makes sense, it makes contact before meaning, it is a modality of approach before thematization. To relate to things solely on the level of the Said is to reduce the Other to a theme and to dissociate language from its elementary stratum as relational: "Language as *saying* is an ethical openness to the Other; as that which is *said*—reduced to a fixed identity or synchronized presence—it is an ontological closure to the Other" (Levinas 1995, 194). Language as Saying signifies signification itself. The Saying is an expression of the preontological weight of responsibility that cannot be recollected into the present, an *anarchic* relation that cannot appear in whole in the Said but is still involved in its signification: "The responsibility for another is precisely a saying prior to anything said" (*OB,* 43). The Saying, as the signification of an unrepresentable relation, is therefore what grounds the possibility for the representation materialized in the Said.

Using a linguistic metaphor, Levinas describes the Said as a "noun": naming, designating, identifying. Complementing the metaphor, Levinas describes the Saying as a "verb": signifying language as a modality of response-ability, as a process of "languaging." In speaking or writing, one is addressing one's words— and oneself—to the Other and thereby putting oneself in the position of a potential addressee, exposed to the Other's questioning. Through language, I am exposed to the Other's teaching, to a discourse bringing me more than I could already contain. Writing and speaking—communicating—is dissimulation of the "I" both as a unitary subject and as a linguistic construct. "There is *nothing* that is named *I*," argues Levinas (*OB*, 56). "I" is a linguistic index signifying the one who speaks or writes and therefore signifies everybody who participates, in one way or another, in language; "I" denotes nothing save the transitory position of the narrator. This "I" is not a pure Said since the meaning ascribed to it is not pre-given in language but always determined by its use. Put differently, the semantic meaning of "I" is purely pragmatic.[9]

Defying conversion into a noun and the Said, "I" already bears the elementary relational mark of language. Once a speaker or writer states "I," what is effectively stated is an expression of response-ability taken by occupying the position of a discourse initiator. Speaking and writing may then imply a responsible involvement by putting oneself on the line and inviting responses and questions. Thus, in addressing the Other, in Saying, I do not merely emit signs but also express vulnerability to the point of making myself an expressive sign. "I" am/is a sign of responsibility, "For it is a sign given of this giving of signs, the exposure of oneself to another, in proximity and in sincerity" (*OB*, 56).

In proposing the notion of the Saying, Levinas draws attention to a relation that cannot be thematized by language but nevertheless transpires through language:

> Saying is communication, to be sure, but as a condition for all communication, as exposure. Communication is not reducible to the phenomenon of truth and the manifestation of truth conceived as a combination of psychological elements: thought in an ego—will or intention to make this thought pass into another ego—message by a sign designating this thought—perception of the sign by another ego—deciphering of the sign. The elements of this mosaic are already in place in the antecedent exposure of the ego to the other, the non-indifference to another, which is not a simple "intention to

address a message." The ethical sense of such an exposure to another, which the intention of making signs, and even the signify-ingness of signs, presuppose, is now visible. The plot of proximity and communication is not a modality of cognition. The unblocking of communication, irreducible to the circulation of communication which presupposes it, is accomplished in saying. It is not due to the contents that are inscribed in the said and transmitted to the interpretation and decoding done by the other. It is in the risky uncovering of oneself, in sincerity, the breaking up of inwardness and the abandon of all shelter, exposure to traumas, vulnerability. (*OB*, 48)

Communication is not reducible to the process of transmitting messages from one ego to another as a serial process, from thought in ego, through transmission and reception of signs, receptions by another, to deciphering and reconstructing original meaning. This process, which corresponds with many traditional conceptualizations of communication, is completely subsumed in the Said. But not only the mechanistic models of communication are criticized here, but also other conceptions circumscribing communication as the "manifestation of truth" (either subjective or objective) or reducing it to the "intention to address a message." It would be safe to say that most of the traditional conceptions of communication, including those analyzed in the previous chapter, fall under these rubrics, as they are largely invested and involved in the study of communication as the Said. Levinas puts forward the idea that communication is not only the process of giving signs; its effect transcends its content, for communication is always for someone and therefore already involves an unarticulated expression of relation. Thus, for Levinas, communication is ultimately irreducible to its contents.

An Intricate Relationship

The Said and the Saying reveal the different dimensions of language but the two do not comprise a conceptual dichotomy identical, for instance, to the *langue* and *parole* of Saussure (1993). Although the Said may correspond with the predetermined linguistic aspect of language characterizing *langue,* and the Saying may be analogous to the participatory element of language, to *parole,* the two couplets are comparable only to this extent. The main difference lies in that, for Levinas, the relationship between the Said and the Saying is anything but structural. Whereas, for Saussure, *langue* is the linguistic basis of language, for Levinas the basis lies in the preoriginal relation expressed in the Saying. But this relation, which gives rise to the Said, is not exhaustible in the meanings it conveys.

The Said and the Saying are entwined in language; the Saying addresses the Said to another and the Said in itself is a linguistic manifestation of that relation. Yet the Saying is not synchronous to the Said in language but antecedent to the "verbal signs it conjugates, to the linguistic systems and the semantic glimmerings" (*OB,* 5). The proximity expressed in the Saying inspires the Said but does not inhabit it, for the only thing the Said cannot thematize is the Other who is addressed. And yet, every Said resonates the antecedent address of the Saying, an "already said" (*déjà dit*), that can be heard only through a Said. It seems that the reduction of the Saying to logos is essential to the articulation of that very Saying. This is the toll of every articulated expression: "The correlation of the saying and the said, that is, the subordination of the saying to the said, to the linguistic system and to ontology, is the price that manifestation demands" (*OB,* 6). Language thereby allows, although not without a certain betrayal, the manifestation of responsibility. In "carrying" the Saying, the Said nonetheless betrays the preoriginal Saying animating it.

This betrayal, however, does not take place seamlessly. Language permits complex thematization, including this very attempt to describe the indescribable and to say the unsayable encompassed in the Saying. Still, the transcendence of the Saying, which is compromised in the Said, leaves its imprint on what has been said: "The plot of saying that is absorbed in the said is not exhausted in this manifestation. It imprints its trace on the thematization itself" (*OB,* 46–47). The Saying leaves its *traces* on the Said; it does not obliterate the Said nor does it contradict its assertion. This relationship cannot be captured under the rubrics of action-reaction or cause and effect; it is much subtler. A trace comes to pass as an incision, fissure or lapse in the Said. It is a "presence of that which properly speaking has never been there, of what is always past" (*TO,* 358). Hence, it cannot be captured as such, transferred into the Said, or made manifest in any straightforward manner. Neither presence nor absence, a trace causes interruption; it intervenes in the present by leaving an unrepresentable imprint upon the discourse of the Said.

The concept of the trace, which is perhaps one of the more obscure ideas in Levinas's work, might find manifestation in one of the concepts analyzed above: the face. As above, the face of the Other signifies behind the person's portrait or persona (also "mask" in Greek): "The beyond from which a face comes signifies as a trace" (*TO, 355*). Like the face, the trace's intervention is not violent—it does not throw the logos into disarray; instead, it opens ruptures through which the Saying may arise. This rupture in the logos is not the beginning of irrationalism but what makes possible every logos and every rationalism (compare Derrida, *VM,* 97–98). It thus follows that a lack of traces may call for further scrutiny: since the Said can never completely consume the Saying, the disappearance of traces can mean effacement or denial. And it is precisely here that Levinas sees the importance of contemporary philosophy: not in thematizing the world but in exposing the traces, or the lack thereof, left on the surface of Western philosophy, revealing thereby, as Jacques Derrida deduces, "that what was taken for its solidity is its rigidity" (*VM,* 90).

Levinas mentions three main producers of the discourse of the Said: the State, medicine and philosophy. These are probably as metaphorical as they are concrete, but the intuition behind this postulation is to allude to the apparatuses that exercise their power by rendering every discourse logical and reparable by logic whenever ruptured. The rule of reason is not derived from the truthfulness or internal coherence of the discourse produced but rather from the power vested in the various apparatuses of the State, medicine and philosophy (as the discourse of knowledge), which ensures the universality of the discourse of the Said while repressing the Saying. Nothing can interrupt this discourse: every contention or interruption would be immediately incorporated within its logic, effectively allowing for its resumption. Hence, the one who fails to yield to that logic "is threatened with prison or the asylum or undergoes the prestige of the master and the medication of the doctor" (*OB*, 170). Rendering every discourse a discourse of the Said is, therefore, a violent act. Although denied, the mark of interruption is still maintained to a certain extent in the discourse endeavoring suppression, despite itself. The "knots" made in the discourse attempting to thematize the interruption, in a "dialogue delayed by silences, failure or delirium" (*OB*, 170), may then be taken themselves as traces of traces.

In sum, the Said and the Saying share an intricate relationship. Whereas the Said seeks closure, the Saying remains open-ended, offered to the Other. In attempting to bring the world into language, the Said moves in Ulyssean circles: it sets out only to return to its origin, to the self. The Saying, conversely, sets out on a journey without return; like Abraham, it is forbidden from ever coming back to its place of origin. But the Said and the Saying are tied, comprising the irreducible nature of communication. The Said emanates from the Saying, which communicates nothing but the desire to communicate. Yet the Said is indispensable because it performs an ancillary function: in thematizing, it lets the Saying leave its traces, even if these traces become immediately thematized. The Saying needs the Said in order to realize its signification; it requires a Said in order to mark itself as its "beyond" (Ziarek 1989, 231). The Saying inflects the Said and errs in it.[10] The Said and the Saying are, then, interdependent: the Saying can appear only as a certain "betrayal" in itself, that is, through the Said. However, the Saying can never be totally engulfed in the Said: it remains beyond by both stimulating the Said and rupturing it.

Ethical Language

There are moments when the Said falls short, fails, or ceases altogether to correlate words meaningfully. In such moments the Saying is exposed, separated from the Said. "One is called to the deathbed of a parent, and one, facing her, does not know what to say. Yet one has to say something" (Lingis 1994, 107). One seems to be lost for words but still feels obligated to say something: "It will be all right," while reflecting on the meaninglessness of what has been said, and on the incapacity of words to offer solace when most needed. One is at the limit of the power of language, at the limit of the Said. In moments like this, the rift between the Said and the Saying opens up. The Said collapses precisely when there is still so much to be said.

If the relation to the Other is not reducible to and thematizable in the Said, then, how can one write, speak and philosophize about it? Furthermore, if Levinas is "right" in his analysis, does it not mean that he is already "wrong," that the unthematizable is already thematized and the unrepresentable is already represented within his writing?[11] How can he write (and speak, lecture, comment) about ethical language without falling into the same trap he warns us against, the trap of the selfsame? Is it possible to write about the Saying while using the Said? Levinas's language—the way in which he writes and expresses his ideas—may then be a "case study" for his general analysis and for the intricate relationship between the Said and the Saying.

One's first impression when reading Levinas may be of disorientation. His writing is convoluted, involving words that appear to be familiar but seem to denote something different from the way they are usually understood. The terms "responsibility," "proximity," "sensitivity," "exposure" and "openness" all appear frequently in his texts but do not quite mean one thing in particular; they are used to set out on an elliptical path describing the relation to the Other. The relation itself cannot be conceptualized, inscribed, or encompassed in a theme, only approximated. Nevertheless, the exploration itself takes place within the Said while using propositions that may resonate with ontological language; after all, Levinas, like anyone who speaks or writes, uses the word "is." For instance, when describing the Saying as exposure to the Other, he writes: "The subjectivity of a subject is vulnerability, exposure to affection, sensibility, a passivity more passive still than any passivity." (*OB,* 50). Later, he states: "The overemphasis of openness is responsibility for the other to the point of substitution, where the for-the-other proper to disclosure, to monstration to the other, turns into the for-the-other proper to responsibility. This is the thesis of the present work" (*OB,* 119). Still later: "Proximity, difference which is non-indifference, is responsibility. It is a response without a question, the immediacy of peace that is incumbent on me. It is the signification of signs. It is the humanity of man not understood on the basis of transcendental subjectivity. It is the passivity of exposure" (*OB,* 139). What *is,* then, subjectivity, proximity and responsibility? What *is* the thesis of his work?

Levinas's writing does not define, delimit or circumscribe its concepts; instead, it sprawls, swerves and spreads outward centrifugally. Responsibility is proximity is sensitivity is openness is exposure, and so forth. But this is not a mere repetition, as the itinerary of the sentence does not return on its tracks in order to re-engrave what was already said. Levinas's elliptical phrasings run close to each other but never converge. There is always a certain difference between them, a difference that cannot be described or inscribed independently, yet is made manifest through the gaps opened between the phrases. Difference is neither presence nor absence, neither "is" nor "is-not" (here the Said already breaks down), but comes to pass as a disruption of such dichotomies. It emerges from the fissures of the Said as an *anarchic* trace that cannot be re-presented. Thus, at a certain moment it seems that the "is" erodes to the point that it could be replaced by "as": responsibility as proximity as sensitivity as openness as exposure, and so on. This textual proximity, which is not a simple juxtaposition of statements, appears to be interrupting itself, its stability and order. Its work is not contradictory or dialectical: it unsettles, disturbs order "without troubling it seriously" (Levinas 1987, 66).

A similar recurrence takes place on a larger scale in Levinas's key text *Otherwise Than Being, or Beyond Essence,* which is the main philosophical source of this work. The itineraries charted across its pages engage with the issues of proximity, sensitivity, subjectivity and Saying from different angles, re-saying (*redire*) the Said each time differently. Jacques Derrida describes such writing with respect to Levinas's earlier work (yet only at "its decisive moments") as moving along the cracks opened up in the Said and revealing the "wounding of language" (*VM,* 90). Jean-François Lyotard adds that "perhaps Levinas's writing is the testimony of the fracture, of the opening onto that other who in the reader sends a request to Levinas, of a responsibility before that messenger who is the reader" (1988, 113). Enticing the Saying from the Said discloses the author and removes him or her from their author-ity so as to welcome the Other. It therefore seems that Levinas employs language otherwise: his writing is not exclusively a framework of knowledge as it is also an approach, a drawing near, an expression of a heightened sensitivity to what cannot be included within it, that is, the one who is addressed. He proposes his text to the reader, to the absolutely Other, as an offering: a Saying, slightly betrayed, entwined in a Said.

Dislocating Communication

Emmanuel Levinas's thought, writes Derrida, "summons us to a dislocation of the Greek logos, to a dislocation of our identity, and perhaps of identity in general; it summons us to depart from the

Greek site and perhaps from every site in general, and to move toward what is no longer a source or a site" (*VM,* 82). The philosophy of the Other, of *hors sujet,* invites a reexamination of the traditional site of language—the logos and the Said—and speculation on a way of approaching the Other while moving away from any foundation. The ethical relation to the Other lies in the proximity that unsettles order, allowing the face to appear and question. Moving toward the Other implies the questioning of oneself and being questioned by the Other, possible only when departing from the security of either conformity or individualism. It means, in a word, dislocation.

Dislocation does not imply moving to an alternative site from which the relation to the Other could be relaunched—dislocation is not relocation. Instead, it is the unsettling of one's own location and of a location in general. The self approached by the Other "does not posit itself, possessing itself and recognizing itself; it is consumed and delivered over, dis-locates itself, loses its place" (*OB,* 138). The relation to the Other as portrayed by Levinas is utopian in the original sense of the word: a relation of nonplace, a "u-topian" relation, one that is displaced and displacing and therefore always out-of-place. Being put in question by the Other is thus both dis-location and dislocation: the renouncing of any foundation and the interruption of every preestablished procedure or norm. In order to encounter the Other as a face, in proximity and exposure, one must abandon all alibis given by the State, law or religion, or acquired through knowledge and experience. Encountering the Other face-to-face requires the dislocation (in both senses) of oneself and of the means by which one approaches the Other.

This, however, does not amount to advocating nihilism. Dislocating the relation to the Other does not imply abolishing stability or rigidity merely for the sake of destruction. Its purpose is, rather, to expose the responsibility for the Other that underlies sociality but which might be stifled by the weight brought about by organization and routinization in social relations. This philosophy, as Derrida notes, calls for the dislocation of the modes of language that appropriate and thematize the relation to the Other, thus producing an uninterrupted discourse—that is, a Said divorced from Saying. Such is a logocentric discourse reducing the Saying to the Said while attempting to disqualify and delegitimize the Saying. In this sense, positing language exclusively as the Said is an exertion of violence in a way that denies that very act. Herein lies a most provocative insight: that what sustains the coherence and consistency of the discourse of the Said is precisely the suppression of the trace of the Saying. And this insight, fundamentally, sets the groundwork for recasting the relation between ethics and communication, for it could now be shown that the success of the Said may in fact be connected to the repression of the Saying; or, alternatively, that the folding of the Said may not necessarily mark the end of communication as empathic contact but rather its beginning, a different beginning to be sure, which calls upon the preoriginal configuration of communication in the Saying.

And yet, does the preoriginal Saying, which is prior to the emergence of language qua the Said, mean that some form of communication had already taken place before the Said? Is the Saying another modality of "communication before communication" characterizing many of the traditional concepts of communication? How can communication be prior to the content proposed without already establishing a common foundation?

Communication as Contact

According to one Jewish custom, when a young child starts learning the Hebrew alphabet, honey is dripped on the letters and the child is then allowed to lick it from the letters, so that he will always associate the letters of Torah with sweetness. The young child is initiated into language not through aural or visual experience but through contact, and a most palpable one. The words of the Torah are therefore not only sacred and wise, they are also sweet; and the letters of language do not only have shape and sound, they also have taste, smell and texture. Before knowing the form of the letters, let alone of the actual words, the child undergoes language in a most tactile way. What is perhaps intimated by this custom is that language is not only the content it holds. Language, words and letters, are felt before becoming instrumental, and they are palpable and sensual before being submitted to an abstract structure. Languages touches, both tangibly and metaphorically.

In addressing oneself to the Other, one does not only use language to deliver information: language is for a speaker or a writer a means of signification. Language is first and foremost a way of approaching and addressing someone, and only later a linguistic structure that outlasts any particular address. Language is a means of signification before it is a means of thematization, or better, it signifies through (and despite) thematization. The Saying, still entwined in the Said, impresses before it makes sense, it affects before it effects. Language is a manifestation of a relationship with a singularity that is not thematized in language but is still approachable through language. By addressing something to someone, speech and text signify the very act of signification, of Saying: "The first word says the saying itself. It does not yet designate beings, does not fix themes and does not mean to identify anything" (*LP,* 125). Before making sense, the first word makes contact, and once addressed, one is touched by the Other before one comprehends the message—an apprehension that precedes and enacts comprehension.

For Levinas, touch is the most fundamental sensation of the relationship with that which surrounds. Like language, the sensory is also irreducible to the information it extricates from the world: "The visible caresses the eye. One sees and one hears like one touches" (*LP,* 118). The eye and the ear may indeed objectify what is sensed, but this operation is preceded by an immediate experience of "touch." By describing subjectivity as sensitivity and exposedness, Levinas effectively posits the sense of touch as the elemental experience of the outside. Touch is the elementary sense, the arch-sense or metasense, and in that respect all other senses operate first as a skin touched by light, sound, scent or savor, and only later as distinct sensory organs. Skin, as the meta-sensory organ of the body, is not only protective of an organism but is also the surface of contamination and exposure, of susceptibility itself. Sensory experience transcends the data attained by the senses, as it also constitutes the ability to be affected by and derive pleasure from the outside. For Levinas the sensory experience is positive and nourishing: the eye is caressed by the visible, the ear by the audible, the skin, the mouth and the nose are immersed in various sensations consuming the world.[12] Yet the fact that one can derive pleasure through the senses is precisely what exposes and makes one vulnerable and dependable. The sensitivity that animates subjectivity and provides *jouissance* is also what allows one to be approached, touched and questioned by the Other.

Contact is therefore the elemental relation, the foundationless foundation of ethical relationship. Language now appears also to make contact and touch in a similar manner:

> [This study] has conceived together language and contact, in analyzing contact outside the "information" it can gather on the surface of beings, in analyzing language independently of the coherence and truth of the information transmitted, in grasping in them the event of *proximity. . . .*
>
> The contact in which I approach the neighbor is not a manifestation or a knowledge, but the ethical event of communication which is presupposed by every transmission of messages, which establishes the universality in which words and propositions will be stated. This contact transcends the I to the neighbor, and is not its thematization; it is the deliverance of a sign prior to every proposition, to the statement of anything whatever. Language is a battering ram—a sign that says the very fact of saying. (*LP,* 125)

Language touches the Other in a nonideal way: it does not form a union with another but makes a first impression, a contact, which only later becomes intelligible, like the way a young child encounters the Hebrew letters for the first time. The first word, which says the Saying itself, reveals that which underlies language: the relation of proximity. Unconvertible into language yet upon which every transmission and exchange are already dependent, proximity is "the original language, a language without words or propositions, pure communication" (*LP,* 119). Language strikes "like a battering-ram" (*LP,* 122), thus upholding the possibility of entering into a relationship independently of a system of signs common to the interlocutors. Rather than reinstating the structure according to which it operates, language pushes its own envelope outward, thereby allowing it "to break through the limits of culture, body, and race" (*LP,* 122). The very beginning of language, the contact made by the first word, is already the breaking up of the stability and coherence of what is said.

Language as a form of communication upholds the tension between what is addressed and the act of addressing; it touches and makes contact (sweet like honey, painful like a battering ram) by proposing logos to another. To communicate therefore entails opening oneself beyond acceptance of contents delivered. It implies an openness that exceeds recognition of, or agreement with, another. Contrary to those who seek for communication a "full coverage insurance" (*OB,* 119), which would invariably lead to the seeking of closure, certainty and comfort of solidarity in an original "We," Levinas stresses that communication involves *uncertainty*. Rather than the empirical situation of exchange, Levinas deems communication in exposure to the Other that precedes and exceeds correspondence of minds. Renouncing any a priori foundation or commonality, Levinas thus portrays communication as being "at the risk of *misunderstanding*" and "at the *risk of lack of and refusal* of communication" (*OB,* 120; italics mine). Communication as an event of proximity, as the ethical event of communication, is "an adventure of a subjectivity," attainable only as a "dangerous life, a fine risk to be run" (*OB,* 120). To communicate means to cross an abyss without ever arriving at the other side: it involves leaping toward what is beyond existing boundaries—beyond what is already represented, comprehended and thematized—in order to instigate and to further allow communication.

Community of Interruption

Levinas's philosophy, as outlined thus far, offers a radical reevaluation of subjectivity, ethics and communication as distinct subjects of investigation. Yet its significance lies in further revealing the way in which the three are interrelated. Without being reduced to a fully conceptualized framework, the relationship among subjectivity, ethics and communication seems to culminate in one point: interruption. In what follows, I will attempt to circumscribe interruption as a possible correlative between communication and ethics. The notion of interruption also occasions bringing Levinas together with two of his interpreters-interrupters, Maurice Blanchot and Jacques Derrida.

Being a self means being exposed to the Other, to the interruption provoked by the face causing the self to lose its "sovereign coincidence with itself, its identification, in which consciousness returned triumphally to itself and rested on itself" (*TO*, 353). But interruption also marks a unique kind of solidarity with the Other, one that is not characterized in union or identification, rather in responsibility. To discover this orientation in the self is to reclaim the responsibility for ethics, the responsibility for responsibility. Interruption as a form of communication, or communication as a form of interruption, means losing one's identification with oneself and responding to the absolutely Other. Being predisposed to communication insofar as interruption, the self may be regarded as an elemental site of interruptions. The interruption evoked by the Other is not made present in the relation, it is not re-present-able in language, but comes to pass by rupturing it. Even when encountered face-to-face, the Other manifests him or herself without manifesting themselves completely; there is always something that escapes presence, that is, the Other's alterity. Interruption thus signifies a certain absence, a withdrawal from presence: "It insinuates itself, withdraws before entering" (Levinas 1987, 66).

Following Levinas, Maurice Blanchot defines three sets of relations. The first is governed by the law of the same: "Man wants unity, he observes separation" (*IC,* 66). Whatever is deemed different—be it subjects or objects—is sought, not without struggle and labor, to be comparable and made identical with the Same. Comparison and identification therefore provide the means for constructing a whole whose truth is reaffirmed by reducing the Other to the Same: "In this case, unity passes by way of totality" (*IC,* 66). In this relation, the Other is perceived as a function of the Same and is approached with the intention of subsuming the Other into the structure of the Same. The Other is regarded as a contraption to ascertain the solidity of the whole in which she or he is encountered (as an identical self, as an alter ego, or as an object of knowledge).

The second kind of relation also strives for unity but one that is attained dialectically. The Other is affirmed only to be immediately immersed in synthesis, either by dividing the self or by dividing the Other. This relation is one of coincidence and participation in which differences reconcile: "The Self and the Other lose themselves in one another: there is ecstasy, fusion, fruition" (*IC,* 66). The unity thus achieved transcends both self and Other, producing a higher order that is beyond the sovereignty of both. Here the relation to the Other seeks to transform incompatibility into combination, from difference to the complacency of "a familiar address that forgets or effaces distance" (*IC,* 77).

Relation of the third kind, conversely, is one that does not end in unity, neither totalizing nor transcending the Other. Contrary to the two relations above, in which the Other is annexed either by objectification or by merger, in the third relation the Other remains outside any relation that culminates in unity. This relation is characterized by a foreignness that nevertheless "unites." Akin to Levinas, a relation without relation is as follows:

> Now what "founds" this third relation . . . [is] the *strangeness* between us: a strangeness it will not suffice to characterize as a separation or even as a distance.
> —Rather an interruption.

> —An interruption escaping all measure. But—and here is the strangeness of this strangeness—such an interruption (one that nei- ther includes nor excludes) would be nevertheless a relation; at least if I take upon myself not to reduce it, not to reconcile it, even by comprehending it, that is, not to seek to consider it as the "fal- tering" mode of a still unitary relation. (*IC,* 68)

The relation of the third kind does not imply being removed from the Other by the "strangeness between us" to the point of indiffer- ence. This relation is based precisely on what differentiates self from Other coming to pass neither as inclusion nor as exclusion but rather as interruption. In this relation, "the one is never compre- hended by the other, does not form with him an ensemble, a dual- ity, or a possible unity: the one is foreign to the other, without this foreignness privileging either one of them" (ibid., 73). Interruption, as Blanchot insists, is still a relation, yet one that unsettles the con- struction of a new order, any order, and of order in general.

For Blanchot, this relation is upheld in language: the Other does not belong to language (insofar as the Said) as he or she always remains beyond, addressed in the Saying. An experience with lan- guage therefore means an interruption of subjectivity. Language is the already-foreign in which the Other interrupts me—the Other needs language in order to breach my self-sufficiency because lan- guage maintains the possibility of situating me beside myself (Bruns 1996, 136). This irreducible experience of language entails a certain mode of alienation, a displacement—or better, disloca- tion—in relation to the Other. Yet it also implies that language pro- vides a means of access through which one is interrupted by the Other so as to invite further communication—interruption is rudi- mentary to communication, "interruption permits the exchange. Interrupting for the sake of understanding, understanding in order to speak" (*IC,* 76). Blanchot thus invites interruption to interrupt by deferring to the ruptures and intervals it puts in language and between self and Other. In the relation of the third kind, "there is in the field of relations a distortion preventing any direct communication and any relation of unity" (*IC,* 77). But the dislocation evoked by the arrest of the exchange, by silence, blanks or gaps, is not exhausted in such manifestations because it invites a fundamental reevaluation of the relation itself. It summons a radical change in the structure of communication, "A change such that to speak (to write) is *to cease thinking solely with a view to unity*" (*IC,* 77).

In "At this very moment in this work here I am" (*AM* 1991), Derrida attempts, among other things, to draw out the ways in which Levinas sets his writing in *Otherwise Than Being, or Beyond Essence* without presenting himself as a self-present author. The title is a combination of three phrases that repetitively appear in Levinas's text precisely when he reflects on how his work works. But the proposition and use of such phrases is doubtless incongruous with ontology, intimating a certain absence (of the writer, of Levinas), an unbridgeable distance, which, as Derrida affirms, "does not forbid, on the contrary, proximity" (ibid., 12). "Here I am," "at this very moment" and "in this work" do not signify a closure of the discourse produced by Levinas but its openness: by repeating these phrases as an ontological Said, a certain dislocation has taken place. Through these phrases, suggests Derrida, it is possible that the ultimate interruption occurs:

> The "metaphors" of seam and tear obsess his text. Is it merely a matter of "metaphors," once they envelop or tear the very element (the text) of the metaphorical? It matters little for the moment. In any case they seem to be organized as follows. Let us call by one word, *interruption* (which he uses often), that which regularly puts an end to the authority of the Said, the thematical, the dialectical, the same, the economical, etc., whatever is demarcated from this series so as to go beyond essence: to the Other, towards the Other, from the Other. The interruption will have come to tear the continuum of a tissue which naturally tends to envelop, shut in upon itself, sew itself back up again, mend, resume its own tears, and to make it appear as if they were still its own and could return to it. (Ibid., 26)

When writing about interruption, the fabric of the text must remain ruptured: interruption can never be circumscribed as a theme within a text so as to allow it to pass through and rupture. The way Derrida describes Levinas's writing may also correspond to the mode adopted when writing on interruption: "interrupting the weaving of our language and then by weaving together the interruptions themselves, another language comes to disturb the first one" (ibid., 18). Interruption reveals itself as it acts upon language, thereby revealing itself as a manifestation of communication that is beyond its contents. Interruption instigates communication and goes on to interrupt the communication thus instigated. Yet writing must then proceed otherwise: rendering the traces left by interruptions apparent, logos loosely knotted, "another way of retying without retying" (ibid., 28).

*   *   *

The philosophy of Emmanuel Levinas offers a radically different perspective from which to explore questions relating to communication and/as ethics. Its import, I argue, lies in liberating ethical communication from the empirical reality of exchange and from reciprocity of message circulation. A way of conceiving communication beyond the integration of minds is extended instead. While traditional views have often regarded the limit of communication as tantamount to its annihilation and consequently to an ethical quandary, this discussion has proposed that the limit of communication may present an opportunity for encountering alterity point-blank. What is opened at the end of discursive capabilities, at the limit of the discourse of the Said, is a space of exposure and susceptibility, a space for the Other to intervene. The end, then, marks a beginning in a different sense—the beginning of communication as an ethical event.

My reading of Levinas has proposed the concept of interruption as a possible correlative between communication and ethics.

Interruption intimates a heteronomous relation, one that transcends both juxtaposition and synthesis, and transpires within the difference between self and Other. Interruption comes to pass in the Saying's puncturing of the Said, in the double-bind of language, in the constant tension between the linguistic potential to thematize and the primary modality of approach toward the Other. Critically speaking, interruption is precisely what is denied in the discourse of the Said, in the logos seeking coherence and solidity. As such, the suppression of interruption would be on a par with effacing the Other's face, with precluding the possibility of being called into question by the Other. Ethical communication would therefore be missed in the putting of minds *en rapport;* it would be found instead in the interruption of rapport—or better, in a rapport of interruptions. Neither identification nor alienation, such is the fraternity of responsibility, of friendship. This ethics, which puts the Other at the locus of regard, would renounce all imperatives, all perhaps except for the two words ending Jacques Derrida's text on Levinas: "Interrupt me" (*AM,* 46).

Three

Traces of Babel

All true language is incomprehensible, like the chatter of a beggar's teeth.
—Antonin Artaud, *Indian Culture and Here Lies*

"And the earth was of one tongue, and of the same speech."
With these words begins the biblical story of Noah's descendants. As they journeyed from the east and found a land, they set out to do the insurmountable, to transcend themselves, to build a tower, "the top whereof may reach to heaven." They ventured to make their name famous before being scattered into all lands. God then came down to see the city and the tower and said: "Behold, it is one people and they all have one tongue: and they have begun to do this. Neither will they leave off their designs, till they accomplish them in deed." God descended on the city and confounded their language, "that they may not understand one another's speech." He confused the language so they could no longer understand one another, abolishing the enterprise and scattering them into all lands. He then named the city Babel "because there the language of the whole earth was confounded."

The biblical story of the confusion of languages upholds in a uniquely rich way many of the fears and longings associated with language as an experience of social life. It is no coincidence that numerous volumes reflecting on the meaning and nature of language reverberate directly or indirectly with this story, specifically, the hopes and the perils both in having a universal language and in the fallout of linguistic quandary. The theme of this chapter is the relationship between language and ethics as reflected by the story of Babel and by what it has come to signify. However, my intention is not simply to show that this story inspires or figures the ways in which this relationship has been conceived; such a claim would belong to a mythological analysis, which is beyond the scope of the present study. Instead, I propose to regard the story of Babel as the touchstone by which traditional and current questions about the nature of human communication together with the solutions they dictate have been defined and explored. As will become evident in the following pages, traces of Babel are found in the various levels of this discussion.

The lessons derived from the confusion of languages point toward two major approaches. The first regards the linguistic reality after Babel as a problem to be overcome, as the diversity of idioms prevents the creation of greater understanding. The confusion is to be undone by perfecting language as a means of communication beyond the specificities of individuality, culture and nation. The second approach, conversely, deems linguistic multiplicity as both intra- and interlinguistic, that is, immanent not only between languages but also within each language. The difference between speakers and languages indicates something essential to linguistic interaction in particular and to communication in general, which should be acknowledged and even safeguarded. The theoretical, intellectual and ethical motivations of these approaches are at the focus of this chapter.

The first section will discuss two of the main scholarly endeavors toward establishing a universal language: Esperanto and Basic English. The two extend from elaborate philosophical and ideological perspectives associated with Ludovic Lazarus Zamenhof's work in developing the artificial language of Esperanto and with C. K. Ogden's exploration of a simplified version of the English language. The following section will propose an alternative interpretation of the linguistic confusion associated with Babel. The story will serve as an entry point for approaching questions of language and ethics from a deconstructive perspective while circumscribing the event of incomprehension as bearing a special ethical significance. The irreducible incompatibility of languages and speakers gives rise to the challenge of translating, an issue that will be further explored in the next section focusing in particular on the accounts of Walter Benjamin and Franz Rosenzweig. I will attempt to outline translation as a paradigm of communication that implies a special involvement with alterity. Finally, I will turn to Tzevetan Todorov's historical account of the conquest of America, which I believe might reverberate most acutely the main themes of the discussion.

Undoing Babel

The construction of a universal language has been a theme accompanying modern thought as early as the seventeenth century, following Latin's demise as the international language of educated Europe. Consequent attempts to construct new international languages were closely associated with development in knowledge, science, philosophy and education (Knowlson 1975, 4; Steiner 1975, 201–3). Descartes's suggestion for a language based upon "true philosophy" and Leibniz's proposal for a *characteristica universalis* are two examples often mentioned in relation to these endeavors. Among others who shared similar aspirations were Voltaire, Montesquieu, Fourier and Tolstoy (Eichholz and Eichholz 1982, 13). As James Knowlson shows in his historical account of universal language schemes in Europe from 1600 to 1800, the enterprise shared by many scholars was to construct a common language that could restore the role of Latin. As he further contends, most contemporary projects of universal language saw their mission in achieving a unity undivided by difference in color, race, nation and belief. The goal of many projects was to "remedy Babel," that is, to provide a cure to the biblical confusion of tongues (1975, 9). Such projects often converged with reformative aspirations striving for the reunification of the churches held especially among Protestant groups throughout Europe. The preoccupation with universal language was therefore the meeting point for rational and scientific knowledge and religious fervor, as expressed by Comenius, a Moravian reformer who looked forward to the invention of a "language absolutely new, absolutely easy, absolutely rational, in brief a Pansophic language, the universal carrier of light" (ibid., 10).

The search for a universal language also reflects the orthodox disputes regarding the nature of language from Plato onward. The main question was whether words conveyed the essence of things they designated or whether they were purely arbitrary signifiers. For many biblical commentators, the book of Genesis was the ultimate account of the true nature of language. According to that view, humans had once possessed a deep understanding of the world and of the true nature of things, which has been unattainable ever since. Although the majority of seventeenth century universal language planners did not see themselves as excavators of a *lingua humana* (the primitive yet pure language of humankind before Babel), the idea of the lost language capable of conveying something of the essence of things probably influenced their work, and as Knowlson suggests, more than they cared to recognize (ibid., 12–13). Either way, the leading motivations of most attempts were clarity, simplicity and transparency of signification, and these ideals were readily associated with an ideal arrangement of social harmony.

This intellectual preoccupation grew in accordance with progress made in science and knowledge beginning in early modernity through the Enlightenment to late modernity. The number of suggestions for artificial or planned languages increased steadily: 41

during the seventeenth century, 50 in the eighteenth, 246 in the nineteenth and 560 during the twentieth century (Nuessel 1996, 372). Mundolingue, Balta, Bopal, Langue bleue, Spelin, Universal-Sprache and Veltparl are just some of the language projects that appeared between 1863 and 1899 (Gordon 1988, 338). One prominent effort was Volapük, a language invented in 1880 by the Catholic priest Johann Martin Schleyer. Although his notion of universal language was not markedly different from that of his contemporaries, Schleyer was one of the first to link the scientific and technological development of the late nineteenth century to the possibility of creating a linguistic tool that could unite individuals across the world:

> Thanks to railways, steamships, telegraph and the telephone, the world has shrunk in time and space. The countries of the world are in effect drawing closer to one another. Thus the time for a small-minded and fainthearted chauvinism is forever over. Humankind becomes daily more cosmopolitan and increasingly yearns for unity. The amazing universal postal service system is an important step towards this splendid goal. With respect also to money, weights and measures, time zones, laws and language the brothers and sisters of the human race should move to unity. (Schleyer, cited in Kim 1999, 133)

Out of the many proposals there are two attempts that stand out: Esperanto and Basic English. Like earlier projects of universal language, both Esperanto and Basic English emerged from specific intellectual, material and ideological contexts that have influenced their development and acceptance. However, unlike the others, they represent relatively successful attempts to turn a theoretical idea into a social practice. Both have acquired supporters (as well as critics) while inciting the interest of intellectuals and practitioners alike. Esperanto and Basic English are much more than mere linguistic constructs as they have transcended the community of their speakers, contributing to the ongoing debate on the role of language in ethics, philosophy and politics.

The Language of Hope

The general definition of Esperanto as it appears in the *Oxford English Dictionary* is: "an artificial language designed for world use." Among other qualifying adjectives are "auxiliary," "constructed," "created," "international," "planned," "synthetic," "universal" and "vehicular" (Nuessel 1996, 371).[1] The grammar of Esperanto consists essentially of 16 rules, which can be easily learned by heart. There are no irregular verbs, only one definite article is used for all genders, numbers and cases, and all spelling is phonetic. The language's vocabulary is based on word-roots taken from modern languages and in some cases directly from Greek and Latin. Based on a system of affixes, Esperanto makes it possible to form as many as 40 words from a single root. These and other features make up a highly economical structure allowing for further development of new words and terms as well as for an easy and quick learning of the language (Eichholz and Eichholz 1982, 17; Forster 1982, 375–78).

Esperanto is one of the few languages with a specific date of origination. It was invented and developed by the Polish oculist Ludovic Lazarus Zamenhof (1859–1917) during the last quarter of the nineteenth century. Zamenhof debuted the language in 1878 in Russian and soon after editions appeared in Polish, French, German and English. Initially, Zamenhof's project did not bear a name. A declaration appearing on the second page of his book, in which he gave up all his rights to the language, stating that an international language is common property, was signed by the pseudonym "Doktoro Esperanto," namely, "the one who hopes" (Privat 1963, 44). Zamenhof not only gave a name to the project but also a motivation that is still very much shared by its speakers and often associated with the cause of world peace (see Forster 1982, 3).

Assessing Esperanto's significance would be incomplete without noting the background from which it emerged. Zamenhof often mentioned the reasons that stimulated him to undertake such an ambitious task, as he expressed on one occasion:

I was born in Bielostok, in the province of Grodno (Russia). This scene of my birth and childhood determined the trend of my future aspirations. In Bielostok the population contains four different elements—Russians, Poles, Germans, and Jews. Each of these sections speaks a different language, and is on bad terms with the other. . . . I was educated to be an idealist; I was taught that all men were brothers, while, all the time, everything around me made me feel that *men* did not exist; there only existed Russians, Poles, Germans, Jews, and so on. This state of affairs was a continual torment to my young mind. (Zamenhof, cited in Long 1913, 11)

According to Zamenhof's biographer, Edmond Privat, this strife witnessed firsthand by young Ludovic was the primary motivation for devising a solution in the form of a universal language. Eagerly learning German, French, English, as well as Greek and Latin, Zamenhof originally envisioned reviving one of the latter two classical languages, which were Europe's lingua franca during the time of Alexander the Great and the Middle Ages. Yet he quickly realized that both were relatively difficult to learn and largely inadequate for modern use, so he opted instead for the construction of an entirely new artificial form of speech that would be easy, simple and logical but also flexible and expressive. The intuition leading Zamenhof was that if everyone would learn a neutral language in addition to their own, people could come into direct communication with each other, thereby bridging individuals of different races, religions, cultures and languages. As Privat recounts, the picture that was developing in the mind of the young Zamenhof was: "Break down, break down the walls between the peoples! . . . They are puppets controlled by unknown wire-pullers. Misunderstanding due to mutual ignorance must cease!" (Privat 1963, 25–26).

For Zamenhof, Esperanto was a crucial part of a larger view regarding the ideal structure of social life. He expressed his ideological credo in a short pamphlet published anonymously in 1906 entitled *Homaranismo* (Esperanto for the belief that one is first and foremost a member of the human race):

> *Homaranisimo* is a teaching which, without tearing a man away
> from his natural fatherland, language, or religion, will enable him to
> avoid falsehood and contradiction in his national and religious prin-
> ciples, and put him into communication with men of any language
> or religion upon a neutral basis, on principles of mutual brotherhood,
> equality, and justice. (Zamenhof, cited in Privat 1963, 65)

Early twentieth century eastern Europe, an area divided by race,
religion and language, was for Zamenhof a paramount example for
the problems facing the modern world. However, his intention was
not to replace indigenous languages with Esperanto but to establish
this language as auxiliary, that is, as a neutral means of expression
when meeting people of different origins and creeds. In that way, he
believed, one would not impose one's mindset and biases on the
other, ultimately eradicating the causes of conflicts and violence.

Although not stated as such, Zamenhof's approach nevertheless
reveals his belief that people are essentially the same but divided by
the objective conditions into which they are born and raised. These
various social, religious, cultural and linguistic characteristics are
precisely what prevent individuals from realizing their fundamental camaraderie, and once such walls are removed, companionship
will be restored. Esperanto may therefore be the vehicle through
which humans may re-create and effectively actualize the latent
communality they already share. As a neutral instrument of communication, Esperanto offers people of all origins the opportunity
to meet others halfway: while no one would be required to relin-
quish their mother tongue, communication would by carried out by
means of an auxiliary, unbiased language. For Zamenhof, then, the
way to a harmonious social existence runs through the establishment of an independent and external means of communication: an
interlinguistic language.

The turn of the twentieth century saw many supporters for the
construction of Esperanto as a universal language. One British
Esperanto enthusiast, Bernard Long, expresses the necessity for
this language, especially in the context of modern progress. Long

criticizes what he deems to be a common view according to which the multitude of languages is a situation to be endured indefinitely. For him, the reluctance to accept and use the possibilities supplied by Esperanto reflects a condemnable defeatism: "In other spheres than that of language we do not assume this helpless attitude in the face of natural difficulties. We tunnel through mountains, we bridge rivers, we lay telegraph cables in the sea" (Long 1913, 5). Thus, resistance toward the very idea of international language has to be overcome in order to realize its full potential, as this enterprise would ultimately facilitate a greater good for all. Still, like Zamenhof and other Esperantists, Long stresses that the aim is not to interfere with national speech, sentiments or other private opinions. Rather, learning and using this auxiliary tongue is essential for anyone who desires to see fuller and more effective international cooperation in modern progress.

According to this enthusiast, Esperanto is based on the rationale of immediate simplification of international intercourse, one that is already prevalent in "such diverse matters as music, marine signaling, mathematics, and scientific classification" (ibid., 6). Like Schleyer, the inventor of Volapük, Long correlates linguistic simplicity and functionality with the linear progress of science and knowledge, a link that also upholds the possibility of creating harmony and goodwill. Here Esperanto is not merely a language; it is an emblem for the potential unity between modern progress and peace. As Long further asserts, "The international character of modern progress is leading us to see that in the commonwealth of nations the good of each unit is identical with the good of all, and people of similar tastes and occupations are everywhere combining in world-wide alliance for the furtherance of mutual interests and ideals" (ibid., 7). For Long, as well as for Zamenhof and other Esperantists, the fundamental commonality among all people is the basis from which such auxiliary language draws both its moral legitimacy and its linguistic substantiation. Nevertheless, Long's text also marks a more pragmatic vision elaborating on the advantages of this language for trade, tourism and scientific collaboration.

Almost from its inception, Esperanto was more than an imaginative linguistic experiment; it was equally a community of speakers, supporters and organizations, in short, a social movement. As sociologist Peter Forster (1982) contends, Esperanto may be viewed as a particular social movement whose members share similar values and ideals, which are in turn pursued and disseminated through symposia, publishing houses and other international organizations. This movement has traditionally expressed a lukewarm and even hostile attitude to governments as sources of support; the emphasis has been on recruiting individuals directly to the cause (5, 9).[2] The Esperanto movement, adds Young S. Kim, helped to generate an ideological framework of "one-worldism" by providing a transcendent basis for cooperation and common identity at the global level (1999, 147). And as Frank Nuessel notes, some Esperantists even refer to each other as "samideano," or "adherent to the same idea" (1996, 374).[3] It follows that to be an Esperantist means at once being a speaker of the language and a member of the Esperanto community. But is there not an inherent contradiction in this constellation of ideology and praxis? Is one not already predisposed to sympathize with members of this speech community by virtue of committing to the very idea of Esperanto, its logic, credence and promise? Or alternatively, can the language constructed to bring people together beyond color, race and religion do so without having already set aside such differences before any exchange commences? It would seem, then, that approaching another in Esperanto means accepting an anterior communal fellowship, and as such it would probably entail more than a coincidental propensity for a congenial exchange with fellow Esperantists.

Recently, some of the original arguments in favor of Esperanto have reemerged in the context of the growing processes of globalization. Esperantists have customarily regarded their enterprise as universal and their ideological vision as universalism. This view corresponds with what Zygmunt Bauman (1998) identifies as the idea of universalization, which, like other early and classic modern notions such as "civilization," "development" and "consensus," conveys the hope, the intention and the determination of order making on a universal scale. Esperanto clearly aligns with the traditional modern views of progress and development, and for contemporary advocates the issue of universal language is ever more poignant in a time when communication technologies connect individuals and countries across the world.

Following that vein, Ronald Glossop's (1988) account of language policy for a universal community provides an assessment of the promises of embracing Esperanto as a universal language. According to Glossop, worldwide adoption of Esperanto as a second language is the most fair and rational path to be followed with regard to language policy for the world community. Glossop argues that the Esperanto movement provides a particularly good example for a working global community because it presents the ultimate combination of language policy and the creation of a just world order: "[I]f everyone in the world knew a neutral language such as Esperanto a sense of world community would be fostered which would tend to undercut nationalism, one of the most significant contributing factors to war" (1988, 396). Glossop does not fail to mention the practical benefits of the language to "economic well-being," social justice and political participation. For him, all these concerns apply equally to Third World countries, like India and several African countries, where the language of a former colonial power was adopted as a national language. A neutral language such as Esperanto may offer, according to Glossop, an opportunity to discard the languages of former conquerors and struggle against the continuing domination of world powers. In the long run, he proclaims, the demands of living in a global community will eventually mean the end of most, if not all, major national languages. The remaining question would then be: which one will it be, English or Esperanto? (398, 403).

In sum, the creation of Esperanto proposes a vision combining an artificial linguistic construct and a utopian ideology. At its base is the belief that by providing a simple and neutral means of communication, individuals of different linguistic, religious, national and cultural backgrounds could relate to each other with greater compassion and understanding. For many advocates, Esperanto comprises the ultimate means for liberating suffocated sentiments of harmony and peace. Yet this hope arises from a presupposition accompanying Esperanto since the early writings of Zamenhof that holds that ethical relationships are based on and consist in commonality. In the epistemology of Zamenhof and his followers, differences are inconsequential insofar as an ethical relation is concerned. The essential unity of all people is both presupposition and goal: underlying apparent ethnic and nationalistic schisms, it might reemerge by using a unifying means of communication. Esperanto, both as a language and as a social movement, epitomizes an eminent modern ideal: the hope of establishing an enlightened universalism through a common vernacular.

Back to Basics

Basic English was the brainchild of British philosopher and critic Charles K. Ogden. Ogden began developing a simplified, error-proof version of English with an easily mastered vocabulary in the early 1920s. Unlike Zamenhof, Ogden was initially less concerned with the moral and political issues involving the construction of a universal language. His preoccupation was with a problem Jeremy Bentham (one of Ogden's main inspirations) called "the eels of language"—the slipperiness of verbs, which due to their complex nature and elusive meaning inevitably lead to inaccurate expression and thought (Gordon 1988, 337–38). The product of his work, published in 1930, included a list of 850 words which, according to Ogden, are equal in efficiency to approximately 5,000 and could do the essential work of as many as 20,000 (Ogden 1940, 10). Divided into three classes, this restricted vocabulary consisted of 600 names and nouns, 150 adjectives and 100 of what Ogden called "opera-tions." The last are of special importance because they represent an attempt to solve the problem of "the eels of language" by limiting the number of verb forms, or operators, to a minimum of 18. Together with words designating relation, direction and other par-ticles, these operators could replace the meaning of verbs in full English (for example, "to come in" takes the meaning of "to enter"; "to give thought" or "to take thought" of "to mediate"; "to get for a price" of "to purchase," and so on). Like Zamenhof, Ogden did not advocate the trading of indigenous languages with Basic, but rather for the employment of Basic as an auxiliary means of com-munication. Yet, the project of distilling the essentials of English into a compatible language encompasses much more than an intel-lectual exercise in efficiency and succinctness. It is the product of an elaborate study into the nature of language and meaning under-taken by Ogden together with the British critic I. A. Richards in their magnum opus *The Meaning of Meaning* (1972).

Appearing in more than ten editions since first published in 1923, this study sets out to unravel what the authors regard as the fundamental misconceptions about language. One of the major issues discussed in the study is the power of words to obscure thought and to obstruct communication. The aim of the project is to devise a "science of symbolism" that would purge language of confusion and misunderstandings. Ogden and Richards identify the main difficulty with the mixing of symbolic and emotive uses of words. Failure to distinguish between these two functions of language has been, according to the authors, a source for much confusion in thought and research. Moreover, many traditional controversies were actually the result of a linguistic jumble, allow-ing for a situation wherein "the same words being used at once to make statements and to excite attitudes" (ibid., viii). Their declared task is to formulate rules to "determine the right use of words and reasoning," and make language a more reliable instrument of com-munication (ibid., 107).

Ogden and Richards trace the predicament of language back to the "superstition that words are in some way parts of things or always imply things corresponding to them" (ibid., 14). According to the authors, the belief that words have power over things signified, so prevalent in early cultures and religious thought (a belief also associated with the language medieval scholars called *lingua humana*), has not disappeared during the modern era. As they observe, "The persistence of the primitive linguistic outlook not only throughout the whole religious world, but in the work of the profoundest thinkers, is indeed one of the most curious features of modern thought" (ibid., 29). In the modern era, stress Ogden and Richards, the problem became even more widespread. Owing to "the development in the methods of communication, and the creation of many special symbolic systems, the form of the disease has altered considerably . . . [and] now takes more insidious forms than yore" (29). Ogden and Richards's main motivation in developing a new theory of meaning is to liberate language from the primitive relics of the past, from its limitations and imperfections. And modern progress in science and technology has made the flaws of language even more apparent: "Tens of thousands of years have elapsed since we shed our tails, but we are still communicating with a medium developed to meet the needs of arboreal man" (26). For Ogden and Richards, the misuse of language in modern times is the result of an unsuccessful process of "natural selection"; linguistic imperfections are therefore to be shed like an atrophied tail.

Ogden and Richards's perspective reflects a deep-seated suspicion of language pursuant to a long British tradition of distrusting the elusive nature of words found in the works of Bacon, Hobbes, Locke, Hume, Bentham and Russell (Peters 1999, 13). "Words," they assert, "whenever they cannot directly ally themselves with and support themselves upon gestures, are at present a very imperfect means of communication" (Ogden and Richards 1972, 15). In their analysis, a successful process of communication is one that does not fall victim to the deceit of words. It transpires once communicators reach unity-in-mind beyond the predicaments constantly arising in language: "a language transaction or a communication may be defined as a use of symbols in such a way that acts of reference occur in a hearer which are similar in all relevant respects to those which are symbolized by them in the speaker" (ibid., 205–6). Communication takes place between minds rather than between individuals. Nevertheless, since words are all that communicators have, it is imperative to devise a method to control meanings and hence the importance of clear and exact definitions. A language purged of emotive and metaphorical obscurities would not only make a desirable scientific design, it would be also generally advantageous since "in most matters the possible treachery of words can only be controlled through definitions, and the greater the number of such alternative locutions available the less the risk of discrepancy" (206).

Attaining accurate communication despite the "treachery of words" is therefore Ogden and Richards's ultimate goal. For them, language is first and foremost a means of thought exchange, a "transaction" through which one consciousness may gain access to another. Some 40 years before McLuhan they propose: "language, though often spoken of as a medium of communication, is best regarded as an instrument; and all instruments are extensions, or refinements, of our sense-organs" (ibid., 98). Basic English may then be regarded as the realization of Ogden's philosophical inquiries into the "science of symbolism": a clever linguistic instrument designed to allow an efficient and undistorted exchange (compare Gordon 1991). The economy of an 850-word vocabulary seems to emanate directly from the proposition: "It is not always new words that are needed, but a means of controlling them as symbols" (Ogden and Richards 1972, 19).

Whereas Esperanto is based upon a rather limited and idealistic epistemology of human nature, Basic English draws upon an elaborate philosophical and linguistic research very much attuned to practical aspects of modern life. Indeed, when advocating Basic

English as an international common language, Ogden presented it as "a system in which everything may be said for all purposes of everyday existence: the common interest of men and women, general talk, news, trade, and science" (Ogden 1940, 91). To him, Basic English was the only rational way to make sense in a world getting smaller through discoveries in science and technology. The radio, he writes, "is now putting Babel in the houses of those who have no knowledge even of the names of the languages they are hearing" (ibid., 171). Communication technology amplified what he and Richards called "verbomania," an ill they identified distinctively with the modern misuse of language (Ogden and Richards 1972, 40). The reality of too many words and too many speakers was antithetic to Ogden's economy of speech. In his view, only regular use of Basic—also the acronym for British, American, Scientific, International, Commercial (noteworthy is that each word in the acronym represents an empire or a metanarrative, or both [Peters 1999, 13])—would help cure such modern ills and create a sense of a genuine world community. For instance, one of the ideas Ogden entertained was a worldwide news service, day and night, in Basic English. A five-minute report, every hour on the hour, would be enough, according to Ogden, "to give everyone the feeling that this little earth was pulling itself together. And with that feeling would come a new hope for all the forces moving to peace" (1940, 172).

In *Basic English and Its Uses* (1943), I. A. Richards proposes a supportive account of Ogden's enterprise. For Richards, Basic English presents a most useful means to bridge the gap opened between technological progress, on the one hand, and the constraints exerted by the existing social and political structures, on the other. The modern discrepancy between progress and war, argues Richards, is the outcome of misusing technological innovations. Situating his reflections in the context of World War II, or what he refers to as "the immense collective crimes of the present," he calls for reevaluation and reconstruction of some positive and permanent goals:

One of these goals is a reasonable degree of communication spread out more evenly over the planet. . . . It is a necessity now; necessary for human progress, necessary perhaps for human survival. We can no longer risk letting any large section of the human race live in separation, cut off from the fullest possible communication with the rest. When the separated section is powerful, we know what happens. It develops a warped understanding of its own interests, from which must come designs against the interests of the rest of the planet. National aggressions are no accidents, no local freaks of evil inspiration. They are outcomes of spiritual separation. (1943, 5)

Richards deems catastrophic the employment of communication technology (he especially mentions the radio) in cultivating nationalist sentiments, and proposes instead a more even degree of "communication spread." This suggestion puts him in line with the early instrumental understanding of communication as propaganda associated mainly with Harold Lasswell. The battle, then, is against exclusive loyalty to one group, which for Richards is synonymous with "disloyalty to the planet" (ibid., 6). He stresses the necessity of balancing the effects of new technological inventions, such as the airplane and the radio, by equal developments in the means of "mental transport" and in the spreading of "common truths which would make antagonism and disloyalty harder to cultivate" (ibid., 6). The idea of Basic as a universal medium falls readily into a 1940s communicational mindset and terminology. Like other modes of communication, it can be used for constructive or insidious ends, depending on the context and purpose.[4]

Basic English attracted supporters and enthusiasts of many kinds, including Ezra Pound, Laurence Durrell, Winston Churchill and H. G. Wells. The latter went so far as to emphasize the literary potential of Basic, predicting that the twenty-first century would be the golden age of Basic (Gordon 1988, 339). But a writer who had a special involvement with Basic was George Orwell. His initial interest in the idea of an international language stemmed from dissatisfaction with the English class system, which made it difficult for working- and middle-class populations to learn foreign languages and restricted them exclusively to English. Orwell was displeased with Esperanto, which he regarded as too artificial and as an ideology more than a language. Opting instead for the promise presented by Basic, his initial explorations included, among other things, correspondence with Ogden on promoting this language (Bolton 1984, 117). In late 1942, while working for the BBC, Orwell produced a program on the Indian Service in which he pronounced his ambition to make Basic English a popular idea, "particularly useful as between Indians, Chinese and other Orientals who don't know one another's language" (Orwell cited in Bolton 1984, 117). He embraced the idea even further when proclaiming: "In Basic, I am told, you cannot make a meaningless statement without its being apparent that it is meaningless—which is quite enough to explain why so many schoolmasters, editors, politicians and literary critics object to it" (ibid., 117). In September 1943, Winston Churchill, in a speech at Harvard University, quoted Franklin Delano Roosevelt on the merits of Basic, announcing ominously: "The Empires of the future are the Empires of the mind" (Fink 1971, 156). Becoming convinced of the need for a lingua franca between the Allies, Churchill set up a special War Cabinet Committee to study its potential; shortly thereafter, the British government bought the rights to Basic from Ogden (Bolton 1984, 116).[5] One of the committee's recommendations was that a substantial part of the BBC's overseas transmission should be broadcasted in Basic. Among the people assigned to the job was George Orwell, still working at the BBC's Indian Service.

Orwell's faith in Basic's capability to solve problems of international communication, argues W. F. Bolton, diminished considerably in the years following the war (1984, 118). Turning back to full English, Orwell wrote in 1948 his famous political novel *1984* featuring an artificial language employed by the dictatorship of Oceania: Newspeak. Views on whether the literary creation of Newspeak is based on Orwell's previous preoccupation with Basic are divided. Critics like Fink (1971) and West (1985) argue that Basic is indeed the inspiration behind Newspeak, while others like Bolton (1984) and Gordon (1988) cast doubt on such speculations. Indeed, while Basic was devised to clarify thought and meaning, Newspeak's design is to diminish the range of thought and to destroy unwanted meanings. Newspeak's syntax and extensive use of euphemisms ("joycamp" for forced-labor camp, for example) reflect some additional differences (Bolton 1984, 152–53). And yet there are some remarkable similarities: a simplified and reduced vocabulary (especially striking is the use of antinomies: good-ungood, straight-unstraight, for example), regularized word morphology, the contraction of verbs (Syme, the Newspeak expert, says that the great wastage is in the verbs) and the utilization of an artificial language on a universal scale.[6] But more importantly, both actual and fictional creations posit language, for better or worse, as an organizing tool in social reality. In both accounts, language is primarily an instrument used to make a specific reality accessible while rendering other undesirable realities inaccessible.

To recapitulate, Basic English presents an erudite attempt to surpass the limitations of language by developing a simplified version of English for world use. Extending from Ogden and Richards's philosophical explorations in *The Meaning of Meaning,* Basic is a theory taken into practice by means of re-enacting language's constructive elements while ferreting out the superfluous ones. On the linguistic level, Basic constitutes a scientific attempt at regulating and reorganizing meanings. On the practical level, it offers a nuance-free lingua franca for commercial, scientific and international use. Recently, some have resumed interest in the language for human-computer communication (Gordon 1988, 340). Nevertheless, the point to be made here is that Basic—much like its literary twin, Newspeak—eliminates misunderstanding by decimating the messiness involved in human speech. The production of a pure, error-free, accessible linguistic apparatus entails, at least in principle, viewing speakers as similar if not as identical. Dissatisfied with the way language "evolved," Ogden sought to remedy some fundamental linguistic imperfections, which he associated mainly with past misconception regarding the nature of language. His faith in Basic is perhaps best expressed in the epigraph to his introductory book to Basic English, which features the story of the tower of Babel in Basic. The first line reads: "Now the earth had only one language, and the number of its words was small" (1940, i).

In conclusion, Esperanto and Basic English are perhaps two of the most prominent attempts to devise and practice planned languages for universal use. Preceded by a history of projects motivated by practical, scientific and religious ambitions, they join both scholarly and popular aspirations in simplifying and purifying communication. Notwithstanding their linguistic and applied differences, the two languages share a few common characteristics. First, both projects originate from an instrumental perspective deeming language as a mere means and thus promoting discussion of its utilization. This view corresponds with the expansion of technological, scientific and commercial considerations in modern society, which are largely dependent upon a systematic integration of communication processes. The employment of these languages is still a central issue in the ongoing discussions on "global community" (Fettes 1991; Glossop 1988; Kim 1999).[7]

Second, both Esperanto and Basic English are committed to creating a greater understanding and concord regardless of speakers' identities, characteristics and beliefs. Universal language is expected to transcend diversity and join individuals despite differences. Indeed, their inverters' notions of like-mindedness diverge: Basic English, according to Ogden, is an attempt to bring together people's minds, whereas Esperanto, as Zamenhof declared in one of his speeches, brings together their hearts (Privat 1963, 75). Zamenhof and Ogden were not mute about the relationship between language and ethics as both expressed faith in the ability of a common language to create greater understanding and compassion between speakers. Nevertheless, in both projects commonality (either presupposed or prospective), rather than difference between speakers, is the underlying principle insofar as the relationship between language and ethics is concerned.

Finally, the emphasis given in both Esperanto and Basic to a successful completion of the exchange suggests, in effect, the reduction of language to a mere information circulating device. It seems that the more clear and transparent language becomes, the more likely it will employ a closed, self-referential and impersonal system of signification. Absent from this scope is what cannot be represented, thematized or carried into language, the alterity that is forever beyond language but still approachable only through language. Constructing a universal language resolves the paradox of language and alterity by cutting the Gordian knot rather than untying it. Such an approach toward human interaction, to use Levinas's term, is the ultimate incarnation of the discourse of the Said.

Deconstructing Babel

The myth of the tower of Babel has infiltrated the epistemological underpinnings of many of the projects for the construction of a universal language. For the creators and practitioners of Esperanto and Basic English in particular, the confusion of tongues provides a looming omen and hence an incentive to rectify the existing linguistic reality. This approach, as I argue above, consigns language to the task of recreating a lost harmonious community. It therefore entails a particular interpretation of the myth, which possibly also colors the way language is viewed in general. In order to unpack further this issue, I return to the tower of Babel and explore a different interpretation of the biblical story. In so doing, I hope to pursue an alternative theoretical approach, one that emphasizes the relation between alterity and language.

The construction of the tower of Babel undoubtedly represents a most impertinent enterprise, a most precipitous outstretching to God—reaching to him directly, without mediation, penetrating the

divine sphere by a manmade brick tower. It resonates almost immediately with the concept of Greek hubris, which forbids excess and
surfeit of any kind, advocating instead the principle of *meden agan:*
all in moderation. Jacques Ellul (1970) contends that Babel did not
crumble under the lightning flash; the problem was spiritual and
Babel was only a symbol. It symbolized the desire of humans to
make a name for themselves, to transcend, and the city and the
tower were merely vehicles toward that end. Babel, as a paramount
example of the sin of excessive pride, would therefore suggest that
the gift of pure language was put to a malevolent purpose. Yet the
story unfolds stressing that the whole earth was "of one language"
before the scheme to erect the tower was hatched. And it is here, I
would argue, that a deeper meaning might lie, for it is, and possibly before all other things, a story about language.

"And the earth was of one tongue, and of the same speech." In
Hebrew this first verse has a somewhat different meaning, which is
conveyed more fully in the following translation: "The entire earth
had one language with uniform words."[8] Here the translation of the
Hebrew words *dvarim achadim* into "uniform words" resonates
more closely with the original. Many Jewish scholars have pon-
dered the meaning of this exceptional verse, holding the opinion
that no repetition in the biblical text is meaningless. Several exege-
ses expound that there was broad agreement among the Babylonians because their language enabled them to agree on the nature of
all representations of things. And so language was not only one but
uniform: a language that did not permit misunderstanding. Thus,
when saying to each other, "Let us make a city and a tower," the
meaning and the objective were clear—there was no doubt.

When taking a closer look at the text, another facet is disclosed:
"And each other said to his neighbor . . . And they said: Come let
us make a city and a tower, the top whereof may reach heaven: and
let us make our name famous." So they spoke, they conversed. God
responded, not by acting but rather by speaking back: "And He said:
'Behold, it is one people and they all have one tongue.'" The text

does not emphasize action but verbal exchange. A peculiar tension then arises: the people speak and God speaks—not to one another, but unto themselves. Clearly, the tower grew from this one language: its structure and purpose were discussed before the people turned to its building. It was the product of the sharing of one language, yet it was also the language's extension, a realization of what an all-embracing language might accomplish. And indeed, when God struck down, it was not on the tower—the product of language—but on language itself. God recognized their power through their language, their insurmountable ability, as if he were hearing something associated with himself. "Come ye, therefore, let us go down," so God announced and struck at the heart of the people's might—their language. He confused the language and so they could not understand one another, abolishing the enterprise and scattering them into all lands. God then named the city "Babel," "because there the language of the whole earth was confounded." Babel stems from the Hebrew verb *balal,* namely to confuse, to scramble. Hence Babel is the opposite of what Noah's descendants had hoped for it to be: it was not an emblem and a beacon for their unity but rather a testament to a radical disarray.

It is difficult to imagine what it would be like to be torn away from a reality in which all representations are transparent, clear and nonbiased, and to be flung into a world in which language is opaque. All that had made sense, all that had been known (in the most basic sense of the word) was now in havoc. The language they had used before was their tool, or in Martin Buber's terms, the ultimate "It": it was used "outwards," in order to reach to the sky, to build a tower, to make themselves a name. The people of Babel employed language in the realm of the It—and in this realm alone—thereby making their world perception complete, total, shadowless. Or, in Emmanuel Levinas's terms, their language was the ultimate incarnation of the Said: a complete reduction of language to the circulation of information, a language addressed to everyone in general but to no one in particular.

Before God struck, the Babylonians wished to make a name for themselves; afterwards, they avowed for the first time that they had *proper* names—without a common language they could see each other as separated, distinguishable, and still, incomprehensible. Before, they could grasp things together as if they were members of the same body; after, they suffered from in-com-prehensibility—they could not comprehend together, were no longer in communion. Before, they lived in the realm of the Said without the Saying; after, they articulated a pure Saying warped in an obscure Said. Before, every time they called each other they articulated a perfect message, grasped in the same way from both ends; after, they were not in control anymore, quite the contrary—language (or rather the confused situation) controlled them. Radical misunderstanding was reinstated and became the order on earth, a linguistic disorder, which introduced a unique ethical moment—language could not be used anymore for the duplication of one mind into the other; it came to an impasse, abruptly exposing speakers to the otherness around them. The confusion caused the people of Babel to retract their gazes from the tower to one another's faces, acknowledging, maybe for the first time, that they were different, finite, separate—a dialogue of baffled faces. Never before were the Babylonians so close and yet so far as in this moment. Is there a moment wherein one is more exposed to the Other's otherness?

In the essay "Des Tours de Babel," Jacques Derrida also takes up the biblical story of Babel. Derrida's interpretation highlights two points: the violence embedded in the employment of a universal language and the special challenge introduced by the aftermath of the confusion of languages, namely, the challenge of translation.

> In seeking to "make a name for themselves," to found at the same time a universal tongue and a unique genealogy, the Semites want to bring the world to reason, and this reason can signify simultaneously a colonial violence (since they would thus universalize their idiom) and a peaceful transparency of the human community. Inversely, when God imposes and opposes his name, he ruptures the

rational transparency but interrupts also the colonial violence or the linguistic imperialism. He destines them to translation, he subjects them to the law of a translation both necessary and impossible. (*TB*, 253)

According to Derrida, Babel does not merely figure an irreducible multiplicity of tongues; it also exhibits "an incompletion, the impossibility of finishing, of totalizing, of saturating, of completing something on the order of edification, architectural construction, system and architectonics" (*TB*, 244). The Babylonians ventured to build a universal empire while imposing their tongue on the universe. God punished them with "confusion": he interrupted the linguistic order by making one speech incommensurable with another. From that moment, exchange was no longer given; it had to be recreated. Yet by condemning the people to a state of confusion, a full and complete restoration was not only impossible but also forbidden. The interruption of the universal language condemned speakers to *translation*—in order to communicate they would have to transform meaning in one language to the other. Translation then becomes both necessary and impossible: necessary, since this is the only way one idiom may come into communication with another; impossible, because of the irreconcilable difference put in language, thus making every translation lacking and incomplete; otherwise, it would not be translation but duplication. The interruption of the linguistic order renders every translation partial and thereby necessitates further translations. Interruption instigates translation, or as Maurice Blanchot comments, "interruption permits the exchange. Interrupting for the sake of understanding, understanding in order to speak" (1993, 76). Interruption (confusion) and understanding (translation) are therefore interrelated. It follows that any kind of understanding is always provisional and deficient; understanding and misunderstanding are not antonymous but mutually contingent and paradoxically imply each other.

The paradox of translation appears most evident in the word "Babel." As pointed out before, the word stems from the Hebrew

verb *balal,* to confuse or scramble. Nevertheless, according to
another exegesis, mentioned also by Derrida, the word is a combination of the Oriental *Ba-bel,* which means God the father; still
another interpretation suggests the ancient Akkadian *Bab-el,* which
signifies the Gate of God. By naming the place "Babel," God effectively imposes his name on the city. Thus, Babel is already both a
proper name (the name of and given by God) and a common noun
that means "confusion" (which, incidentally, found its way also to
English in the form of the verb *to babble,* to German as *babbeln,*
and to French as *babil*). But the word "Babel" itself is untranslatable: "at the very moment when pronouncing 'Babel' we sense the
impossibility of deciding whether this name belongs, properly and
simply, to *one* tongue" (*TB,* 252–53). This word, argues Derrida, at
best comments, explains, paraphrases, but does not translate.
"Babel" bears the trace of the interruption of languages, as it does
not exclusively belong to one and only one language. Its meaning
cannot be contained in one language or be fully transported into
another—it "spills-over," always requiring additional approximation and explication.[9]

"This story," concludes Derrida, "recounts, among other things,
the origin of the confusion of tongues, the irreducible multiplicity
of idioms, the necessary and impossible task of translation, its
necessity *as* impossibility" (*TB,* 250). The tower of Babel might
then stand for a linguistic construct in which words were bricks and
verbs were mortar, a linguistic construct that collapsed. Yet Babel
was not demolished, it was not destructed, but rather *decon-
structed.* God destines translation as law, duty and debt. He leaves
his mark on language in the very name of Babel, a translatable-
untranslatable name, which at once belongs and does not belong to
one language. The rupture he decreed, maintains Derrida, has first
teemed within his name: divided, polysemic, ambivalent—"God
deconstructs. Himself" (*TB,* 249). God put his mark on language,
rendering it innate in-com-prehensibility, wrapping it in ambiguity,
in a perpetual tension of proximity and separation; at Babel,

language imploded. The "tower" collapsed, it lies in ruin, and these ruins are here, now, in this sentence, they are *in* language.

To summarize, the interpretation suggested here points out the following: it is precisely in moments of inconsistency that otherness might present itself most invasively and hence call for a response exceeding any general or standard code of exchange. Approaching another qua Other means being at the wake of Babylonian exile: exposed to irreducible communication gaps, to breakdowns, failures and lapses; yet these do not mark the end of communication but rather an opening to otherness through communication. As Geoffrey Bennington contends, "Something is communicated to me in a strong sense, or *there is* an event of communication, only when I do not have immediately available to me the means to decode a transparent message" (1994, 1–2). This implies that there is communication only when there is a moment, however fleeting or minimal, of nonunderstanding, of disorientation, or even of stupidity with respect to what is said. I am in a situation of communication in a deep sense only when I do not understand what the Other says. Here the space of communication is most radically open for the Other's intervention, and it is here that communication is perhaps most radically itself. This reveals the danger in the attempt to render the universe monolingual, since striving for a linguistic unity implies overriding the irreducible difference of speakers and obliterating intervals of inconsistency. Perfecting language as a means of communication—and thereby reconstructing a lost archetypical community—circumscribes linguistic aporia as a problematic condition to be scrutinized and ultimately resolved. When relegated to the downside of constructive exchange, misunderstanding and incomprehension are consequently excommunicated from what might fall within the boundaries of any legitimate communicational spectrum. If there is a lesson to be learned here it is merely that the irreconcilability of tongues and speakers, which in itself gives rise to the opportunity of facing otherness pointblank, does not denote the termination of meaningful communication but rather its very initiation. It is from here that communication truly worth the name would involve a special challenge, namely, the renewed endeavor of, and the ethical commitment in, translating.

Translation as a Paradigm of Communication

Two German translations of poetry books appeared between 1923 and 1924: Walter Benjamin's translation of Charles Baudelaire's *Tableaux parisiens* and Franz Rosenzweig's translations of 60 hymns and poems by the medieval Jewish poet Yehuda Halevi. In addition to the translated texts, each book contains an essay on the philosophy of translation. Benjamin's introduction, "The Task of the Translator," and Rosenzweig's afterword not only comprise two rich and complex approaches to the act of translation but also suggest some provocative insights into translation as a paradigm of communication. Both Benjamin and Rosenzweig would later comment on these essays as the pinnacles of their intellectual pursuits.[10] Although written in reference to two very different texts, the two essays share many theoretical similarities; there are also, of course, some important differences. In the following, I confine my discussion to the ways they conceptualize the act of translation, emphasizing particularly its significance within the wider issue of communication as an ethical involvement.

Walter Benjamin: Translation Is a Mode

Walter Benjamin opens his account by positing the basic problematic of translation: the relationship between the original text and the translated one, between original and recipient language. The essential quality of translation, argues Benjamin, is not in the imparting of information. Translation that intends to perform a transmission function cannot offer anything but information and hence something inessential to the original. For Benjamin this is the hallmark of bad translation—venturing to state the same thing in another language. But if the work contains something more than information, something that is fundamentally unfathomable, mysterious, "poetic," untranslatable, it can be reproduced only if the translator is also a poet. This is the cause for yet another kind of bad translation, one that is intended to accommodate the reader, to render meaningful the alien text in the proverbial idiom. Such translations revere the target language by attempting to make the foreign familiar. Translation is therefore in a bind between original and target language; serving either one or the other is inevitably to lose the "essential quality" of the work.

"Translation is a mode," contends Benjamin, and this mode is expressed in the work's translatability (1969, 70). This idea corresponds with Benjamin's broader approach to language according to which language primarily communicates itself; it is a medium of communication in the purest sense—language communicates communicability.[11] For Benjamin, translatability is the essential feature of certain works, which in themselves call for translation. This is not to say that such works should or even could be translated; rather, it means "that a specific significance inherent in the original manifests itself in its translatability" (ibid., 71). Translatability issues from the original: it enunciates a claim for a continued life (or rather, after-life, since translation comes later than the original), for a renewed meaning, a claim for truth (for Benjamin, the ultimate example for translatability is the Holy Scripture). Yet if certain works imply this elusive quality, only through translation is it liberated and made manifest. Translation is charged with a mission: to safeguard a feature that is noncircumscribable within any single language. It is not oriented toward the original nor toward the translating language, but rather toward something that is in each language as well beyond each (Galli 2000, 22). Translation is a mode pointing toward "pure language."

Benjamin further explicates the unique role of translation by suggesting: "Translation thus ultimately serves the purpose of expressing the central reciprocal relationship between languages. It cannot possibly reveal or establish this hidden relationship itself;

but it can represent it by realizing it in embryonic or intensive form" (1969, 72). Translation discloses the interrelation between languages, as what is stated in one language can be, at least potentially, stated in another. While lying beneath every single language, this relation becomes evident only *between* languages, in the attempt to translate from one to the other. Translating from language A to language B, as George Steiner notes, makes tangible the implication of a third, active presence (1975, 64). Languages share a special kinship, they are "not strangers to one another, but are, a priori and apart from all historical relationships, interrelated in what they want to express" (Benjamin 1969, 72). Before and beyond imparting information, languages share an intention to express, an expression of their expressibility. This kinship of languages, which can be manifest only in translation, is not accomplished "through a vague alikeness between adaptation and original. It stands to reason that kinship does not necessarily involve likeness" (ibid., 73–74). Translation does not constitute a meltdown of single languages into one linguistic fusion. The kinship of languages (that is, as individual members of the same family) rests in the intention underlying each one, an intention that no single language can attain by itself but which "is realized only by the totality of their intentions supplementing each other: pure language" (ibid., 74).

This leads to the acknowledgment that translation inevitably has a special involvement with alterity, but one that insists neither on domesticating the foreign nor on absorbing it into itself. Translation involves more than recognizing or tolerating alterity, as Benjamin writes:

> This, to be sure, is to admit that all translation is only a somewhat provisional way of coming to terms with the foreignness of languages. An instant and final rather than a temporary and provisional solution of this foreignness remains out of the reach of mankind; at any rate, it eludes any direct attempt. . . . Although translation, unlike art, cannot claim permanence for its products, its goal

is undeniably a final, conclusive, decisive stage of all linguistic creation. In translation the original rises into a higher and purer linguistic air, as it were. It cannot live there permanently, to be sure, and it certainly does not reach it in its entirety. Yet, in a singularly impressive manner, at least it points the way to this region: the predestined, hitherto inaccessible realm of reconciliation and fulfillment of languages. The transfer can never be total, but what reaches this region is that element in a translation which goes beyond transmittal of subject matter. This nucleus is best defined as the element that does not lend itself to translation. (Ibid., 75)

Translation implies an involvement with a foreign element, with otherness, which in itself remains forever elusive. It strives to achieve a pure linguistic state, a "final, conclusive, decisive stage of all linguistic creation," but this goal, ipso facto, is unachievable. Herein lies the paradoxical nature of every faithful translation: while being inspired by "pure language," it can neither dwell there nor enter it completely. "Pure language" can never be actualized, only gestured toward. At best, a translation might touch the original only lightly and at infinitely small points, just as a tangent touches a circle, thereupon pursuing its own linguistic path. Reminiscent of a Sisyphean motif, translation yields to something it cannot fully capture. The task is never complete and translation is imperative precisely for that reason; it is necessary and impossible, necessary because impossible.

Jorge Luis Borges's story, "Pierre Menard, Author of the *Quixote,*" recounts a radical feat of translation. Menard, a twentieth century poet, took upon himself a most Herculean task: to reproduce the already extant *Don Quixote* without consulting the original. "Needless to say," writes Borges, "he never contemplated a mechanical transcription of the original; he did not propose to copy it. His admirable intention was to produce a few pages which would coincide—word for word and line for line—with those of Miguel de Cervantes" (1964, 39). Menard's task was, therefore, one of total translation—to become in tune with Cervantes to the point of assuming the sum of components that had produced the original. For that end, he converted to Catholicism, studied seventeenth century Spanish, learned the rules of chivalry, and forgot the history of Europe after 1602. Among Menard's project bibliography were also early texts on universal language, including Leibniz's *characteristica universalis*. Astonishingly, Pierre Menard was able, at long last, to produce a few fragments identical to the original. Yet although indistinguishable verbally, Menard's lines, expounds Borges, are infinitely richer and subtler than Cervantes's. Whereas Cervantes's writing was in his own culture and language, for Menard, reproducing a few fragments (and the key line: "truth, whose mother is history") three centuries later meant transgressing a human boundary—the negation of time and space. Even identical words might have different meaning in different times, and this is one of the reasons every generation produces its own translations of the same originals.

Diverging radically from Menard's feat, Benjamin defines the task of the translator as "finding that intended effect [*Intention*] upon the language into which he is translating which produces in it the echo of the original" (1969, 76). Translation does not attempt to replicate, transcribe or transubstantiate the original; it does not attempt to follow Menard on the path to remedy Babel. Rather, it endeavors to reverberate the original's intention in the target language, and in order to produce that effect the translator has to search for a spot within the target language that would resound the foreign one most distinctively. The task of the translator, Benjamin concludes, is to "release in his own language that pure language which is under the spell of another, to liberate the language imprisoned in a work in his re-creation of that work" (ibid., 80).

Benjamin's notion of translation upholds much of the complexities and challenges instituted by the encounter with otherness. To be sure, this aspect of translation is only latent in Benjamin's text, as it is mostly concerned with the actual textual practice. Still, I highlight this aspect in Benjamin's account because it captures something of the elusiveness of the ethical involvement with alterity. Specifically, this account assigns the translator to the irreducible point of contact between familiar and foreign while neither rendering the familiar foreign nor making the foreign familiar. The task of the translator lies in *interrupting* his or her own language, finding in it traces of otherness, and thereby exposing and expressing the fundamental relation of one language with the other. The original affecting the translated text does so only indirectly; it is quite close but infinitely remote. It is in this proximity of languages that translation transpires. Herein translation institutes the underlying relation between languages by expressing, rather than effacing, their differences. This relation, ineffable as such and in itself, is expressible only in the singular approach of one language to another.

Franz Rosenzweig: All Communication Is Translation

A translation of Yehuda Halevi's works, states Franz Rosenzweig, does not aim to make the reader believe that Halevi composed in German. These translations are nothing but translations. For Rosenzweig, the point of translation is completely misguided if the translation attempts to make the original speak in the language into which it is translated. This is not to say that in such a case the content of the translation would be incorrect. If a German merchant receives an order from Turkey and sends it for translation, it is likely that the translation would be accurate enough to execute the order. Yet the problem, Rosenzweig argues, is not accuracy—such a translation may indeed be German enough but not Turkish enough. The translation of the business letter is done in the German that is "already there," and its understandability is dependent upon that very transaction. By contrast, the task of a genuine translation is to "reflect the foreign tone in its foreignness: not to Germanize what is foreign, but rather to make foreign what is German" (Rosenzweig 1995, 170).

Absorbing the foreign original in the native language renders translation a mere technical transformation. Such a translation makes no demands on the target language, as it leaves it intact; it remains as it was before the translation. Yet the problem Rosenzweig identifies in this action is much deeper, for it represents a view that deems language a mere instrument of communication. By allowing the original to appear as if it were actually written in the translated language, language "rigidifies to a means of communication, which any Esperanto can completely bring about" (ibid., 171). Technical translation that aims to make what is beyond the boundaries of a single language intelligible within those very boundaries is comparable to the work of a universal language, which for Rosenzweig epitomizes the annihilation of the tension between the foreign and the familiar, Other and Same—a linguistic lobotomy. Technical translation might be similar to the work of a Babel fish, the leechlike creature in Douglas Adams's *Hitchhiker's Guide to the Galaxy* (1992): by popping it into his ear, the galactic hitchhiker could understand any language he came across, allowing him to use his own idiom even in the remotest parts of the universe. Such reconciliation between origin and target languages, it should be noted, would be radical to the point of making the initial translation the final and the only one.

Rosenzweig's account preserves a special role for the translator, which bears in itself an important ethical commitment:[12] "The translator makes himself the mouthpiece of the foreign voice, which he makes audible over the gulf of space and time" (ibid., 171). Through translation, she or he allows the foreign voice to express itself in its own tone, tenor and accent. Nevertheless, the translator is not a mediator or a representative of that voice; he or she does not assign himself or herself to the task of enunciating something in the place of the original. This would still be within the realm of technical translation (like the role of Adams's Babel fish). The effect of the foreign voice as expressed in its translation is manifested by transforming the target language: "If the foreign voice has something to say, then the language afterwards must appear different from before" (ibid., 171). The language into which one translates must undergo a certain renewal by making what is indigenous somewhat alien and thereby approaching the foreign voice from within. In other words, it must be ruptured and interrupted.

The fact that such a renewal of one language through a foreign one is at all possible indicates that each single language upholds the expressive potential of others. Parallel to Benjamin's approach, Rosenzweig claims: "One can translate because in every language is contained the possibility of every other language" (ibid., 171). To Rosenzweig, all languages stem from the same germ cell and are therefore united in the things they can express. "There is only one language," he asserts. Yet the oneness of all languages is not monolithic—it is not one in the structural or foundational sense but, rather, in the sense that every language trait of one language can evidence itself, at least in principle, in others. The mutual translatability of languages reveals an underlying bond between languages that becomes evident only through the efforts and the effects of translation, in the move toward another language, but still within the multiplicity of languages and peoples (Galli 2000, 18).

Translation may then be regarded as an individual involvement guarding against the establishment of a unitary linguistic structure, as expressed allegorically in Franz Kafka's "The Great Wall of China." In Kafka's tale, a mysterious high command has decreed the building of a Great Wall by means of a piecemeal system. The command was never fully understood save by an ancient book expounding that the wall would eventually provide a secure foundation for the tower of Babel, which had failed because of the weakness of its foundations. "How can the wall," asks the narrator, "which did not form even a circle, but only a sort of quarter or half-circle, provide the foundation for the tower?" (1960, 77). Still, the construction spanned through generations and was carried out by many people who contributed to its building piece by piece, working together dispersedly, never completing a continuous structure. The fragmentary wall of Kafka's story, much like the work of translation, would never come full circle, and precisely for that reason the wall provides the foundationless foundation for the unrealizable goal of reconstructing Babel.

Rosenzweig's account also presents the opportunity to rethink the meaning and the place of understanding in communication in terms of translation. In a letter to a friend, he writes, "I myself understand a poem only after I have translated it; a compromising confession" (Rosenzweig, quoted in Galli 2000, 18). What Rosenzweig intimates here is that translation augments the original by adding new meanings: through translating, the original takes up shades and nuances previously concealed by its native idiom. By brushing against a foreign language, the original is enhanced and extended. At the same time, translation changes the target language, causing it to stretch out and grow. Translation reveals the fundamental dialogical aspect of language, exposing the fact that language is never complete within itself as private or national. The translated text may therefore appear as the pretext upon which one language touches the other without converging. It is here that the greater goal of translation lies, as Rosenzweig writes: "one should translate so that the day of that harmony [*Eintracht*] of languages, which can grow only in each individual language, not in the empty space 'between' them, may come" (1995, 171). Cultivating a language in the empty space between languages—precisely the Esperantist and other universalistic aspiration—abolishes the very prospect of translation. Such attempts ultimately culminate in producing an essentially monological language. The understanding generated through translation, on the other hand, is always in process: while aiming for the day in which all languages exist in harmony, it is always in the state of "not-yet," like Kafka's Great Wall. This harmony is the horizon of communication—never actually reached yet still dictating the general direction, an inspiration that always exceeds actuality.

This leads to the deeper level translation occupies in Rosenzweig's philosophy of language. An excerpt from a text written in 1926, "Scripture and Luther," presents succinctly the kernel of his approach:

Translating means serving two masters. It follows that no one can do it. But it follows also that it is, like everything that no one can do in theory, everyone's task in practice. Everyone must translate, and everyone does. When we speak, we translate from our intention into the understanding we expect in the other—not, moreover, some absent and general other, but *this particular* other whom we see before us, and whose eyes, as we translate, either open or shut. When we hear, we translate words that sound in our ears into our understanding—or, more concretely, into the language of our mouth . . . in speaking and hearing, what is asked is not that the other possess our ears or our mouth—in that case translation would be of course unnecessary, as indeed would be speaking and hearing as well. And in speaking and hearing between peoples it is not asked that the translation be either the old original—in which case the hearing people would be superfluous—or a new original—in which case the speaking people would be annihilated. Only a mad egoism could desire either of these. (Rosenzweig 1994, 47–48)

The two masters that translation serves, according to Rosenzweig, are thus the original and the target language, one's own tongue and the foreign one. Translating is described as *serving* the two rather than using them—a task that is at the same time indispensable and unattainable, indispensable because unattainable, a task that escapes rigid theorization, veering instead to actual practice. For Rosenzweig, translation is not merely a textual activity, it is the fundamental action of every communication, including a spoken exchange. Translation precedes and enacts understanding: when speaking one translates from one's intentions to the Other, a particular Other, who accompanies the process and "whose eyes, as we translate, either open or shut." And when hearing, one translates into one's individual framework and context. Still, understanding does not imply transposing one's point of view with the Other's, nor does it necessitate a stable resolution between parties: it is not about possessing the Other's ears or mouth—Rosenzweig's idea of understanding is nonessentialist. By proposing that understanding follows translation, Rosenzweig deflects understanding from both rational and spiritual mindsets, rendering it instead as an exigent task to be carried out only in the pragmatic specificities of each particular exchange.

It therefore seems that by locating translation at the very basis of communication, Rosenzweig draws a direct parallel between language and person: from one language to another, from one person to another (Galli 1995, 325). It follows, then, that translation may provide a model for both speech and writing, a communication paradigm for semiosis, for using signs, for responding to the Other (Gibbs 2000, 292). Understanding, as a prospective outcome of this process, can be achieved only in the response to the Other: from one language to the other, from one individual to the other, from one community to the other, from one nation to the other. Neither subordinating nor subsuming, this relationship is the prerequisite for understanding: unsettling and renewing—contaminating—the familiar by and through the foreign, the Same by and through the Other.

A passage from Italo Calvino's enigmatic text, *Invisible Cities,* offers yet another astute portrayal of the stakes associated with translation. Newly arrived and ignorant of the languages of the Levant, Marco Polo could deliver his reports to Kublai Khan only by using objects collected during his travels, to which he pointed with gestures, leaps, cries, imitations and sounds. Marco Polo's stories were hardly clear to the emperor, especially because objects could have various meanings depending on the story. However, what enhanced for Kublai every piece of news was "the space that remained around it, a void not filled with words. The descriptions of cities Marco Polo visited had this virtue: you could wander through them in thought, become lost, stop and enjoy the cool air, or run off" (Calvino 1974, 38). Over time, words began to replace objects and gestures—"The foreigner had learned to speak the emperor's language or the emperor to understand the language of the foreigner"; but then a strange thing occurred: "communication between them was less happy than in the past" (ibid., 38–39). True, words were more efficient, and yet when Polo began to describe life in the places he had visited, words failed him. Slowly he went back to relying on gestures and grimaces. Again, a new kind of dialogue evolved in which the Khan answered with his own hand gesticulations. As understanding grew, their hands began to assume fixed attitudes and the repertory of gestures tended to become closed and stable.

Calvino's parable, like Marco Polo's objects and gestures, may mean different things at the same time. Yet what the exchange between the two protagonists seems to capture most perceptively is the loomlike motion of translation. Incomprehensibility and communication gaps institute translation as a mode of communication. The role of translation is irreducible to the information delivered— it is quite possible that Marco Polo's descriptions were completely misunderstood by Kublai Khan. Paradoxically, the operation depended on its incompletion because once a shared code was achieved there was no need for translation, or as Calvino insinuates, when the exchange was most clear and lucid it was also "less happy." Renewing the dialogue involved rupturing communication and thereby reinstituting the role of translation, but as soon as a new exchange pattern set in, the role of translation withered. When denotation and connotation became one, communication ceased, leaving Marco Polo and Kublai Khan mute and motionless.

In conclusion, I have attempted to explore translation as a communication paradigm involving a constant engagement and negotiation with alterity. The two accounts by Walter Benjamin and Franz Rosenzweig provide a gateway to the task of translating. The accounts differ in many respects, and I do not intend to suggest they share the same view of translation. However, I wish to consider a few points that resonate between them. First, for Benjamin as for Rosenzweig, language is much more than an instrument of communication. Both suggest, in different ways, that language expresses first and foremost expressibility itself. Language articulates primarily an approach to another, or, to use John Stewart's (1995) phrase, it is a form of articulate contact. Translation reveals the dialogical nature of language, its answerability, to use Bakhtin's (1990) term, which inspires every exchange. Both accounts claim that languages are not strangers to one another because every language contains the possibility of every other language. This is what makes translation possible in the first place. But the relationship between languages is not one of convergence, of all languages meeting at the same point. Languages constitute a relationship based on their dissimilarity: the multiplicity of languages is precisely what introduces at once the necessity and impossibility of translation. Consequently, both reject the idea of universal language, Rosenzweig more explicitly than Benjamin. The space between languages is not to be conquered and their bond is not to be actualized. Pure language is forever unspoken.

Translation indicates an inherent feature in every communication. Although usually referred to as transpiring between languages, translation originally occurs within each individual language. Translation, as George Steiner contends, "is a special, heightened case of the process of communication and reception in any act of human speech. The fundamental epistemological and linguistic problems implicit in interlingual translation are fundamental just because they are already implicit in all intralingual discourse" (1975, 414). Translation takes place within language as much as between languages; interlinguistic translation is indicative of a more fundamental intralinguistic translation. Translation as a mode of communication transpires between foreign tongues, even if they speak the same language. Communication depends on the multiplicity and irreducible difference between communicators and languages, for when people are "of one tongue and the same speech," communication effectively reaches a paralyzing halt.

Finally, every act of translation involves an approach from "here" to "there," implying that saying is not only *in* a certain dialect but *saying to* another dialect, context, individual, community. This movement or approach toward something that is always beyond one's linguistic and communicational competence intrinsically involves uncertainty. Translation is an expression that exceeds what it translates; it is an offering, in the strong sense, of a locution that is unstable and incomplete. Translation understood in this way resonates with and bears the ethical significance of the Levinasian idea of the Saying: proposing a proposition from one singularity to another irreducible to either one or to any external common ground. Taken to its limit, this means that translation is neverending, for its objective, ipso facto, is unattainable. Its termination would eventually be determined by the limitations of the specific situation, by the fatigue, constraint or incapacity of the parties concerned. Since no reception is automatic and any understanding is inescapably transient and faltering, translation requires duration incommensurate with the time frame and intentions of the origin or "sender." The concept of translation may then offer a way to approach the question of understanding from the Other's side of the process. For these reasons, translation is a paradigm of communication that is fundamentally Other-oriented.

Interregnum

By way of conclusion, I would like to devote the remaining pages to Tzvetan Todorov's *The Conquest of America: The Question of the Other* (1984). Todorov provides a most telling analysis of the encounter of Europeans and Native Americans as reflected by their usage of language. Yet this work is not merely a historical study but an exemplary history—it turns to the past in order to say something about the present.

Todorov associates Christopher Columbus with a form of communication he calls communication between "man" and the "world." Holding a firm belief in the absolute European-Christian truths, Columbus's actual experiences and encounters with Native Americans served only as an illustration and further confirmation of what he had already known. Thus, for instance, while searching for the location of terra firma, the mainland, he announced that the land he discovered was part of the continent (Asia), discarding information from the natives, who claimed that the land was actually an island (Cuba). According to Todorov, Columbus's goal in his interactions was only to reaffirm his idea of the world, classifying his findings like specimens in a prearranged table. Nothing in the natives' information, character or behavior could have possibly surprised Columbus, as his conviction was always anterior to his experience. It seems, therefore, that Columbus's travelogue does not reveal his exploit as the discovery of America but rather as rediscovery, as finding it exactly as he had already conceived it to be.

Columbus's addressed his language, accordingly, directly to nature, to the referent. To him, words and things were tied together, circumventing the dimension of intersubjectivity and the reciprocal value of words. Even when translating from the Native American language, Columbus was much less concerned with what a specific word signified in the natives' conventional and relative hierarchy. His objective was to see to which Spanish word it corresponded (Todorov 1984, 29). Failing to recognize the surrounding linguistic diversity, the only two possible, and complementary, forms of behavior adopted by Columbus upon encountering a foreign tongue were to acknowledge it as a language but to refuse to admit it was different, or, to acknowledge its difference but to refuse to admit it was a language (ibid., 30). Columbus, as Todorov concludes, constitutes the figure of the enslaver to whom the natives were, at best, subhuman. In Columbus's view, there was no human subject on the other side. His use of language, which was heedless of the existence of an Other, was the harbinger of the violent subjugation of Native American cultures, religions and languages to European conventions.

Hernando Cortés's approach might appear prima facie as opposed to that of Columbus. Unlike Columbus, Cortés wanted to comprehend the world of the "Indians." The first most important action in his quest for information was employing an interpreter, a woman known by the name "La Malinche" (ibid., 100). Fluent in

Aztec and Mayan languages as well as Spanish, she constituted Cortés's point of contact with the native population. Cortés was extremely intrigued by the native Other: he admired Native American culture, customs and art; he endeavored to immerse himself in the foreign civilization, in its language, social and political structures. He wanted to slip into the Other's skin. The objective, nonetheless, was still power and control. Cortés, as opposed to Columbus, constitutes the figure of the colonizer. Indeed, for him the "Indians" were not mere objects but rather an exotic and fascinating people; however, in his scope they were individuals or subjects only insofar as they were producers, manufacturers, of objects and artifacts. Cortés's colonialism reflects a purely instrumental approach. The capacity to come to terms with the Other becomes a question of profitability rather than merely a quest for domination.

This leads to Todorov's staggering conclusion: it was precisely the ability to understand the Other that furthered the European conquest, leading ultimately to a most terrible termination. "This extraordinary success is chiefly due to one specific feature of Western civilization which for a long time was regarded as a feature of man himself, its development and prosperity among Europeans thereby becoming proof for their natural superiority: it is, paradoxically, Europeans' capacity to understand the other" (ibid., 248). Cortés's superior understanding did not prevent the brutal annihilation of Aztec civilization and society; quite the contrary, this destruction became possible precisely because of his understanding. It was Cortés's superior understanding (which at times bordered on overt admiration) that facilitated a quick takeover of Mexico. Levinas's observation that comprehension involves seizing or taking [*prendre*] something that is Other into the Same, takes in Todorov's account a most tragic twist: "There is a dreadful concatenation here, whereby grasping leads to taking and taking to destruction" (ibid., 127). Understanding does not safeguard the Other from calamity, and as Cortés's case shows, it might even introduce further violence. Such is the understanding that kills.

However, several figures came closer to acknowledging the Native Americans as moral human beings, as Others. Among them was Bartolomé de Las Casas, a colonizer who withdrew his aspiration to assimilate the natives and developed in his old age an esteem and even love for the natives not as a function of his ideals but of theirs. Another figure was Albar Nuñez Cabeza de Vaca, a conquistador whose explorations brought him to a view external to both Christian and Native American universes. His descriptions of interactions with Native Americans introduced a third pronoun, "we," which indicated the blurring of his identity (ibid., 199). But most interesting in this respect were Diego Duránd and Bernardino de Sahagún, two scholars who studied for decades native culture, history and society. Their pursuits for knowledge, as opposed to Cortés's, led them to the acknowledgment of the Other, which, in turn, interfered with the initial rationale of their pursuits.

According to Todorov, Duránd constitutes a form of cultural hybridization. His initial explorations into the Other's universe were shaped by the broader effort to convert the Native American population and battle paganism. Duránd noticed that the natives had inserted segments of their old religion into the Christian practice. Holding a purist idea of Christianity, he began comparing the two cultures, an involvement that led him to find the alien rites and rituals strikingly similar to those of the Christians. But this conclusion only caused him to be even more attentive to the natives. Duránd's book on Aztec religion consequently includes two points of view, Spanish and Aztec. In examining some discrepancies between the two, he made use, inter alia, of a manuscript written in the Native American language, Nahuatl, which he translated into Spanish. "He who translates a history," writes Duránd in this text, "is only obliged to reproduce in a new language what he finds written in the foreign tongue" (ibid., 213). Having intimate knowledge of both cultures, he assumed the role of the translator. Duránd's goal was not truth, historical or otherwise, but fidelity to a foreign voice.

Sahagún, argues Todorov, represents an approach emphasizing the exteriority of the Other's voice. Like Duránd, he also set out to explore the foreign culture with the intention of propagating the European. Sahagún, a grammarian and Latin professor, was deeply committed to the dissemination of Christianity (ibid., 219). To facilitate its expansion, he learned the native language Nahuatl, and in his writings he went on to portray the Native Americans as potential converts. But his later work on the spiritual and material life of the Aztecs before the conquest marks a radically different perspective. He desired not only to know the Aztec culture but also to preserve it. Sahagún started to compile testimonies he found most trustworthy, and in order to guarantee their truthfulness he presented them in the original Nahuatl, to which he added his own translation. The result was a work of great complexity combining Spanish and Nahuatal, as well as drawings. Sahagún's approach of letting the different voices speak and then adding his commentary was intended to achieve a greater fidelity to the alien voice. Both Sahagún and Duránd, concludes Todorov, represent an affirmation (though in different ways) of the Other's alterity, which goes hand in hand with the recognition of the Other as a moral subject.

What distinguishes Sahagún and Duránd is their indeterminate position: neither Spaniard nor Native American, neither obliviousness nor symbiosis, neither here nor there. To demarcate this position, I borrow the Latin word *interregnum,* which originally means a period between two sovereigns or regimes, to denote more figuratively the space or interval between authorities, systems or mindsets. Such is also the position of the translator: as a writer and a speaker—communicator—she or he is in the interregnum of languages, communities, and cultures, not merely "in-between" but simultaneously inside and outside, both within and beyond. The translator is at once an interpreter and an interrupter. The translator's task is not accomplished in bringing one into the other, but in the approach from one *to* another, from here *to* there, and vice versa. In this light, Levinas's words resonate even more distinctively: "A sign is given from one to the other before the constitution of any system of signs, any common place formed by culture and sites, a sign given from null site to null site" (*LP,* 122).

*   *   *

"As efficient causes of expressions that convey information," writes Alphonso Lingis, "we are all interchangeable. Our singularity and our indefinite discernibility is found in, and is heard in, our outcries and our murmurs, our laughter and our tears: the noise of life" (1994, 92). As effective carriers and relayers of information, the Babylonians were all variants of the Same: members of a transparent community that ensured that what was formulated in the mind of each one was also formulated in the minds of all the others. Forged by the alliance of sameness, Babel was a city purged of noise. It was the confusion of languages that infused Babel with the noise of life, the babble of noise, the noise that would forever become tantamount with the name "Babel."

The story of Babel has provided a rich metaphorical repository for those striving to reconstruct a universal speech community. According to such schemes, which usually venerate communal identity, fate and goal, the construction of a common vernacular would ultimately contribute to the construction of an idyllic world community. But such attempts might equally signal a nascent violence operating under the cloak of perfect communication, more specifically a form of colonial violence subjugating linguistic peripheries to totalizing schemas. In calling attention to the otherness eclipsed by the breaking down of linguistic barriers, I do not wish to present a view valorizing the gaps accompanying, for better or worse, any kind of communication. My aim has been, rather, to draw out the otherness that inheres in every linguistic exchange but emerges most viscerally in instances of misunderstanding, inconsistency and incomprehension. These borderline incidents at the frontier of linguistic capabilities are precisely where ethical possibilities may lie. The ethical position involving language and the Other implies a nonalienating foreignness: a relation preceding and exceeding any common ground, site or lingo. Both snugness in the familiar, on the one hand, and radical immersion in the strange, on the other, might mark heedless and even detrimental disregard for otherness. An ethical relation, in contrast, is a nonassimilatory relation consisting in an exposure to the Other, in proximity, in a nonunifying affinity. To approach another qua Other intimates a tentative contact, from one singularity to another singularity, in piecemeal fashion. Such is the task of translation: an involvement irreducible to either side, which implies the precariousness in the interregnum of speakers, languages and cultures. That Babel can never be undone is precisely what inscribes communication with an ethical mark.

FOUR

Incommunicable Boundary

What hampers communication is communicability itself;
humans are separated by what unites them.

—Giorgio Agamben, *The Coming Community*

J ohn C. Lilly's *The Mind of the Dolphin* opens with the following statement: "Communication, when it succeeds, is one of
man's greatest assets, and when it fails is his worst enemy" (1967,
19). "The best communicators," he adds, "are those who are the most
mentally healthy, happy, natural, spontaneous, disciplined persons"
(ibid., 19). Emphasizing the correlation between successful communication and mental health, Lilly, an accomplished psychiatrist,
has ventured to combat "man's worst enemy" by means of facing
the ultimate challenge: interspecies communication. To Lilly, such
an exploit could serve as a template for human problems—*inter*-
species communication as a parable of the *intra*species condition.
Thus, by traversing the border between human and nonhuman—the
boundary between the familiar and the utterly foreign—an invaluable truth about the generality of communication might be revealed.

The challenge, Lilly stresses, is a momentous one: "For the mental health of each one of us, for the national and international peace of all of us, communication is a paramount and pressing issue" (ibid., 22).

Lilly's approach may indeed be extraordinary in its candor or simplicity, but its epistemology hardly constitutes an exception. It reflects three sides of a conceptual triangle that will be the focus of the following discussion: (1) the relationship between mental and social well-being and communication; (2) the dangerous or even disastrous effects associated thereby with communication failure; and (3) the relegation of incommunicability to the perimeters of ordinary processes. As I hope to show, these three facets do not merely form a simple conjunction, but are in fact causal and inter-dependent insofar as they work to constitute a conceptual frame-work of communication that is predisposed to the regulative ideal of transparent interaction. What this causality entails, then, is situating the incommunicable boundary at the edge of existing possibilities, at the divide between ordinary and extraordinary and hence as the next frontier to be conquered. Thus, the location and the locating of that boundary introduce questions of liminality and heteronomy, of transgressing and traversing the interface between Same and Other—in short, the makeup of an encounter with alterity.

As a way of intervention, I turn to a phenomenon that is perhaps the ultimate manifestation of a communicational boundary: autism. By examining the ways in which autism has become an object of knowledge in disciplines concerned with mental and social life, I will unpack the modes by which communicability and incom-municability have been perceived, distinguished and deployed in clinical, scientific and social research. The theme of communica-tion is an Ariadne's thread that runs through some key works on autism, which I weave out in order to discover what this phenom-enon has come to denote. The next section addresses the ethical challenge introduced by an alterity that insists on remaining beyond communication. Turning to Herman Melville's *Bartleby the Scrivener,* I will unravel a tangle of risks and possibilities instituted by an encounter with a figure that prefers not to interact, a singularity that upsets binary classification and calls for an equally singular response. Extending from the literary case of Bartleby, the following section proceeds to generalize on the possibility of failure in communication. Drawing on speculations by Derrida and Levinas, I propose that the risk of failure is a necessary and positive condition of communication, and, consequently, that incommunicability is in fact intrinsic to and constitutive of communicability. Such reconceptualization, I argue, recalls the relation with the Other back into communication and summons an encounter with alterity.

Autism: A Brief History of a Communicational Boundary

The term "autism" was originally coined by Swiss psychiatrist Eugen Bleuler in 1911. Stemming from the Greek *autos* for "self" or "same," the term denoted a special disorder Bleuler associated with severe cases of schizophrenia (another term he coined) manifested in detachment or escape from reality. Bleuler's definition seemed to have captured a condition that presumably had been floating around long before it was circumscribed as such. One early and well-documented case was the Wild Boy of Aveyron, a feral child who had been found wandering naked in the forest in the winter of 1800. The child, named by the Parisian press "Victor," looked to be about 12, unable to speak, highly irresponsive and incapable of explaining who he was or where he had come from. A physician named Jean Itard took the boy into his home and devoted the following five years to teaching the silent boy to speak. Despite Itard's efforts, "Victor" never learned to speak, except for some sign language (Itard 1962). However, he seemed to be very particular about certain mundane activities, especially household rituals such as setting the table. It was also reported that the boy used to spend hours a day wrapped in a blanket and rocking back and forth. An observer commented that the boy had "no sense of gratitude towards the man who feeds him," while another added: "I am dismayed to see natural man so egotistical" (Dolnick 1998, 173). "Victor" seemed to be living in a universe of his own, barely aware of other people. The discovery of the wild boy quickly became a hot topic in Parisian salons and cafés, falling readily into the period's debate about society's impact on the individual and the image of the "noble savage."

The Other Mind

The person who is most associated with the modern classification of autism as a separate syndrome is Leo Kanner, an Austrian-born child psychiatrist working at Johns Hopkins University. In 1943, Kanner published "Autistic Disturbances of Affective Contact," a seminal paper that is still widely regarded as a defining piece in autism research. Kanner's study was based on eleven children seen in his clinic (eight boys and three girls) of mixed personal and social backgrounds. In addition to diagnosis, Kanner's report also contained parents' views of their children's behavior, including descriptions such as: "self-sufficient," "like in a shell," "happiest when left alone," "acting as if people weren't there," "perfectly oblivious to everything about him," "giving the impression of silent wisdom," "failing to develop the usual amount of social awareness" and "acting almost as if hypnotized" (1973, 33). Although the children had some resemblance to those suffering from schizophrenia, the lack of common characteristics, such as early onset, hallucinations and precedents in family history, led him to believe that these children shared a common, previously unreported, disorder. This disorder, concluded Kanner, was the children's *"inability to relate themselves* in the ordinary way to people and situations from the beginning of life" (ibid., 33; italics in the original). In contrast to Bleuler, who used the term to describe a disorder associated with schizophrenia, Kanner claimed that autism was a separate phenomenon: "There is from the start an *extreme autistic aloneness* that, whenever possible, disregards, ignores, shuts out anything that comes to the child from the outside" (ibid., 33).

In studying these children, Kanner focused on three key characteristics: social interaction, communication impediments and insistence on sameness. Almost 60 years later, these remain the defining characteristics of the disorder.[1] Unlike cases of childhood schizophrenia, which are sometimes manifested in withdrawal from preexisting relationships, these children never formed relationships in the first place (Mesibov, Adams and Schopler 2000, 639). "The children of our group," writes Kanner, "have all shown their extreme aloneness from the very beginning of life, not responding to anything that comes to them from the outside world" (1973, 41).

Eight of the eleven children had acquired the ability to speak while the other three had remained mute. The speaking children were capable of clear articulation and presented no difficulty in naming objects. Kanner noted that most parents reported that the children had learned at an early age to repeat inordinate numbers of nursery rhymes, prayers, list of animals, rosters of presidents, the alphabet forward and backward, and even French lullabies. These unusual abilities clearly reflected a nascent intelligence and a remarkable rote memory (these and other abilities were portrayed most conspicuously in the Hollywood movie, *Rain Man*). Kanner inferred that these extraordinary talents might have been the result of parents saturating the children with information so as to entice them to interact. Although unsure whether parents' behavior contributed essentially to the course of the psychopathological condition, he conceded that "it is also difficult to imagine that it did not cut deeply into the development of language as a tool for receiving and imparting meaningful messages" (ibid., 35). Diagnosing their conversational abilities, Kanner described the children's understanding as literal, noting in addition an unusual tendency to repeat pronouns, often retaining the intonation of the speaker. His diagnosis was that "from the start, language—which the children did not use for the purpose of communication—was deflected in a

considerable measure to a self-sufficient, semantically and conver-
sationally valueless or grossly distorted memory exercise" (ibid., 34).

The third characteristic observed by Kanner was insistence on
sameness, or as he put it, "The child's behavior is governed by an
anxiously obsessive desire for maintenance of sameness that
nobody but the child himself may disrupt on rare occasions" (ibid.,
36; italics in the original). The children appeared to be particularly
sensitive to intrusions such as loud noises and abrupt movements,
to which they frequently responded with horror. Yet, according to
Kanner, it was not sounds or motions themselves that were dreaded
but the intrusion, or the fear of intrusion, upon the child's aloneness.
Thus, changes in everyday routine like furniture arrangement, pattern of behavior, a change of clothing, as well as broken and dis-
mantled objects, often drove these children to despair. The dread of
change and incompleteness seemed to be connected to the monot-
onous repetition observed in the children's expressions and behavior. These children were avoiding any threat to their extreme
aloneness, which resulted in an obsessive desire for consistency.

Kanner remained ambiguous as to the cause of the disorder. His
paper ends by asserting the existence of an innate disability he
identifies as "inborn autistic disturbance," while suggesting at the
same time that parents might have also contributed to the development of the disorder.[2] Others allowed for much less complexity.
Bruno Bettelheim was undoubtedly one of the most visible authorities on autism during the 1960s. His professional profile included
dozens of books and articles, commentaries and many television
appearances. Bettelheim's credo on autism was presented most
fully in his magnum opus, *The Empty Fortress*. Bettelheim left no
doubt as to whom he considered to be the cause of what he called
"infantile autism": "I believe the initial cause of withdrawal is
rather the child's correct interpretation of the negative emotions
with which the most significant figures in his environment approach
him" (1967, 66). Kanner's suspicion of the parents' contribution,
which includes descriptions like "perfectionist," "obsessive" and

"lacking humor," is gentle in comparison to Bettelheim's attribution of cause.[3] Pointing a blaming finger at the parents' behavior, especially the mother's, Bettelheim argues that the origin of infantile autism lies in a detached, unresponsive or otherwise depressed mother who generates in the infant a sense of frustration that ultimately leads to the child's withdrawal.

Yet, it was not only the pathological condition that evoked his lifelong fascination with autism. Bettelheim maintained that studying the problems posed by autistic children might have implications far beyond the particular disturbance:

> Beyond the many "scientific" reasons that make it important to study this severest arrest of personality there was also a personal bent to my interest. What first disturbed me and aroused my interest in these children was how deliberately they seemed to turn their backs on humanity and society. If their experience of reality was such that it led to a total rejection, then there was a terribly important lesson to be learned about reality, or whatever part of it provoked their rejection. (Bettelheim 1967, 6)

Bettleheim's preoccupation with autism, or what he called his "personal bent," originated from a distinct experience in his life, which can hardly be overestimated, on his understanding of autism. Bettelheim, an Austrian-born Jew, was a survivor of two concentration camps, Dachau and Buchenwald, before fleeing Europe to the United States in 1939. His wartime experience, so he argued on many occasions, provided him with the crucial clue to understanding this affliction: "I had experienced being at the mercy of forces that seemed beyond one's ability to influence. . . . It was an experience of living isolated from family and friends, of being severely restricted in the sending and receiving of information" (ibid., 8). Retaining a scrutinizing eye during captivity, Bettelheim postulated that the extreme conditions experienced in concentration camps caused some people to suffer from emotional depletion, to avoid any contact with their surroundings, and eventually to retreat into themselves. This "near-autistic" behavior (as he dubbed it) often marked an imminent demise. "Could there be any connection," he asks, "between the impact of the two kinds of inhumanity I had known—one inflicted for political reasons on victims of a social system, the other perhaps a self-chosen state of dehumanization?" (ibid., 7).

Bettelheim's controversial contention was that there were some important parallels between the behavior he had witnessed in concentration camps and that of autistic children, most distinctively an acute withdrawal and social isolation resulting from overwhelming circumstances. Viewed from this perspective, the autistic child's mysterious symptoms would not seem so mysterious. It was an extreme response to an extreme situation, as what was an "external reality for the prisoner is for the autistic child his inner reality. Each ends up, though for different reasons, with a parallel experience of the world" (1967, 65). [4] But if the perpetrators of the prisoners' distress were SS guards, those responsible for the child's were inevitably the parents. The child who develops autism, he declares, "seems to feel about himself and his life exactly as the concentration camp prisoner felt about his: deprived of hope, and totally at the mercy of destructive irrational forces bent on using him for their goals, irrespective of his" (Bettelheim, quoted in Dolnick 1998, 183). [5]

When discussing the dynamics of autism, Bettleheim states that "autism begins as a breakdown in communication" (1967, 78). According to his reasoning, the process whereby one is compelled to retreat from social reality begins in the communication between infant and nursing mother. Even at that early stage, he argues, things can go tragically wrong as the infant might misread the mother's anxiety or discomfort, or correctly read her negative feelings and so "may retreat from her and the world" (ibid., 72). Communication breaks may therefore be a result of both misinterpreting "the signals he receives in terms of his anxiety or hostility" or interpreting these signals only too correctly and consequently withdrawing from contact (ibid., 73). In any case, it is the "degree and persistence of the person's failure to send and receive messages correctly that accounts for the degree and persistence of his emotional disturbance" (ibid., 73). Thus, communication breaks in the interpersonal inflict breakdown in the intrapersonal; and the more communication is obstructed, the less contact there is with others, and the more one must rely on his or her inner experience to interpret reality.[6] For Bethlehem, communication breakdown leads to difficulty in interpretation, to solipsism, and ultimately to autism.[7]

While Bettelheim's psychoanalytic theory of autism was gaining support, some initial contradictory observations were nevertheless being made. For one thing, many autistic children had perfectly normal siblings who seemed unaffected by the syndrome originating from their allegedly ill-natured parents. Further studies found that parents of children with autism demonstrated as much warmth and sociability as parents of children with other disabilities.[8] Most recently, autism has been viewed as an organically rather than psychologically based syndrome.[9] Since the exact cause of autism remains unknown (although some argue it is genetic), several scientists have recently opted to study and describe the nature of the syndrome rather than to inquire into its origin. A most notable attempt along these lines is the cognitive psychology approach, Theory of Mind.

Although developed by a few scientists, the work of Simon Baron-Cohen is probably among the principal contributions to the development of Theory of Mind (ToM). The basic tenets of his approach are presented in his celebrated text, *Mindblindness: An Essay on Autism and Theory of Mind* (1995). The work's premise is based on a growing understanding among cognitive scientists of the dependence of human behavior on the individual's ability to interpret others' behavior and intentions. In other words, effective social relations require that one fills in the blanks when dealing with others, that is, be able to "mind read" others' actions and intentions. On this view, mind reading is a natural and innate capability that enables social contact to take place: "We mindread all the time, effortlessly, automatically, and mostly unconsciously" (1995, 3). Mind reading does not connote a paranormal or telepathic knack; it is a fundamental, yet impressive, capability underlying human mentality. This ability, according to Baron-Cohen, is the result of a long process of evolution during which the increase in brain size gave rise to "the ability to process information about the behavior of others and to react adaptively to their behavior" (ibid., 13). Mind reading is therefore an instinct that allows one to make sense of and modify one's behavior vis-à-vis other social interpreters:

> Like the chess expert, we are social experts. Our social reasoning process has become automatic and effortless—possibly as a result of years of daily practice, possibly also because, right from the beginning of life, the human brain is programmed to automatically and effortlessly interpret social behavior in this way, as a result of millions of years of evolution. Perhaps we never go through a stage of finding social interaction an effort to decode. Rather, we are born understanding social chess, or at least we have many of the basic principles that we will need in order to make sense of and take part in the game. We have some key neural mechanisms that allow us to "see" the solution to a social situation intuitively. (Ibid., 19–20)

Mind reading and communication, argues Baron-Cohen, are closely connected. Referring to the linguistic theories of Grice and Austin, he suggests that aside from "decoding the referent of each word (computing its semantics and syntax)," the key feature of communication is imagining "what the speaker's communicative intention might be" (ibid., 27). Thus, when communicating, one goes beyond the words one hears or reads to hypothesize about the speaker's or author's mental states. According to Baron-Cohen, this faculty, ipso facto, is what enables communication: "Our mind-reading fills in the gaps in communication and holds the dialogue together" (ibid., 28). Mind reading, in short, both complements and is dependent upon communication. This is true in yet another sense: "for communication to succeed, the speaker must monitor whether the meaning of an utterance has been received and understood as he or she intended it to be, or whether rephrasing is required to resolve ambiguity" (ibid., 29). An utterance like "Shall we?" will not, in most contexts, be enough to make sense and will require further elaboration so that the hearer will be able to understand the message. That such contraction of meaning is at all possible is because "language functions principally as a 'printout' of the contents of the mind" (ibid., 29). "Successful communication," then, entails a constant feedback check between communicators to verify whether the interpretation produced by one side corresponds with the other. The role ascribed to communication within this theory is of sharing information, or alternatively, of curbing misunderstanding due to incorrect or insufficient information.

Baron-Cohen identifies four separate mechanisms that comprise a mind reading system: Intentionality Detector (ID), Eye-Direction Detector (EDD), Shared-Attention Mechanism (SAM) and Theory-of-Mind Mechanism (ToMM). These four mechanisms are "hard-wired" in the brain and activated by experience, each corresponding roughly with what he designates as the "four properties of the world: volition, perception, shared attention, and epistemic states" (1995, 31). The functions of these mechanisms are as follows: ID is the perceptual device that interprets motion stimuli in terms of mental states of goal and desire; EDD detects the presence of eye stimuli, direction and target; SAM's key function is to build triadic relationships, that is, relations between the self and a third object; and finally, ToMM is the mechanism responsible for inferring the full range of mental states from behavior or, in other words, for employing Theory of Mind. According to Baron-Cohen, the four mechanisms share a complex relationship that develops throughout early childhood, by the end of which ToMM reaches its full functional capacity.

Proposing this elaborate theory of mind allows Baron-Cohen to focus consequently on autism as a special case study. According to his analysis, autistic children have normal ID and EDD but suffer from a deep impairment of SAM and ToMM. Less cryptically, this means that autistic children's "primitive" faculties of detecting others' intentions and eye signaling function normally, whereas their developmental faculties of shared attention and inferring others' mental states are severely impaired. Whereas "normal" minds possess the innate capability of mind reading, autistics are deprived of this crucial faculty. Thus, as the title of his essay suggests, autistics suffer from "mindblindness"; that is, they cannot read adequately other peoples' minds.

The cognitive description of operational systems of ToM and mind reading could equally be, as Baron-Cohen indicates, "a description of an organism with 'natural intelligence' (e.g., *Homo sapiens*), or it could be a description of an 'artificially' intelligent system (a robot or a computer)" (1995, 85). The only difference is that in the former the "wetware," as he dubs it, in the human neural brain takes the role of "hardware" in the machine. In keeping with this rationale, Baron-Cohen also speculates about the existence of mind-reading systems in the animal kingdom, considering the possibility that higher primates might also possess some ToM mechanisms. Baron-Cohen is not, of course, the first to muse about nonhuman communication (organic or mechanical) in attempting to learn about the human situation.[10] Such attempts were mostly based on the premise that control and communication systems are immanent in organisms both biological and artificial, thereby making the distinction between human and nonhuman dimmer.[11]

What is at issue, then, is a comprehensive schema of interactivity, of units-in-a-system, which, once constituted as such, is immediately mobilized to examine the most radical case of its own dysfunction. And yet, is it not equally possible to read autism, or more precisely "mindblindness," the other way around? That is, constitutive of Theory of Mind rather than explained by it? Could this theory of mind be consistent independently of its negation? Clearly for Baron-Cohen, autism is a paradigmatic case of system dysfunction, not just another mental disorder (he does not refer to any other examples, not even to schizophrenia, the "usual suspect"), but a critical collapse of ToM mechanisms. Yet by marking the edge of this epistemology, autism effectively validates the very concepts by which it is probed. Without autism, Theory of Mind would simply make no sense, and without the idea of "mindblindness," mind reading would be equally meaningless. To the extent that this is true, autism does not merely constitute a "case study" but the very foundation of ToM, precisely because it defies the theory's functional integrity. Autism plays the role here of the archetypical inverse, or the radical negative, which nonetheless completes the picture and thereby supports the epistemology, logic and structure of the theory.

My intention in adducing the Theory of Mind approach is not so much to challenge its truthfulness or scientific rigor but to cast doubt on its reasoning about "normal" communication and its use of autism to that end. Baron-Cohen is not the first to situate autism as a corroborating contrary, as it were, to a unified theory of mind (compare Minsky 1986). But in being unaware of, or willfully blind to, the historical context of its vocabulary (computer and communication engineering), the cybernetic depository it mobilizes, and the teleological bias governing his reasoning, he effectively surpasses his predecessors in defining autism as a paragon of incommunicability. As Donna Haraway has suggested, defining deviant behavior as a kind of communication breakdown that requires "informational therapies" is a product of the mid-twentieth-century marriage between psychology and cybernetics (1989, 105).[12] As a principal case of communication breakdown, autism is perhaps the most radical case of deviant behavior insofar as the communication system is concerned. Yet by positing this condition as insurmountable and irreparable—but still definable—in terms of the system, what is implied is that all other variants of interpersonal and social contact fall, in one way or the other, within the realm of the communication system.

The foregoing discussion reflects only a fraction of the extraordinary scientific preoccupation with autism. It is remarkable that such concern was devoted to a disorder whose occurrence for many years had been estimated at a rate of about four to five cases in every ten thousand.[13] Such statistics, at least prima facie, would hardly suggest a conspicuous terrain for intensive scientific research. As one professional attested,

> this syndrome has attracted the attention of clinicians and researchers far out of proportion to its incidence. It has drawn the attention of some of our most talented persons. . . . Articles and books on the subject number in the hundreds each year. . . . There is even a new journal *The Journal of Autism and Childhood Schizophrenia* devoted to it. . . . I know of no parallel in psychiatry or medicine where so much attention has been given to a relatively uncommon disorder. (La Vietes, in Sullivan 1976, 43)

This fascination might find explanation in the proposition I wish to advance here: namely, that autism is not merely a disorder but also a paradigmatic case of arrest in communication, socialization and development, and as the ultimate impasse it constitutes the antipode against which the medical-scientific discourse measures its rational tools for accessing another mind. Some of the titles of books and films on autism might be taken as a further indication to its special position in the discourse: *The Child in the Glass Ball, The Empty Fortress, The Siege, Your Child Is Asleep, The Ultimate Stranger, The Out-of-Synch Child, Invisible Wall, Far from the World, The Wild Child* and *Search for the Lost Self* (Sullivan 1976, 47). It is therefore possible that autism attracts attention because it marks an epistemological boundary, and as such bears high stakes for what Thomas Kuhn (1970) calls "normal science" in fields such as medicine, psychology, psychiatry and cognitive science.

My point, in sum, has to do with the ways the delineation of autism reflects back on ordinary situations of communication. What I propose is that the medical-clinical-scientific involvement with autism as a paramount phenomenon of incommunicability may be viewed as laying a knowledge claim not only with respect to autism but also with respect to the common condition.[14] The accounts above differ in many respects, but it seems that they all converge when it comes to describing "normal" communication. Kanner, Bettelheim and Baron-Cohen seem to regard successful communication as closely related to normalcy, to mental health, and to nourishing relationships. Autism, by contrast, marks the boundary of this discourse by portraying it as a pathological result of communication breakdown or a malfunctioning communication system, be it external (relation with parents) or internal (either self-imposed or inborn). More generally, what such perspectives imply is a dichotomous and mutually exclusive understanding of the relationship between communicability and incommunicability, the latter being relegated beyond the realm of the ordinary, "normal," processes. Incommunicability is deemed exterior to whatever might fall within the realm of typical and constructive relations. Yet it is precisely this exclusion, which involves a hierarchical arrangement of the opposition, that endows the typical with positive meaning. Thus, without retracting from the severity of the condition, which might nonetheless correspond somewhat with its pathological diagnostics, the various ways in which autism has been categorized might also indicate something about the discourse produced around it, and particularly about the manner "communication" has been deployed therein. The variety of characteristics used to describe autism may therefore reveal the medical-clinical-scientific stance—one that undoubtedly bears a significant authority—as intrinsically equating normalcy with effective communication.

Handling the Refractory Element

While striking root in medical science as a disorder associated with a single mind, autism has also permeated the metaphorical and conceptual vocabulary of students of culture and society. One of the earliest examples is Harold Lasswell, who used the term as early as 1930 in his study of psychopathology and politics to denote a behavioral pattern he called "autistic reveries," indicating a non-adjustive approach to reality (1930, 226). Some eight years before Kanner's classification, Lasswell employed this category in a paper entitled "Collective Autism as a Consequence of Culture Contact" (1935). In this study, Lasswell investigated the impact of intercultural contact between Western culture and Native American communities along the Rio Grande River. These communities have been in contact with Spaniards, Mexican and Americans since the sixteenth century and have been relatively persistent in preserving their ceremonial practices and cultural unity. The cultural crisis suffered by all, almost simultaneously, was the cult of peyote, a drug produced from a cactus, which was brought from the plains of Oklahoma. The introduction of the drug marked an increase in "autistic events": the widening scope of fantasy and individuality instituted through the adoption of the cult, which was deeply anathematic to the prevailing collectivistic culture of Native American pueblos. The community that was more successful than others were in maintaining its social and cultural structures was the Taos pueblo, which practiced what Lasswell calls "collective autism": the consumption of the drug in the company of others. Lasswell's conclusion is that "we have to do with a situation in which a collectivistic, Apollonian, and formalized culture subjected to restriction by individualistic, Dionysian and autistic cultures, has responded by increased collective autism" (1935, 245).

While Lasswell employed "autism" mostly as a symptomatologic notion, for prominent social psychologist Theodore M. Newcomb it was an essential attribute existing in the intrapersonal, interpersonal and social. In "Autistic Hostility and Social Reality" (1947), Newcomb sets up a conceptual link between pervasiveness of communication breaks and harboring of hostile attitudes. The reasoning is quite straightforward: "the likelihood that a persistently hostile attitude will develop varies with the degree to which the perceived inter-personal relationship remains autistic, its privacy maintained by some sort of barriers to communication" (1947, 69).

Starting with the most fundamental level, a personal disorder might be regarded in itself as the result of restricted communication. Thus, for instance, the impossibility of communication caused by social and cultural taboos (such as sex) is responsible for psychopathological repression. Through psychoanalysis, Newcomb argues, "certain areas of the patient's life are restored to communication." In this way, "full two-way communication becomes possible. . . . [The patient] becomes more realistic—i.e., less autistic—in his interpretations of the other's response to his own behavior . . . it is a removal of barriers to full communication" (ibid., 70, 74). A successful process of communication with a substitute object of hostility (that is, the therapist) may accordingly alleviate one's hostile attitude toward oneself and one's significant others.

In Newcomb's view, the interpersonal is of special significance because it is the locus wherein "a process of maintaining normativeness occurs" (Newcomb 1947, 70). And the "therapeutic" quality of communication is equally true for the generality of interpersonal relations. According to Newcomb, isolation from interpersonal communication constitutes a crucial condition for the development of hostile impulses. Moreover, it is often the case that an initial impulse creates barriers to further communication, thereby perpetuating initial animosity. And yet, maintaining an exchange with others is not necessarily enough to prevent the perpetuation of hostile attitudes: employees may still sustain interaction with a boss they resent and spouses may spend years in a state of mutual mistrust. What is barricaded in such cases, Newcomb maintains, is not the process of communication itself but the individual's frame of reference. Sustaining a fixed frame of reference, which renders certain meanings inaccessible, is more surreptitious, indeed more insidious, a mode giving rise to barriers behind which hostile impulses might teem. To Newcomb, such barriers to communication prevent the possibility of seeing another as reasonable rather than hostile, or in George Herbert Mead's words, taking the role of the other (Mead 1967, 161). The only remedy is, as expected, reconstituting an effective two-way communication, which, in due course, may bring one back to social reality and even dissolve the most persistent frame of reference.

This reasoning sets the ground for a discussion of autistic hostility to others as members of different social groups. According to Newcomb, the principles at work on the individual level also apply to the social level and to the creation of what he identified as "socially shared autism" (Newcomb 1947, 78). The only difference is that while individual hostility is mustered up by individual defenses, collective insulation is created and reinforced by social agencies. Hostile attitudes toward minority groups, for instance, do not usually follow personal experience but are acquired through social interaction within the majority group. Hence, effective intragroup communication is essentially responsible for erecting barriers between groups, and the more invasive the intragroup processes the more persistent the intergroup barriers. In Newcomb's view, such mechanisms characterize racial segregation laws and practices in the United States, which restricted interaction between dominant and minority groups to conditions in which meanings were fixed in advance. But social isolation may equally be the product of group preference, perhaps the acme of which, Newcomb remarks, "was achieved by the Jews of old, who prescribed such rigid eating codes that it became almost literally impossible for any repast to be shared with a non-Jew" (ibid., 80). As a possible solution, socially constructed hostility is most likely to be reduced when institutionalized barriers to communication with members of other groups are crossed. A more pervasive attitude change, however, may be achieved by appropriating existing channels, which have already proved their effectiveness in producing group isolation, to transform an intragroup frame of reference. Hence, the same systems that serve to sustain group autism may as well serve to modify it.

Perhaps the most challenging case for Newcomb's approach is the introduction of the press and radio as the mass media of communication. For Newcomb, the very nature of telecommunication spells a serious problem since "distance and strangeness them-selves make communication difficult" (1947, 82). While being physically separated, groups and communities across the world learn about each other mostly through the mass media. Here, the key determinate of hostility is the social belief system, or what Walter Lippmann called "the picture in our heads," which deter-mines the context into which information concerning distant peo-ple is fitted and retained (Lippmann 1957). Taking the role of the other becomes even more problematic if other groups are referred to in terms of a threat by leaders or by the media in which one has confidence, or both. There is reason to suspect, then, that rather than working to change "the picture in our heads," the media actually contribute to its assimilation. And since the malady of socially shared autism is similar in all relevant respects to that of individual and group antagonistic barricading, the diagnosis is essentially the same: find the barriers to communication and work to remove them.

Newcomb's multilevel analysis outlines a causal link between barriers to communication and the rise of hostile attitudes toward others both immediate and remote. As such, it supposedly pro-vides a blueprint for solving the meta-problem of human violence: the formation of animosity between individuals and groups. For Newcomb, communication is a crucial factor in both creating and alleviating hostile attitudes, a factor whose lack or misuse may account for the creation of autistic communication patterns. Communication in a closed circuit might then result in a short-circuit: by feeding on itself, socially shared autism might give rise and even elevate antagonistic attitudes. It follows that to counter-act hostility means to fight autism at any level, that is, to seek out indications of barriers to communication, to examine their cause and logic, and to reassign the misused channels of influence to benevolent ends.

Yet, is such indefatigable insistence on proactive communication not hostile in itself? Is such unrelenting compulsion to communi-cate not at the very least as hostile as a refusal to communicate? Is it not possible to turn the table on Newcomb's argument precisely with respect to the link between communication and hostility? Not only do I believe that Newcomb's approach betrays its own premise when associating hostility solely with autism, but I would even go further to claim that this approach might be in itself hostile when proclaiming to uncover practices by which hostility is being cultivated. Such an adamant reproach of an inability to take the role of the other, arguably characterizing instances of individual and socially shared autism, only renders itself as indifferent to alterity and as unable to take the role of the Other. For Newcomb the only thing that merits rigorous explication is communication blocks, while communicability passes as self-explanatory, natural and neutral. Since the question revolves around how communication can solve the problem of hostility, rather than whether or under what conditions it actually can do so, the prospect that the imperative to communicate might itself be detrimental remains beyond the scope of possibilities.

Newcomb's analysis seems to resonate with subsequent accounts employing the notion of autism to social research. A study by Newcomb's contemporary, which set out to explore the relationship between social equilibrium and ideological momentum, associated autistic patterns of behavior with rituals that aimed at maximizing *esprit de corps* and internal stability (Pieris 1952). Such were the behavioral patterns of native tribes attempting to counteract European intrusion and preserve their society's equilibrium. On a more ominous note, Pieris suggests that the essence of modern totalitarian societies "is the maintenance of barriers to communication, as was symbolically demonstrated in the Nazi burning of the books" (ibid., 345). According to this scholar, such patterns reveal "one of the most urgent problems of our age—this formation of autistic and mutually hostile social groups" (ibid.). Still others utilized autism as a key category to describe an even wider variety of social phenomena. A short list includes autistic attitudes as characterizing medical-scientific writing (Plaut 1950); identifying unenthusiastic middle-class television viewing habits as autistic (Geiger and Sokol 1959); drawing a direct parallel between symptoms of infantile autism and symbolic behavior of cults and religious groups (Westley 1982); the cold war as a case of mutual autism of superpowers (Galtung 1989); collective autism as constitutive of rigid social boundaries (Zerubavel 1991); and finally, autism as cultural *Geist* in modern thought and literature (Glastonbury 1997). A common thread in these speculations is the circumscription of an insolent pattern of behavior that seems to defy a normative convention about the role of communication in social life. Setting up the refractory element for further scrutiny signifies the beginning of a process by the end of which resistance could be tagged, evaluated and possibly resolved.[15]

Bartleby's Contra-diction

Up to this point, I have tried to problematize the axiom by which reciprocal communication constitutes a natural tendency leading to convivial relationship, and to point out the nascent intolerance that such an unambiguous axiom might carry. This is not to say that a reciprocal exchange is not worth striving for, nor to suggest that once achieved such an exchange would necessarily entail encroaching upon another's autonomy. Rather, what is at issue here is the a priori attaching of positive value to reciprocal interaction and the subsequent privileging of this type of relation insofar as the event of communication, and its possible consequences, are concerned. Such preference, I believe, runs the risk of expunging prematurely an event laden with ethical possibilities, namely, the challenge presented by alterity. In the following, I attempt to unpack an instance that exceeds classification and transcends the conceptual grid setting communicability apart from incommunicability. Being highly invested in categorizing phenomena, scholarly and scientific accounts like those analyzed above can hardly accommodate such elusiveness and conceptual ambiguity. Indeed, this is precisely what gives rise to the problematic pointed out in the previous section. A more discerning eye is likely to be that of a novelist, a case in point being Herman Melville's short story *Bartleby the Scrivener* (1853), to which I resort as a device for elucidating previously overshadowed complexities.

Bartleby, a pallid and introverted scrivener, is hired to do arduous copying work for the narrator, an elderly Wall Street lawyer. At first, Bartleby produces an extraordinary amount of work. He copies continuously from first light to dark, not pausing even for a minute while assuming the same serene and silent posture. But when asked to join his employer in examining the accuracy of his work, the scrivener responds, "I would prefer not to." Puzzled by the peculiar reply, the lawyer repeats the demand only to receive the same abstruse line. A few days past, a similar occurrence takes place when Bartleby is called to help examine copies of an important suit, to which he replies unwaveringly, "I would prefer not to." Stunned and outraged, the lawyer exclaims, "*Why* do you refuse?" to which Bartleby answers as innocently as before: "I would prefer not to" (Melville 1997, 13). "But there was something about Bartleby," recounts the narrator, "that not only strangely disarmed me, but, in a wonderful manner, touched and disconcerted me" (13).

Both curious and irritated by Bartleby's eccentricity, the lawyer decides to try befriending the odd copyist and in this way reason with him. Yet this also is to no avail: upon being asked to run an errand on an exceptionally busy day, Bartleby again emits his usual line. "You *will* not?" reproaches the lawyer; "I *prefer* not," repeats the scrivener composedly (17). He subsequently remains fixed in his hermitage, oblivious to everything but his own particular occupation, which he performs diligently. Dropping in the office one Sunday morning, the lawyer realizes that Bartleby has been actually living in his corner for quite some time. The disconcerting discovery brings him to surmise that the lonely man is suffering from an "innate and incurable disorder" (22). Approaching Bartleby empathetically, he implores: "Will you tell me, Bartleby, where you were born?"; "I would prefer not to," replies the scrivener. "Will you tell me *anything* about yourself?" "I would prefer not to," is repeated. "But what reasonable objection can you have to speak to me? I feel friendly towards you . . . What is your answer Bartleby." "At present I prefer to give no answer," says the odd man and retires into his hermitage (23). Bartleby's unreasonable behavior vexes his employer, who finds it disdainful—moreover, ungrateful—considering the indulgence given to such idiosyncrasies.

Before long the scrivener comes to a standstill: he declines to do any more writing. "I have given up copying," he answers in response to the lawyer's inquiries. Now having no service to the office, Bartleby is asked to leave the premises. But he remains there a week later like a fixture in the office, preferring not to budge. It is obvious that something must be done, but Bartleby's passivity keeps disarming any severe measure from being taken against him. Since there seems to be no way of removing the copyist who would prefer not to, the lawyer elects to move his business elsewhere. Bartleby would still remain in the office when a new renter takes over the lease. While at his new location, the lawyer learns that Bartleby was removed to a prison called the Tombs as a vagrant (yet another of the story's absurdities: a vagrant who would not budge). Bartleby dies in prison a few days later. But the mystery behind this character keeps preoccupying the lawyer, who hears that Bartleby was previously a subordinate clerk at the Dead Letter Office in Washington. The job of stacking these lost letters, which on "the errands of life" sped to death, speculates the narrator, must have had a deleterious impact on the man's emotional state, and he concludes somberly: "Ah Bartleby! Ah Humanity!" (41).

Melville's story has inspired various Marxist, psychological, theological and existential commentaries speculating on the meaning of this mysterious character (see Vincent 1966). Some have attempted to determine the psychopathological nature of the scrivener's infliction, and one has even argued that it is possible to identify his behavior as "infantile autism in the adult phase" (Sullivan 1976, 44). Although valid within their own contexts, such interpretations tend to overlook the significance of Bartleby's unique position and particularly the irreconcilable otherness encompassed in his preference not to communicate. It is not surprising, then, that this story has also attracted the attention of recent critics, for instance, Maurice Blanchot (*WD*), Gilles Deleuze (1997), Jacques Derrida (1998) and Giorgio Agamben (1999a), who each refer to the story to illustrate, inter alia, the stakes in the involvement with alterity.

Some critics have noted that Bartleby's anaphoric response bears a special grammatical (or rather, agrammatical) structure. "I would prefer not to" does not constitute a refusal or the simplicity of a negative response. This line, argues Blanchot, does not fold neatly into distinctions of pro and con, for and against:

> "I would prefer not to" expresses: an abstention which has never had to be decided upon, which precedes all decisions and which is not so much a denial as, more than that, an abdication. . . . This is abnegation understood as the abandonment of the self, a relinquishment of identity, refusal which does not cleave to refusal but opens up to failure, to the loss of being, to thought. . . . "I would prefer not to . . ." belongs to the infiniteness of patience; no dialectical intervention can take hold of such passivity. (*WD*, 17)

Refusal usually follows a cogent choice and is therefore the result of some kind of deliberate action. While it might still be frowned upon, to refuse to copy, to work or to respond, is still graspable within functional coordinates of action and reaction. As the lawyer admits, if there had been any sign of such a renunciation in Bartleby's demeanor, he would have doubtless "violently dismissed him from the premises" (Melville 1997, 12). Had he refused, he could have been regarded as rebelling against his circumstances and as such been ascribed with a social role. But Bartleby's line follows no such reasoning—it resists incorporation without the negative willfulness involved in resistance; it exceeds parameters of affirmation and rejection as it remains beyond such functional distinctions. Bartleby's comment does not conform to the perfunctory order of the law office, to an institutionalized and systematized version of social relations. "I would prefer not to" expresses neither defiance nor compliance but a "negative preference": the irreducible neutrality and the uncontainable passivity encompassed in Bartleby's response.

This "negative preference" (which may swirl upon itself to the point of preferring not to prefer) does not seem to bear a semantic difficulty: it is hardly incomprehensible, as the words appear to follow some kind of logic and denote a specific meaning even if a puzzling one. It is understandable yet still seems to make no sense. Although somewhat jarring, it is neither grammatically nor syntactically incorrect, but its form (ending with a negation and an open-ended preposition) undoubtedly comprises an unusual proposition. Gilles Deleuze argues that Bartleby's line has the form of an agrammatical formula, and this formula ravages itself, everything around it and ultimately language as a whole. This formula enters language uncannily and "hollows out an ever expanding zone of indiscernibility or indetermination between some nonpreferred activities and a preferable activity" (Deleuze 1997, 71). This formula, continues Deleuze, "stymies all speech acts, and at the same time it makes Bartleby a pure outsider [*exclu*] to whom no social position can be attributed" (ibid., 73). Bartleby, whom the lawyer-narrator describes succinctly as "more a man of preferences than assumptions" (Melville 1997, 27), articulates a line that upsets the commonsense assumptions or conventions by which language can designate things and activities. As though running beneath conventional English, the formula carves a kind of foreign language within language, creating a vacuum at the depth of its fixed system of reference. Bartleby's formula ruptures language from within without demolishing the totality of its structure; parallel to the way his presence upsets the routinized order in the office, his formula dislodges language from the inside, making the whole confront its very limit. As Giorgio Agamben adds, by hovering between affirmation and negation, acceptance and rejection, this formula expresses "pure potentiality" (1999a, 254). Instead of the Shakespearean binary "to be or not to be," Melville introduces a third possibility, a heteronomous sphere of potentially that transcends existing matrices of action.

Bartleby withdraws to a point of passivity that might be described as more passive than passive. At first, he submits himself to the passivity of writing: he works incessantly, not just fulfilling the lawyer's expectations of him but in fact exceeding them. His initial posture, which is undoubtedly passive, is still within the realm of cooperation, still within the dichotomous distinction of active and passive. But when asked to abandon this passivity and partake in a demanding exchange that inevitably involves a direct and unmitigated confrontation with the authority embedded in his employer, he quietly prefers not to, and thereby introduces an even deeper kind of passivity, one that resides beneath defiance and compliance. This passivity does not merely refuse the lawyer's authority but altogether *defuses* it, as he admits: "Indeed, it was his wonderful mildness, chiefly, which not only disarmed me, but unmanned me, as it were" (Melville 1997, 19). This "negative preference" makes the lawyer confront the scrivener's otherness *hic et nunc,* an encounter whereby the lawyer is disarmed of his powers and exposed to the asymmetry between his position and the one occupied by the frail scrivener. The disproportion between the two characters is so great that the excess of power on the side of the lawyer brings a deactivation of power, which is instituted, paradoxically, by the utter powerlessness of the scrivener.

While Bartleby's eccentricity assumes a rather stable manifestation, the lawyer seems to alternate between extremes: from curiosity to frustration, from a commanding position to helplessness, from fatherly compassion to murder rumination, from wanting to take the scrivener to his home to fleeing the office while leaving him behind. It seems that confronting Bartleby's uncontainable other-ness instigates a radical redefinition of the entire spectrum of pos-sibilities. Following Blanchot, Ann Smock describes this situation as one in which "nothing you can do is of any use but where there is absolutely nothing you might not do. All your power abandons you, but also every limit that has ever restrained you" (Smock 1999, 1038). In this trying situation, there is nothing one can do, but at the same time nothing that one cannot or might not do—the hori-zon of possibilities opens and shuts simultaneously, transforming what is conceived to be possible and impossible, making the impos-sible possible and vice versa. What is introduced thereby is a radi-cal sense of indeterminacy, which nevertheless marks an unlimited potential for action. The interaction (or, rather, the lack thereof) between the lawyer and Bartleby might be seen as illustrating an encounter with otherness that is at once intimately close and infinitely remote. Bartleby is a figure of the limit, a limit he occa-sionally approaches only to immediately retreat into the twilight of interaction. Here no preset rule of engagement will do: the response, whatever that may be, would have to be both unprecedented and unrepeatable. Bartleby, an intimate stranger, does not only disrupt order but also pleads for an original response, one that has never been issued before. This state of affairs marks a temporary ascen-dancy of the Other vis-à-vis rationality, laws and order, and there-fore an opening for a truly singular response. The lawyer's mournful cry "Ah Bartleby! Ah Humanity!" might therefore be read not as conjoining the scrivener with humanity but rather as the final verdict vindicating the rule of law and reason over the challenge of alterity.

There may be reason to suspect that Bartleby is a madman, a schizophrenic or even autistic. Indeed, as mentioned above, the lawyer surmises that the scrivener might be "the victim of innate and incurable disorder" (Melville 1997, 22), and the odd behavior he displays throughout could certainly entertain such an interpre-tation. This presumably confirms Sullivan's (1976) point that

Bartleby constitutes a case of a highly functioning autistic person, providing thereby an apt explanation both for his peculiar behavior and his ultimate fate. Such an explanation is problematic not only because it ends up presupposing itself, but also because it entails a total reduction of Bartleby's incongruous position. This is because defining it as autistic immediately ascribes it with the role of a negative inverse, consequently evacuating it from its heteronomous and nonassimilatory quality, from its radical otherness. The scrivener's incompatibility indeed opens up a veritable terrain of susceptibility to authoritative practices, to inspection and classification, and to the deployment of oppressive power. And yet, at the same time, his passivity resists analysis, as Derrida suggests: "without saying anything, he makes others speak, above all the narrator, who happens to be a responsible man of the law and a tireless analyst" (1998, 24). The inadequacy of conventional techniques drives the lawyer to despair, as he self-righteously declares: "Nothing so aggravates an earnest person as a passive resistance" (Melville 1997, 15). It is only after deciding to tear himself from Bartleby that civil order, now left to its own devices, resumes control and quickly disposes of the irritation. But as long as they were tied together by a mutually irksome situation, both Bartleby and the lawyer have had their fair share (although in different ways) of bizarre behavior. And as long as ambiguity prevailed, both seem to evoke empathy and disparagement intermittently. Thus, ascribing pathology exclusively to the scrivener only reveals the prejudice by which his condition is viewed.

To recapitulate, Melville's short story allows drawing attention to a point that resists clear-cut classification into binaries such as normalcy and aberration, cooperation and resignation, compassion and malevolence, communicability and incommunicability. As such, it illustrates with great intensity an excruciating encounter with alterity that is at once infinitely remote and parasitically close. This encounter evokes the ambiguity underlying an involvement with the Other, which introduces the ethical dilemma in its full magnitude. Bartley's formula, which refuses to refuse, carves out a space of inconsistency within language: given the option between engagement and disengagement, he would prefer not to, thereby presenting a third option incongruous to fixed interlocutory modes. In so doing, he disrupts the distinction between communicability and incommunicability while still facing in proximity, that is, while still evoking response-ability. Ironically, the copyist, who was initially mired in a mechanical reproduction, ends up being out of circulation—like the letters in the Dead Letter Office in which he used to work. His formula nevertheless articulates an appeal by pushing language to its ultimate boundary—to its ineffable "outside"—while bearing the trace of that which can never be stated. Bartleby's formula might therefore be seen as protracting a temporary suspension in standardized exchange, drawing out the heteronomy that marks an encounter with the Other.

The Question of Liminality

Can Bartleby's situation provide a lesson for the generality of discourse? What bearing might such an incommunicable alterity have on communication as a social practice? The intractability represented by the figure of Bartleby would undoubtedly dissolve under almost any kind of disciplinary system, which would ultimately dispose of the irritation by force of classification and exclusion. Yet discrimination against incommunicability is not exclusive to aberrant conditions, social or mental; it might equally be found in a liberal and rational setting still indebted to the ideal of cooperative communication. Consider, for instance, Bruce A. Ackerman's (1980) explication of the importance of public dialogue to liberal society. According to Ackerman, partaking in conversational practice is fundamental to sustaining liberal society. More specifically, it is rational discourse operating under certain basic rules that provides the framework for political participation, sensible civility and responsible negotiation between individual freedom and social obligation. However, a fundamental problem arises when it is impossible to convince someone of the logic of that framework. This framework reaches its ultimate limit, and consequently its breakdown, when it is impossible to persuade a prospective participant to verbalize his or her agenda, to talk about his or her problems. The point whereupon such conventional techniques collapse, argues Ackerman, marks the rise of a violent obstinacy:

> There is nothing I can say to persuade you to adopt Rationality that is not mocked by your blank stare. . . . I can use neither force nor reason to impose dialogue upon you. All I can do is ask my question and await your reply. If you try to stare me down and impose brute force upon me, I will act in self-defense. If, instead, you answer my questions, I will answer yours, and we will see what we will see. The choice is yours. (1980, 373–74)

For Ackerman, a situation in which one does not comply with the conventional rules of reasoning, that is, participating in reciprocal communication, spells an exertion of "brute force" that justifies, in turn, an act of self-defense. Since there is no practical way of forcing another to reply (although he speculates on rather extraordinary measures such as injecting "talk serum" only to quickly disclaim their legitimacy), an irresponsive stare introduces the ultimate boundary of congenial relation. The invitation to engage in a conversation is open to all those who are willing to abide by certain ground rules (rational argumentation, free access, tolerance to other views, and so on), the most basic of which is to actually participate in such a practice. It is, however, closed to those who cannot, will not, or would prefer not to. Responding is the Other's liability; should he or she opt otherwise, their decision would indicate an abuse of tolerance and goodwill.

Such an argument seems to denote a position restricting responsibility (and response-ability) exclusively to the realm of cooperative exchange, to a situation in which individuals are already interlocutors, present and accessible to each other, already in-communication.

It also introduces most drastically the question of responsibility to and for the Other who always escapes transparent interaction, and who always remains, to a certain extent, beyond communication. Does responsibility end with the termination of reciprocal communication? Does incommunicability draw the final boundary of one's responsibility? More fundamentally, what is the status of incommunicability with respect to one's relation to the Other?

There seems to be a conceptual thread running through the medical-scientific accounts of autism and the social examination of refractory elements. What characterizes such views is a decisive move to draw a line between spheres wherein communication processes transpire naturally and uninhibitedly, and an exteriority that negates the rules and logic governing these spheres. Thus, normalcy, normativity and civility are firmly set apart from their polar opposites, from behaviors and phenomena that seem to defy the immanent integrity of each sphere. Distinguishing the stable "inside" from the erratic "outside" implies a double movement: expulsion of antithetic elements, on the one hand, and reinstatement of inherent consistency, on the other. This effect corresponds with what Jacques Derrida (1981b) describes as the complicity between the *pharmakon* (both remedy and poison) and the *pharmakos* (scapegoat), representing two interrelated "allergic" reactions to the outside. While the first is used to cure the organism (but also involves, by definition, the incorporation of a foreign element to produce a vaccine and hence the risk of poisoning), the latter calls for the sacrificial exclusion of the Other, symbolic or actual. This double movement, which attempts to draw a clear division between the inside and the outside, between pure and impure, involves a constant definition and redefinition of the status of the boundary. A similar complicity was revealed earlier in this discussion with respect to the operation of communication: remedial when complying with the rationale of transparent exchange yet potentially toxic insofar as contributing to "autistic" insulation. The opposition between the two, which determines the locus of the boundary, is then set by way

of excommunicating incommunicability. And this double movement not only prescribes the logic of communicability but also, and
more importantly, instills it with propitious meaning.[16]

Disrupting the apparent stability of this conceptual dichotomy
ushers in the question of communication and alterity, an issue
addressed most explicitly in Derrida's essay "Signature, Event,
Context" (*SEC*). In this text, Derrida unpacks, among other things,
the general problematic of privileging speech over writing, the
question of signification with respect to presence and absence of
communicators, and the indeterminate status of context in relation
to meaning. Here, however, I would like to restrict my discussion
to Derrida's critical analysis of J. L. Austin's theory of performative
utterance, which may help to draw out the ethical stakes with
respect to incommunicability. Central to Derrida's discussion is the
status of what he calls "iterability" (Derrida derives *iter* from *itara,*
"Other" in Sanskrit), which sets the sign's potential legibility and
repeatability outside the context of its inscription, in the absolute
absence of its origin. The concept of "iteration" is proposed as a radically different mode of linguistic exchange linking repetition with
alterity and thereby breaking "with the horizon of communication
as the communication of consciousnesses or presence, and as the
linguistic or semantic transport of meaning" (*SEC,* 316). Whereas
traditional notions of communication (Greek logos, Western metaphysics of presence) prescribe the co-presence of interlocutors in a
harmonized social space, a symmetrical relationship between
addresser and addressee(s), and the correlation between meaning
and origin, iteration summons linguistic exchange to an encounter
with alterity, with the Other who always withdraws from presence.
At first glance, Austin's theory of performative utterance[17] seems to
be dealing with the complexity of communication, particularly
insofar as it does not limit itself to a purely linguistic, semiotic or
symbolic concept of communication, to the act of "transporting an
already constituted semantic content guarded by its own aiming at
truth" (*SEC,* 322). And yet, while emphasizing the heteronomy of

linguistic exchange, this theory dismisses the significance of a prospect that is perhaps the most heteronomous of them all, that of a failure.

Derrida points out at the outset that Austin recognizes the possibility of failure, of "essential risk," or "infelicity" as unavoidable in communication, yet at the same time regards that possibility as accidental and inessential to the operation of communication, and therefore irrelevant insofar as the generality of language is concerned. Although acknowledging that all conventional acts of communication run the risk of or are open to failure, such a possibility "is not examined as an essential predicate or *law*. Austin does not ask himself what consequences derive from the fact that something possible—a possible risk—is *always* possible, is somehow a necessary possibility" (*SEC,* 324). Such preclusion, Derrida adds, actually puts Austin in line with traditional linguistic theories from which he tries to distance himself.[18] This brings Derrida to speculate on the possibility of failure (which is already implied in the concept of iteration) not as a possibility that constitutes an exception or accident, but rather as intrinsic to the very structure of communication:

> Therefore, I ask the following question: is this general possibility [of risk] necessarily that of a failure or a trap into which language might *fall,* or in which language might lose itself, as if in an abyss situated outside or in front of it? What about *parasitism?* In other words, does the generality of the risk admitted by Austin *surround* language like a kind of *ditch,* a place of external perdition into which locution might never venture, that it might avoid by remaining at home, in itself, sheltered by its essence or *telos?* Or indeed is this risk, on the contrary, its internal and positive condition of possibility? this outside its inside? the very force and law of its emergence? (*SEC,* 325)

For Derrida, failure or risk, which is always a possibility, always possible, does not mark a circumference around the field of communication. Failure is not an anomaly that constitutes a kind of extenuation, that is, a predicament that must be kept at a safe distance, away from the positive operation of communication. Nor is it external to a secure space in which interlocutors might find themselves carrying out reciprocal exchange while avoiding potential pitfalls. Such a conceptualization, as pointed out before, would involve an exclusion that immediately works to purify a specific paradigm of communication from instances that might defy its rationale, ensuring its complacency within itself. By problematizing the speculations made by Austin, Derrida proposes to take the possibility of failure seriously—as a positive contingency of communication, as an inherent stake in its operation, or in the words of Ewa Ziarek, "as a risk that reveals something essential about the nature of communication and linguistic community" (1996, 99). Rather than exceptional or outstanding, this possibility is very much within communication and always implied in its patterns. And rather than extirpative and hence restorative, it is an internal feature that at the same time remains external to productive exchange, an "outside" that is still "inside," assuming a parasitical-like function. Risk of failure, failure as a risk, is not a particular case of communication breakdown but rather its general rule. By attempting to generalize the possibility of failure, Derrida effectively dissociates the process of communication from the ideal of transparent interchange, from the subjective intention to transport (fixed) meaning from one mind to the other, which ultimately implies the reduction of the Other to a mere recipient of a predestined message.

Shoring up the possibility of failure allows bringing Derrida's deliberation closer to the Levinasian idea of communication as an ethical event. For it is precisely the possibility of failure that permits drawing near the Other and that allows the Other to make a comeback. Levinas writes: "The problem of communication reduced to the problem of the truth of this communication for him that receives it amounts to the problem of certainty, of the coinciding of self with self, as though coinciding were the ultimate secret of communication, and as though truth were only disclosure" (*OB*, 119). As opposed to the attempt to derive communication out of concurrence of minds, which is based on a notion of a subject for whom every other is a potential destination or limitation in the expansion of information, Levinas proposes to consider the radical reverse. It is when facing the Other, in proximity, "at the risk of misunderstanding . . . at the risk of lack of and refusal of communication" (*OB*, 120), that one finds oneself confronted with an inarticulate call for communication of a different kind. This unsettling moment, which punctures the rationalistic ideal of communication, musters up the full onus of responsibility to and for the Other. Communication, now understood as a tentative contact, would involve a necessary uncertainty and would proceed as "an adventure of a subjectivity," always at the risk of failure: "Communication with the other can be transcendent only as a dangerous life, a fine risk to be run" (*OB*, 120). Thus, rather than abolishing responseability, this radical openness to the Other is the very condition of its eventuality. The collapse of patent interaction does not imply the folding of responsibility but instead implies its very beginning. For Levinas, not only does responsibility include the possibility of breakdown, but is in fact constituted upon such a possibility.

It is now that the general question of the relationship between communicability and incommunicability—the question of liminality—arises most distinctively. Following the explication of the possibility of failure and risk extended by Derrida and Levinas, I would like to trouble this seemingly clear-cut dichotomy, and suggest that instead of constituting an opposition, incommunicability is essentially a condition of communicability. The reality of communication means that communication is always imperfect and therefore inherently involves a certain incommunicable element in its operation. For if the self could somehow achieve total communicability, that is, a capacity to transfer meanings from one mind to others uninterruptedly, such a knack would ultimately culminate in the termination of communication itself. Or, as Geoffrey Bennington puts it,

"If the end of communication is the end of communication, then the closer you get to the end, the nearer you are to its end" (2001, 54). Complete interaction is noninteraction. In a situation of perfect communication, there would be no communication; or again, the closer one gets to the regulative ideal of communication, the further one gets from communication. It follows that in order for communication to actually take place, it has to pass through a phase of heteronomy, a phase that transcends the matrix of preset possibilities— a stage of radical uncertainty and indeterminacy. This means that communicability is already imbued with and implicated by a foreign element, an intrinsic component of alterity. And it is precisely here that the condition for responsibility lies in the form of exposure to and opening for the Other. Thus, perhaps a more apt way to describe the interrelation between incommunicability and communicability is *(in)communicability,* as a positive rupture or dehiscence infolded in the operation.

If one allows that communicability and incommunicability are not mutually exclusive, one may consequently call into question what is actually invoked when appealing to the notion of communication. The accounts dealing with the mental and social phenomenon of autism discussed earlier seem to express a common commitment to formulize a functional setting of communicative processes whereby communicability is firmly set apart from incommunicability. Such a move, which entails the repudiation of the parasitic nature of (in)communicability, might now seem more complicit with coercive incursion than with impartial, "scientific," explanation. For if failure is a generic possibility in every communication, rendering the rational-teleological version general would inevitably involve the omission of that very possibility. One may therefore read the appeal to communication in the previous accounts as reducing the nature of communication in the very act of invoking it. The notion of communication continuously being called upon is one that has already congealed into a compatible form, and thus it corresponds perfectly with ideal conceptions of mental and social life. Yet, this seemingly ingrained causality is effectively a contraction attainable only by means of purging prospective procedures from refractory elements (the complicity of *pharmakon* and *pharmakos*). An ideal form of interaction would always entail expulsion of nonconfirmatory elements. Perfect communication would always involve excommunication.

*   *   *

My purpose throughout this chapter has been to trace the status of incommunicability and to specify the ethical stakes involved in consigning it to the edge of an otherwise coherent zone of practice. Through the case of autism, I have tried to problematize the common inclination of several discourses of mind and society to predicate normalcy and sociability upon communicability, and its corollary in deeming the incommunicable aberrational and hostile. In the texts analyzed above, autism constitutes the ultimate boundary of communication, relation and contact; it marks an epistemological circumference separating communicability from incommunicability while rendering the latter exterior to "ordinary" experiences. This fascination with the inexplicable, I argue, has much to do with a preoccupation with an epistemological boundary, one that bears considerable stakes for the study of human mentality and sociality. As such, it reveals some of the most fundamental conceptions regarding the nature of communication within several well-charted academic fields, particularly during the post-World War II period. Most noteworthy in this respect is the extent to which communication itself is deemed explicable, knowable and analyzable in terms and within each individual field of knowledge. There is nothing mysterious about communicability and therefore nothing that calls for further scrutiny; it is only what is perceived to be its negation that requires further unpacking and deliberation.

The two main discursive fields employing the notion of autism discussed here join up in demarcating communicability as both normal and normative. Likewise, they coincide in implicating incompatible phenomena as anomalous—pathological in the medical-scientific, insolent in the social-cultural. The effect of such demarcation is twofold: on the one hand, decontaminating mental and social spheres of communication from incongruous elements, from otherness, and on the other, enclosing these spheres within homogenized and totalized schemas. What consolidates the integrity of this epistemology is the hierarchical order within the dichotomy, an order that renders impasse noxious and interaction remedial. Nevertheless, interaction is desired only insofar as it does not contribute to maintaining closure, that is, to the barricading of communication that may transpire on a broader or higher level of interaction. It is at this juncture that the unstable status of communicability is evidenced most fully. What remains constant throughout, however, is the detrimental function given to impasse, which in turn serves to validate the restorative function of interaction. Such conceptualization, at its most extreme, might itself be unveiled as insular, for insisting on the inviolability of reciprocal exchange may in fact portend disqualifying precisely that which resists such conceptualization of communication. It is in this sense that an inexorable demand to communicate might be as inward-looking as an obstinate opting-out.

Generalizing on the immanence of risk and the possibility of failure, I have attempted recalling the "location" of the boundary back into communication, and propose that risk of failure, lack or even refusal inheres in and is constitutive of communication. This leads to the seemingly paradoxical conclusion that the impossibility of communication is in fact what gives birth to its very possibility. Deeming incommunicability a condition of communicability—hence (in)communicability—introduces a prospect of "positive" rupturing, of a contingency summoning up an encounter with alterity. Such a prospect would designate responsibility as both preceding and exceeding reciprocal exchange, as responsibility begins where reciprocity ends.

FIVE

Silent Demand

Speak, you also,
speak as the last,
have your say.

—Paul Celan, *Speak, You Also*

The language of awaiting—perhaps it is silent, but it does not separate speaking and silence; it makes of silence already a kind of
speaking; already it says in silence the speaking that silence is. For
mortal silence does not keep still.

—Maurice Blanchot, *The Writing of the Disaster*

The right of the individual to freedom of speech has been a central issue in modern liberal thought and an inspiration to numerous moral, political, constitutional and legal deliberations. Having
its roots in the Renaissance, it is tied to the shift in the Western
world from authoritative feudalism and monarchism to a social
organization that guards, and is indeed based on, the dignity, reason
and freedom of the individual. Freedom of speech, a practice based
on the stature of the speaking self and on his or her innate right to
speak, has acquired a prominent place in the liberal lexicon of

social and political rights. Discussions on its operation in modern democracies often involve confronting questions of equality, respect, fairness, liberty and tolerance. As such, its significance and role are presumably informed by the ways liberal thought has conceptualized the relations between speech, individuality, and society.

In this chapter, I attempt to explore the concept and the practice of free speech from a critical standpoint. However, the challenge I wish to propose here is not so much concerned with the positive right to speak or with issues of restricting the right to free speech. It is, rather, the other side of speaking, or the Other's side of this freedom, that is at the center of the following exploration. My purpose is to unsettle the ethical and political credence given to freedom of speech by exposing it to the call for response-ability expressed by the Other. This is with the aim of reconceptualizing the social role of speech and pointing to discursive possibilities ignored by liberal tenets of free speech, foremost among which is speech's disregarded counterpart: silence. A theme running throughout this chapter is thus the status of silence with respect to speech. In drawing attention to the elusive "missing half" of discourse, to silence as an enunciation of alterity, I hope to bring up several ethical and political challenges for further consideration.

The analysis follows three basic arguments for freedom of speech often cited in literature: (1) as a means for attaining the truth, (2) as a means for self-fulfillment, and (3) as a means for maintaining and furthering democracy. The first section explores key approaches to the role of free speech in the social pursuit of truth, focusing in particular on the interrelation between truth and restriction. The ensuing section deals with the role of free speech in the process of self-fulfillment by following two trajectories: calling into question the liberal portrayal of speech as teleological and self-serving, and discussing the primacy given to individual freedom, and resulting issues such as recognition and tolerance. The final section ushers in the question of politics as specified by the role of expression in a democratic political space. At issue is the ethical-political demand for justice and the responsibility to respond to and account for the social production of silence.

Beyond Truth

A most consistent and historically durable argument for freedom of speech is based on the centrality of free expression to the pursuit and discovery of truth. The core assumption is that if free speech, discussion and publication were restricted, society would invariably be prevented from attaining facts relevant for making accurate judgments. Protecting free speech is crucial especially against governmental interference and regulation, which might be motivated by considerations other than the attainment of facts and truth. While making the discovery of truth a primary value, liberal thought has traditionally posited the status of truth as relative, that is, as something that has to be questioned and clarified in relation to other alternatives taking place, as one prominent U.S. judge once remarked, "in the competition of the market" (Holmes, in Barendt 1985, 8). Seeking knowledge about truth is a process through which all sides relevant to the question must be heard, particularly those who are most vehemently opposed to the prevailing opinion. Therefore, the pursuit of truth involves a constant exposure to opposition and criticism, to debate and evaluation and, ultimately, to the risk of being proven wrong.

One of the earliest voices advocating free speech in the name of attaining truth was the English poet John Milton. His famous address to Parliament, *Areopagitica,* has since been a major inspiration and conceptual anchor for numerous deliberations on free speech. Milton's address was concerned with the 1643 order of Parliament that no book should be printed or put on sale unless the authorities first had approved it. While the publication of books was relatively unrestricted during the Middle Ages, mainly because they were deemed inconsequential insofar as their influence, the development of the printing press and the expansion of literacy presented the question of censorship in its early modern form. Milton challenged a restriction that had been in place in various forms since the end of the fifteenth century and that seemed to have transmogrified into a new governmental body. Inspired by the democratic idea of ancient Greece and alluding to Isocrates's discourse, Milton pleaded for the liberty of unsolicited printing, and thereby for the unshackling of Truth:

> She needs no policies, nor stratagems, nor licensing to make her victorious. . . . Give her but room, and do not bind her when she sleeps, for then she speaks not true, as the old Proteus did, who spake oracles only when he was caught and bound, but then rather she turns herself into all shapes except her own, and perhaps tunes her voice according to the time, as Micaiah did before Ahab, until she be adjured into her own likeness. Yet it is not impossible that she may have more shapes than one. (1882, 52–53)

According to Milton, only the abolishing of all forms of censorship and the full disclosure of all aspects and manifestations, including those held to be false, malevolent and evil, could bring Truth to appear. Such an emancipation permits access to the world as it really is: a world in which good and evil "grow up together almost inseparably" (ibid., 17). It is from one apple tasted by Adam that human knowledge inherently involves the knowledge of good and evil "as two twins cleaving together" (18), which for Milton principally means knowing good *by* evil. This equally holds for the quest for Truth, whose shape is rarely readily apparent but possibly multifaceted or even intermixed with manifestation of falsehood. Since "the knowledge and survey of vice is in this world so necessary to the constituting of human virtue, and the scanning of error to the confirmation of truth" (18), the way to discern one from the other is by gaining knowledge of all facts and facets. His faith thus lies in the individual's rational capacity to make sense of the world independently of authoritative dictums. For how else, he asks, "can we more safely and with less danger scout into the regions of sin and falsity than by reading all manner of tractates, and hearing all manner of reason?" (18–19). According to Milton, then, freedom of expression is both the right and duty of every individual, as a rational being, to explore the grounds of his beliefs and actions.

Having set up and celebrated all benefits implied by the practice of unrestricted expression, Milton mentions in passing that all this does not apply to manifestations undermining piety and Christian faith. As he writes: "I mean not tolerated popery and open superstition, which as it extirpates all religions and civil supremacies, so itself should be extirpate," adding immediately to the list that "which is impious or evil absolutely either against faith or manners no law can possibly permit, that intends not to unlaw itself" (Milton 1882, 54). Freedom of speech, the cradle of the quest for Truth, is extended only to those who subscribe to the common faith, excluding a priori all forms of speech that may be deemed impious or dissenting. As Thomas Emerson (1966) notes, among those who might find themselves deprived of the benefits of such freedom are Catholics, atheists and non-Christians. It seems that in Milton's perspective, the views of these groups are not even deemed false, erroneous or evil; they are beyond the realm wherein true and false, good and evil, conflate and compete—they are, so to speak, eviler than any evil and falser than any falsehood. Nevertheless, the exclusion embedded in his reasoning is vague enough to include other groups and individuals who may be found "impious" or "against faith" under certain circumstances. Since these categories do not specify the identity of speakers, someone's views could be tested only when they are heard, and if suitability to exclusion is to be determined in relation to the actual process of expression, then censorship on free speech can be placed, at least in principle, on anyone, and on contents as well as on individuals. Thus, while promoting the ideal of unrestricted expression, Milton's vision of free speech as a means for discovering Truth stops short at meeting its own criteria. By restricting in advance the realm wherein Truth may be found, the outcome of this process can be nothing but a product of that very restriction.

Another classic account of the argument from truth is found in John Stuart Mill's 1859 essay *On Liberty* (Mill 1991). Like Milton, Mill's deliberation on free speech purports that truth can be discovered only when different opinions are aired openly. However, whereas Milton seems to envision a rather autonomous idea of truth focusing on Truth as the ultimate outcome of free exchange, Mill's formulation puts the emphasis on the process through which knowledge may increase, thereby making the process itself a desirable public good. For Mill, putting forth a claim to truth involves putting one's opinion to a continual test presented by other opinions, to a permanent trial of verifiability. This process may not necessarily result in positing "Truth" as the absolute and certain outcome, yet its importance nevertheless lies in identifying error and expounding erroneous beliefs, an effect that constitutes an epistemological advance. As Mill writes:

> The beliefs which we have most warrant for, have no safeguard to rest on, but a standing invitation to the whole world to prove them unfounded. If the challenge is not accepted, or is accepted and the attempt fails, we are far enough from certainty still; but we have done the best that the existing state of human reason admits of; we have neglected nothing that could give the truth a chance of reaching us: if the lists are kept open, we may hope that if there be a better truth, it will be found when the human mind is capable of receiving it; and in the meantime we may rely on having attained such approach to truth, as it is possible in our own day. (Mill 1991, 26)

The necessary condition for accommodating such a propensity for truth is a complete and unconditional liberation of all views and opinions. According to Mill, there is no justifiable cause for silencing someone's opinion because this opinion may very well be true, partly true, or bear a trace of truth. Denying that such a possibility exists entails an unwarranted assumption of infallibility, that is, presupposing that under no circumstance can the opinion held to be true be proven wrong. Having an a priori immunity from being wrong necessarily suppresses the very possibility of discovering truth, for such a discovery can be made only when examining alternative opinions.[1] Taken to the limit, even if all mankind minus one were of one opinion, "and only one person were of the contrary opinion, mankind would be no more justified in silencing that one person, then he, if he had the power, would be justified in silencing mankind" (ibid., 21).

Mill further argues that even if there were a way to ascertain the falsity of an opinion, stifling it would still be an evil. This is because the benefit in an open discussion exceeds its possible outcomes, since through the process those who hold true beliefs will be challenged and called to defend their views. As he writes, "However unwillingly a person who has a strong opinion may admit the possibility that his opinion may be false, he ought to be moved by the consideration that however true it may be, if it is not fully, frequently, and fearlessly discussed, it will be held as a dead dogma, not a living truth" (Mill 1991, 40). Thus, rational confidence in one's views can be achieved only by comparing them to other views, and preferring one opinion to another is justifiable only by acquiring sufficient knowledge about other opinions. Moreover, if one inhibits open discussion, those who hold false opinions may be deprived of completing, correcting and ultimately exchanging error for truth. The discovery of truth is therefore a public concern and not merely a means for ascertaining private certainties. For Mill, the process through which the grains of truth might be sifted from the chaff of error is most fundamentally a social business, benefiting in the long run all parties concerned.

Yet the preeminent social value ascribed by Mill to truth does not come without a cost. As he notes, the cost is an almost unlimited tolerance and even protection to the "most obnoxious opinions" (Mill 1991, 34). By insisting on the essential destructibility of any kind of censorship, Mill gives an automatic priority to procedures leading to the exposure of truth, or at least to the rejection of error, even at the expense of other social interests. This, however, might prove problematic, and as a number of critics have pointed out, it is possible that in some cases truth will actually have a detrimental effect on or collide with equally important social considerations. An often cited hypothetical example is a purported scientific proof that some races are intellectually superior to others (Norris 1976; Schauer 1982; Barendt 1985). Even if such a claim were undisputedly true, making it public might risk setting off racial antagonism, as well as introducing a "legitimate" cause for relying on racial difference in social decision-making processes. A more common problem with Mill's formulation might, however, be introduced by modes of expression such as hate speech, sexist and racist expressions, and other kinds of inflammatory talk. It is likely that such were not what Mill had in mind when calling for the liberation of speech, as his vision of the "marketplace of ideas" was based on rational discourse aiming at rigorous validation of opinions. Still, his objection to suppressing heresy and "obnoxious opinions" is nevertheless a matter of principle and might be seen as a necessary pain to be endured in order to keep systems of exchange open. It may be argued that one way to deal with such modes of expression, a way that is still in line with Mill's approach, is by producing oppositional speech with the aim of criticizing and denouncing these expressions and thereby balancing their effects. Thus, more or better speech may provide a possible remedy against hurtful speech without having to resort to extraneous restrictions. However, such a solution is conceivable only if one accepts that the harm done by speech can be rectified by retaliatory speech, that an offensive statement, and whatever pains it might inflict, can be somehow canceled by a corrective response.[2] In fact, this might even lead to the devaluation of speech itself, first and foremost as a means for the discovery of truth.

It therefore seems that Mill's formulation may live up to its promise only if all parties concerned subscribe to rules of rational argumentation. Yet under this condition, speech would have to undergo evaluation and classification before it could actually be admitted into public discourse. This would mean not only that there are different tiers of speech but also that consequential speech transpires in an elevated social sphere, involving a de facto curtailment of "irrational" forms of speech. Insisting that even "the most obnoxious opinions" be given voice implies that these opinions might have only coincidental relevance to the pursuit of truth and that social discourse is inherently heterogeneous, consisting of views that are better poised to truth (at least at the time of their articulation) than others. Enduring such opinions, which may have some deleterious effects on social life, is integral to the pursuit of truth.

The role of freedom of speech in the discovery of truth is also central in Walter Lippmann's analysis of modern democracy. Lippmann situates the issue in his discussion on what he names "the public philosophy," a political analysis of the challenges facing modern democracies. In brief, his analysis is concerned with the ability of the public—which, unlike in ancient Greece, presently consists of large populations possibly scattered over distance—to participate in a peaceful and meaningful democratic process. To Lippmann, the reality of modern life requires a careful modification of certain democratic ideals, a challenge he undertakes in *The Public Philosophy* (1962). Freedom of speech occupies a special place in his deliberations, for in addition to its traditional role in democratic life it also constitutes an interface between private and public considerations and upholds the problem of discerning between liberty and license. Furthermore, the advent of mass media, which allow the publication of opinions on an unprecedented scale, has considerably amplified the stakes of freedom of speech in modern democracies.

While drawing on the foundation laid down by both Milton and Mill, Lippmann provides a more pragmatic version of the argument from truth. There can be no justification, argues Lippmann, either in principle or in practice, for the existence of an unrestricted right of anyone to utter anything she or he likes at any time she or he chooses. There can be, for instance, no right to deceive a theater

audience by falsely crying "Fire!"; nor should it be permissible to
deceive a customer, an employee or a voter on the basis of one's
right to speak. As Lippmann affirms, the primary reason freedom of
speech has become a central concern for Western societies is the
Greek discovery that dialectics, as demonstrated by the Socratic
dialogues, is "a principle method of attaining truth, and particularly
a method of attaining moral and political truth" (1962, 96). The
method of dialectics allows confronting ideas with opposing ideas
with the objective of ultimately reaching the true idea. Other agen-
das, such as the one ascribed by Aristotle to the Sophists, whose primary concern was winning a case by means of persuasion, are not
contributory to the process and therefore do not warrant tolerance.

For Lippmann, freedom of speech is a necessary yet not
sufficient condition for meaningful public participation in democratic life. Divorced from its original purpose and justification as a
process of dialectical criticism, "freedom to think and speak are not
self-evident necessities" (ibid., 97). It is only from the hope and the
intention of discovering truth that freedom of speech acquires its
justification and public significance. "The right of self-expression,"
he adds, "is, as such, a private amenity rather than a public necessity"
(ibid., 97). Hence, the right to utter words regardless of their meaning and effect—regardless of their truth value—is not a vital concern for modern democracy, certainly not reason enough to merit
unconditional protection. The right to speak freely is a public business only insofar as it follows a dialectical process of criticism. It
is only in that capacity, and not in the individual pleasure of utterance, that freedom of speech is crucial for sustaining democracy.

According to Lippmann, the problem of modern democracies
arises when forms of unconstrained speech threaten to outweigh
earnest and truth-seeking speech, when "the chaff of silliness, base-
ness, and deception is so voluminous that it submerges the kernels
of truth" (Lippmann 1962, 97). The dividing line between liberty
and license runs precisely where free speech is no longer at the service of reason, becoming instead an unrestricted right to take advan-

tage of people's ignorance or to incite their passions. It is then that liberty might turn into "such a hullabaloo of sophistry, propaganda, special pleading, lobbying and salesmanship that it is difficult to remember why freedom of speech is worth the pain and trouble of defending it" (ibid., 98).[3] What Lippmann prescribes in essence is a public obligation to subject speech to the rule of rational debate, as he writes:

> [W]hen genuine debate is lacking, freedom of speech does not work as it is meant to work. It has lost the principle which regulates it and justifies it—that is to say, dialectic conducted according to logic and the rules of evidence. If there is no effective debate, the unrestricted right to speak will unloose so many propagandists, procurers, and panderers upon the public that sooner or later in self-defense the people will turn to the censors to protect them. An unrestricted and unregulated right to speak cannot be maintained. It will be curtailed for all manner of reasons and pretexts, and to serve all kinds of good, foolish, or sinister ends. (Ibid., 99–100)

The important point to note here is that for Lippmann free speech is necessarily a practice that should be socially evaluated and regulated according to rational standards. Free speech truly worth the name is one that is never utterly free but rather subordinated to procedures of critical evaluation of facts and evidences. Unlike Milton and Mill, Lippmann does not shy away from restricting certain modes of expression; instead, for him, such restriction is precisely what makes the practice meaningful.

Perhaps one of the greatest challenges to the practice of free speech in modern democracies is introduced by the mass media. Lippmann is quite skeptical as to the prospect of applying principles of critical debate to the mass media; he asserts, "dialectical process for finding truth works best when the same audience hears all the sides of the disputation" (1962, 99). The problem posed by the mass media (a problem both technical and substantive) is that only rarely, and on very few public issues, "does the mass audience have the benefit of the process by which truth is sifted from error—the dialectic of debate in which there is immediate challenge, reply, cross-examination, and rebuttal" (99). He therefore disclaims almost completely the political role of motion pictures, since "if a film advocates a thesis, the same audience cannot be shown another film designed to answer it" (99). And while conceding that radio and television do permit some debate when letting opposing views be heard equally, he insists that the predicament of mass media lies in the inherent passivity they impose upon the audience, a condition that prevents transforming it from a scattered crowd into an informed and involved public.

The problems that were only implicit in Milton's and Mill's accounts seem to be even more pressing in Lippmann's analysis precisely because of his preoccupation with the pragmatics of the practice rather than with its theoretical aspects. By equating the boundaries of free speech with the boundaries of factual examination, his analysis might risk disqualifying modes of expression that are not necessarily "sophistic" but also not necessarily contributing to the distillation of truth. Thus, for instance, certain types of public demonstrations, strikes or civil disobedience would be regarded as extraneous to the original task of freedom of speech and would probably not be endorsed within his doctrine. This, however, reveals a more fundamental tension in his analysis: on the one hand, Lippmann specifies the challenges democracy faces in the age of mass societies, challenges that require revision and readjustment of traditional democratic ideals. Yet, on the other hand, he resorts to ancient ideas of debate and dialectics, which he imports into a modern setting almost untouched, as the primary criteria for a truthful democratic process. Thus, while attempting to deal with the modern challenges of democracy, Lippmann's perspective is very much indebted to premodern ideals, specifically to the Greek agora, a social space to which all eligible parties (that is, not slaves, women, children, or non-Greek freemen) have equal access, and wherein every single one of them is represented and physically present to the other.

One of the main questions arising from the preceding accounts is the question of exclusion, of the legitimacy in limiting certain modes of expression that are declared inimical to the basis upon which speech could be carried out publicly. The question, in short, is whether, or under what circumstances, abridging freedom of speech might be acceptable. Yet, while being a critical concern for the discussion, the relationship between freedom and restriction is mostly tackled as an exception to a general rule, and as such, as an issue of extenuating circumstance within an otherwise abiding zone of practice. Limitation on expression, so it would seem, is always a subsequent possibility, deleterious for some, necessary for others. However, further unpacking of the relationship between freedom and restriction may offer additional insight into the "positive" value ascribed to free speech, particularly to its role in discovering the truth. In this respect, the work of Stanley Fish (1994) provides an important contribution in demystifying some of the traditional conceptions around free speech.

Fish, a Milton scholar and a First Amendment theorist, has argued provocatively that free speech, as such, does not exist (Fish 1994, 102). "Free speech," Fish contends, is a name given to verbal behavior that serves the issues one wishes to advance; it is the label worn by one's favorites and never by the dissidents. Free speech is not an independent value but a political lever that is endorsed so long as it is at the service of one's own agenda. Yet his argument cuts much deeper:

> I want to say that all affirmations of freedom of expression are like Milton's, dependent for their force on an exception that literally carves out the space in which expression can then emerge. I do not mean that expression (saying something) is a realm whose integrity is sometimes compromised by certain restrictions but that restriction, in the form of an underlying articulation of the world that necessarily (if silently) negates alternatively possible articulations, is constitutive of expression. Without restriction, without an inbuilt sense of what it would be meaningless to say or wrong to say, there would be no assertion and no reason for asserting it. (Ibid., 103)

According to Fish, all forms of free expression follow, in one way or the other, the seemingly insignificant exception made by Milton: that in order for certain types of speech to be heard others have to be silenced. Free speech is not an ongoing, self-regulated practice that might occasionally encounter situations threatening its stability and perhaps even warranting repression. Rather, exclusion is the very basis upon which "free speech" transpires: without exclusion, there would be neither sense nor need of saying anything. The exception to unregulated expression is not a negative restriction but a positive hollowing of space in which assertions occur. The exception to the rule thus becomes the general rule: some form of speech is always being restricted, and that restriction is what renders assertions intelligible. Indeed, employing words such as "limitation" or "restriction" might be misleading because they suggest that an exception came consequent to a practice that was already-in-place. But the fact is, Fish argues, that expression is always a product of constriction, as the very act of saying something, of communicating, is already implicated, constrained, rendered impure—and as such, rendered communicable—by the background context in which the assertion takes place. It thus follows that speech has never been free and freedom has never been general, and it is precisely the background of an originary exclusion that gives freedom of speech its bite.

Fish's critique is aimed particularly against "First Amendment purists" (essentially Mill's position) advocating free expression as a primary value before and beyond other considerations. For Fish, freedom of expression could be a primary value only if what is said does not make a difference, only "if what you are valuing is the right to make noise" (1994, 197). In most ordinary contexts, however, assertions are produced with certain goals, trying to make things operate in one way rather than another. A position endorsing freedom across the board can get what it bargains for only by "first imagining speech as occurring in no context whatsoever, and then stripping particular speech acts of the properties conferred on them by contexts" (108–9) (again, not unlike Mill's tolerance to "obnoxious" views). Clinging to prewritten principles such as the one granted by the U.S. First Amendment reveals, in effect, an avoidance of what is correctly perceived to be the alternative. And that alternative is politics, that is, the realization that what is or is not protected in the realm of expression does not rest on some primary principles but rather on someone's ability to rewrite, recharacterize or recruit those principles in ways that lead to the protection of the kind of speech one wishes to protect and the regulation of the kinds one wishes to silence. "When the First Amendment is successfully invoked," Fish states, "the result is not a victory for free speech in the face of a challenge from politics but *a political victory* won by the party that has managed to wrap its agenda in the mantle of free speech" (110).

The conclusion, then, is that the issue of free speech is always already a political issue, and it is perhaps most political when delimiting politics as an area to be avoided. Ultimately, Fish does not argue either for or against regulation as a matter of a general principle, but proposes instead turning away from any principle to the pragmatic antiprinciple of considering each particular case as it arises. The question whether to regulate or not would therefore always be a local one, and consideration of each case would have to include the risks and the gains implied by alternative courses of action. But in any case, the general right of individual expression cannot be accepted as a primary consideration because it tends to obscure rather than clarify the dilemma. A traditional objection to this could be that restricting one form of speech might lead to sliding on the slippery slope to the restriction of any other. Yet in keeping with Fish's framework, it could be said that some form of speech is always being restricted or else there could be no meaningful assertion in the first place. Moreover, the reality of "free speech" has always been sliding on the slippery slope, as he further declares: "someone is always going to be restricted next, and it is your job to make sure that the someone is not you" (Fish 1994, 111).

While I concur with most of Fish's argument, I believe that this last remark reveals a premise he shares with most of the views he criticizes, a premise that prescribes the problem in terms of an individualistic concern. However issues of speech and freedom are played out, their ultimate shape will abide by the egoistic interests of each potential speaker seeking to safeguard his or her political agenda. Being a political prize, it is a matter to be fought over individually. Thus perhaps at its most political, Fish's argument fails to make what I would consider a crucial political move—the question of the rights and responsibilities with respect to the Other person. It is not merely the production of speech that is a political issue, but perhaps more importantly, the production of silence. An ethical-political commitment would therefore account for what is being excluded from the realm of speech, for the silence of alterity.

In sum, the writings of Milton, Mill and Lippmann situate the pursuit of truth as the primary objective of free speech. The process of discovering truth (or, *mutatis mutandis,* ferreting out error) is guided by the faith in individual reason, which is also the backbone for the execution of a rational public discourse. The claim to truth is what mediates speakers, constituting in itself a prominent social and political goal. While presenting different positions with respect to the question of restriction, these accounts deem freedom of speech an elemental procedure that when left to its own devices would facilitate a social project of trading truth for fallacy. In so doing, they all resort to a general rule for the practice of free speech that precedes the occurrence of each individual utterance (restriction of antifaith for Milton, nonrestriction as a principle for Mill, dialectics and debate for Lippmann). Fish's critical position, however, proposes that restriction is not secondary to an otherwise working procedure but inherent in the very possibility of producing speech, and that restriction is in fact what renders assertions meaningful. It follows that the discovery of truth might be seen in itself as an undertaking that is dependent upon the exclusion of other possibilities, of other truths, rather than on rational excavation, and the process by which it is being sought as a political struggle rather than a linear progress. However, while providing a valuable critique, Fish fails to answer for the silence that he associates with the production of free speech. It is the Other's silence, I would contend, that introduces a radically different set of questions with respect to the social practice of speech, some of which I shall attempt to unpack in the following sections.

Outside the Self

A second major argument for free speech deems it essential to individual development and self-fulfillment. Thomas Irwin Emerson presents a concise description of the argument:

> The right of free speech is justified first of all as the right of an individual purely in his capacity as an individual. It derives from the widely accepted premise of Western thought that the proper end of man is the realization of his character and potentialities as a human being. . . . The achievement of self-realization commences with development of the mind. But the process of conscious thought by its very nature can have no limits. An individual can neither tell where it may lead nor anticipate its ends. Moreover, it is an *individual* process.
>
> From this it follows that every man—in the development of his own personality—has the right to form his own beliefs and opinions. And it also follows that he has the right to express these beliefs and opinions. Otherwise they are of little account. For expression is an integral part of the development of ideas, of mental exploration and of affirmation of self. The power to realize his potentiality as a human being begins at this point and must extend at least this far if the whole nature of man is not to be thwarted.
>
> Hence the suppression of belief, opinion and expression is an affront to the dignity of man, a negation of man's essential nature. (1966, 4–5)

Frederick Schauer offers another apt explication:

Here the ultimate point of reference is the individual, not the state, or society at large. Although society may benefit from the satisfaction of individual interests, the arguments discussed here treat such benefits as incidental to a primary focus on individual well-being. An individual interest in this strong sense remains important even if society might in some way, or on balance, be worse off for recognizing it. Here individual well-being is an end in itself.

The view of freedom of speech as an intrinsic good is most commonly articulated in terms of a particular perception of human nature, and a particular perception of the ideal aspirations of mankind. This approach sees man as continually striving for improvement and self-development, and it sees free communication as an integral part of this objective. (1982, 48–49)

These two characterizations follow a basic tenet inhering in liberal thought since the early writings of Milton and Locke according to which the fundamental and principal unit of consideration is the single individual. It is the particular person, his or her needs, wants and interests, that should be at the focal point of every normative social analysis. Whereas the preceding argument from truth takes a consequentialist approach, that is, treating free speech as a means rather than an end, this view takes an instrumentalist approach in deeming free speech an integral component in individual life and progress.[4]

In this view, restriction on personal expression, on what is permissible to say, write, and also to hear or read, might inhibit the ability of each individual to develop both intellectually and spiritually. Since it is through the exploration of different ideas and perspectives that one forms his or her attitudes and beliefs—thereby forming parts of what one regards as oneself—any kind of intervention in that process is effectively an infringement of individual sovereignty, of the right of each individual to define or fulfill his and her objectives in life.

Beyond Speech

Critique of this argument has often challenged the seemingly causal relation between this freedom and the notion of self-fulfillment. For instance, Fredrick Schauer (1982) argues that freedom of speech (understood in its broader sense as the freedom to communicate) is neither necessarily the definitive method of mental development (mentioning instead experiences like travel, keen observation and work), nor essentially more important than the right to eat, to sleep, or to have shelter. While the point itself might be valid, this critique is still very much indebted to the liberal tenet of regarding the individual as an autotelic entity. Hence, what is at issue here is the status of speech in the constitution of individuality rather than the status of individuality in the constitution of speech, or in other words, questioning not the centrality of the individual within the doctrine of free speech, but the extent to which free speech may validate the already central individual. Since speech is seen first as a means for self-realization (its particular contribution remaining debatable) and only later as a means of communication, the individual continues to occupy a pivotal position in the discussion.

An essential feature of speech in the argument from self-fulfillment is that it is the product (both in the sense of outcome and possession) of the individual. According to this view, speaking is done by a single person who has no necessary relation either to other potential speakers or to the context in which expressions are made. Here the typical model of speech is self-seeking speech—a model having a priori priority over other forms of speech—and concerning itself only derivatively with the community of other listeners/speakers. As Lisa Heldke (1994) maintains, such a conception of speech depends for its legitimacy and cogency upon a particular conception of the nature of the individual and of the nature of the relationship between individual and society. This individual "is unattached to others; it is not formed out of relations to others. Rather, it is an independently-created self·that, for a variety of reasons, chooses or is constrained to enter in relations with others. At its core, this self is discrete, detached" (113). The originary image of this individual is of a self-sufficient autonomous being, of a self emerging out of itself; in short, a self-causative-self (the ultimate *causa sui*). It follows that any relation between individuals of this kind is predicated upon and subsidiary to their self-enclosed being and original separateness as individuals.[5] Insofar as the argument from self-fulfillment is concerned, relation is secondary to individual immanence as one is first a self and only later in relation with other selves. The kind of speech produced thereby is almost by definition teleological and unidirectional.

The problem with this view is indeed its perception of individuality and the role ascribed to speech therein. My intention in the following discussion, however, is to develop a different critical perspective of the argument concerning self-fulfillment, a perspective that does not merely extend the problem of the individual's centrality within the social practice of speech, but seeks to question precisely the nature of speech produced by that individual. It is my contention that subordinating speech to an ideal of self-sufficient individuality effectively produces a decontextualized speaker, and this is by disregarding the context in which every utterance takes place. As I attempt to show below, speech always transpires in a context, and although it may be silent, it is never mute. The idea of self-serving speech may consequently be revealed as indifferent to the context of its production, namely, to the other side of speech, or to the Other's side of this freedom.

As a point of departure, I refer to Martin Buber's philosophy of dialogue. However, I would like to take up a seemingly marginal issue in his discussion on dialogue, yet one that I consider crucial to the recontextualization of speech: the issue of silence as introduced in a short passage entitled "Silence Which Is Communication" (1955, 3). The silence Buber speaks of is not a feature of nonverbal or gestural communication; neither is it lovers' clandestine silence, nor mystical silence shared by avid believers; rather, it is the silence found at the depth of speech. Buber elects to call this elusive silence into presence by way of example: imagine two people sitting beside each other without speaking, looking or even turning to the other. The first is an open and hospitable individual while the other is reclusive and reserved. Regarding the latter, he proposes:

> And now—let us imagine that this is one of the hours which succeed in bursting asunder the seven iron bands about the heart—imperceptibly the spell is lifted. But even now the man does not speak a word, does not stir a finger. Yet he does something. The lifting of the spell has happened to him—no matter from where—without his doing. But this is what he does now: he releases in himself a reserve over which only he himself has power. Unreservedly communication streams from him, and the silence bears it to the neighbor. (Ibid., 4)

What is described in this passage would probably not be regarded by most conventional conceptions of communication as communication. Indeed, objectively speaking, nothing has been transmitted by either one, certainly nothing that could be verified empirically by consulting both sides. And yet, as Buber affirms, something has been communicated here; it is the carrying of one's attentiveness to the other. According to Buber, the lifting of the reticent individual's disinterestedness should not go unnoticed, for it indicates a different, perhaps more fundamental, form of communication. This communication may be described as silent readiness: a potentiality anticipating an exchange, an invitation to a time-space opening in which to meet. Although having no meaning in itself, this wordless silence signifies amenability to the very production of meaning, and it is from this potentiality that speech may emerge.

For Buber, this silent readiness makes manifest an essential fact in human communication: that an utterance is always given to and implicated by the existence of others. According to Buber, communication is constituted upon a relation "rooted in one being turning to another as another, as this particular other being, in order to communicate with it in a sphere which is common to them but which reaches out beyond the special sphere of each" (Buber 1955, 203). The reality of addressing another is not exhausted in uttering words but predicated by turning to another as a particular being, by addressing another as Other. Such is the I-Thou relation: a discourse inclusive of the Other rather than constitutive of the self, a relation that reaffirms the Other in his or her singularity (see Buber 1970). And it is upon this fundamental relation that Buber founds the origin of communication: not merely on an empirical exchange of signs but on an intentional awareness of the existence of the Other, on an Other-oriented attitude that constitutes a discursive sphere in which one is answerable and addressable.

This, however, is not to deny the possibility of non-Other-oriented speech, of forms of self-centered speech commonly referred to as monologue, or as a manifestation of what Buber deems more generally as the I-It relation—regarding other subjects as mere objects, as beings among other beings. Rather, it exposes the fact that the I-It monological relation is secondary to the more fundamental I-Thou dialogue, that self-oriented speech is nothing more than a certain usurpation of speech's originary context; as he writes elsewhere, "Language never existed before address; it could become monologue only after dialogue broke off or broke down" (1965, 114). Here his conception of speech takes up a critical mode:

> Each of us is encased in an armor whose task is to ward off signs. Signs happen to us without respite, living means being addressed, we would need only to present ourselves and to perceive. But the risk is too dangerous for us, the soundless thunderings seem to threaten us with annihilation, and from generation to generation we perfect the defense apparatus. All our knowledge assures us, "Be calm, everything happens as it must happen, but nothing is directed at you, you are not meant; it is just 'the world,' you can experience it as you like, but whatever you make of it in yourself proceeds from you alone, nothing is required of you, you are not addressed, all is quiet." (Buber 1955, 10)

According to Buber, modern knowledge and way of life might be characterized by the expansion of I-It relation at the expense of I-Thou. His reproach is directed most probably to scientific-rationalistic mindsets that reduce social relations to the utilitarian and contractual. Modern knowledge teaches that nothing is required from the subject—or in terms of the current discussion, that nothing is required from the speaking-self whose speech is produced in a space wherein there is no address, in which "all is quiet." Exercising freedom of speech as such, one might regard this space, into which all words are destined, as a vacuum to be filled. And these words are primal, that is, not a reply to a previous call but newly said and radically free.[6] A speaker who cannot be addressed and for whom all is quiet is, therefore, a mutation passing on its enhanced capacity to speak together with numbed hearing devices. This speaker may be called upon but cannot respond: She or he cannot acknowledge an "outsidedness" preceding speech. Where no primary address can be recognized, speech exists alone, and the words produced thereby are the speaker's "property." For when speech becomes ownership, no address can be acknowledged without reward. A speech interested only in its own capacity to speak while denying the possibility of an anterior address (which may very well be silent) is, according to Buber, the modern distortion of speech.

The dialogical status of silence is further conceptualized in Mikhail Bakhtin's work. According to Bakhtinian criticism of modern speech genres, traditional linguistic models (he refers specifically to de Saussure and von Humboldt) view language from the speaker's standpoint, as if there were only one independent speaker who is not related in any way to other listeners or potential interlocutors. Bakhtin argues that what has been ignored by such speculations is the responsive quality of speech communication:

> Still current in linguistics are such *fictions* as the "listener" and "understander" (partners of the speaker), the "unified speech flow," and so on. These fictions produce a completely distorted idea of the

complex and multifaceted process of active speech communication. . . . One cannot say that these diagrams are false or that they do
not correspond to certain aspects of reality. But when they are put
forth as the actual whole of speech communication, they become a
scientific fiction. The fact is that when the listener perceives and
understands the meaning (the language meaning) of speech, he
simultaneously takes an active, responsive attitude towards it. He
either agrees or disagrees with it (completely or partially), augments it, applies it, prepares for its execution, and so on. And the listener adopts this responsive attitude for the entire duration of the
process of listening and understanding, from the very beginning—
sometimes literally from the speaker's first word. Any understanding of live speech, a live utterance, is inherently responsive,
although the degree of this activity varies extremely. Any understanding is imbued with response and necessarily elicits it in one
form or another: the listener becomes the speaker. (1986, 68)

If one were to translate Bakhtin's perspective into cinematographic
language, his camera would probably depict a dialogue in a way
opposite to the familiar. He would zoom in on the listener while
sounding out the speaker, and when the listener takes her turn to
speak, the camera would focus on the one who now becomes the listener; in that way, the entire dialogical sequence would be depicted.
The listener becomes the speaker not because his or her silence sud-
denly begins to "speak"—silence always already "speaks"—but
because here it is being acknowledged and heard. Bakhtin listens to
the Other's listening and finds in it layers of signification—the
speaker becomes the listener and the listener becomes the speaker.
No more do the speaker and the listener occupy opposing positions
within a discourse; no more do they represent the two basic functions of communication (speaker/sender/transmitter versus lis-
tener/addressee/receiver). The dichotomy breaks—the listener
becomes speaker and the speaker listener. Bakhtin thus proposes a
continual swap between the two to the point where it is impossible
to locate positively the reality of speech. Who is the speaker? Who
is the listener? These are merely the asymptotes of discourse

(Pinchevski 2001). Speaking and listening are therefore interchangeable and imply each other as communication transcends its functionality and establishes a response-able relation among interlocutors.

In one of his later notes, Bakhtin introduces an important distinction—the fundamental difference between quietude and silence:

> The disturbance of quietude by sound is mechanical and physiological (as a condition of perception); the disturbance of silence by a word is personalistic and intelligible: it is an entirely different world. In quietude nothing makes a sound (or something does not make a sound); in silence nobody *speaks* (or somebody does not speak). Silence is possible only in the human world (and only for a person). (Bakhtin 1986, 133–34)

Quietude concerns the physical conditions for perceiving a sound: it separates one phoneme from another and allows sounds to travel acoustically; it is the alter-side of language, a nonlanguage, or the negative side of *langue*. Quietude is the substratum of language as a system-of-signs, which enables us to single out one repeatable sign from another in order to retrieve the meaning of an utterance. Silence, on the other hand, concerns the active conditions of speaking and perceiving an utterance in its singularity, and as such it is proper to the human situation in space and time. Silence is the substratum of addressing a particular Other, the "other side" of *parole*. While quietude consists in the nonexistence of signs, or instances in which communication is halted (its opposite occurrence being noise or interference in the external context), silence resides in the evocation and constitution of a dialogical act (or alternatively, in the "failure" of communication understood as the interruption of alterity).[7] Whereas quietude supports the linkage of linguistic elements in language and the transmission process of language as a code, silence is evidenced in the relational, responsive and response-able aspect of communication.

Following Bakhtin, Augusto Ponzio (1993) questions the delineation of communication against the background of quietude,
which is deemed as "the limit, the negation, the annulment of the
objects of linguistics" (ibid., 142). In communicational paradigms
that emphasize exchange of signs ("code linguistics"), speech transpires against a sphinxian background that cannot respond. Calling
attention to the sphere of silence, he proposes that the condition of
freedom of speech lies in a dialogical position that introduces the
possibility of silence as the speaker's choice. Freedom of speech
entails not the mere violation of quietude but the violation of
silence. This is not simply the emergence of speech in a functionally conducive background implied in the transition from nonsigns
to signs (which nevertheless remains on the plane of language-as-
system), but traversing the threshold of silence to the plane of
enunciation, from attentive listening to attentive speaking. There is
no substantial difference between the two states of silence, since
silence that is the starting point of uttering is also the position of listening. Speech is implicit in silence and silence is implicit in speech.

This silence out of which one speaks is revealed in the philosophy of Emmanuel Levinas as coming from the Other and hence as
bearing an ethical significance. His critique of ontology points out
that what does not appear in the entirety of its being within an ontological schema is degraded to nothing, and consequently, and for all
intents and purposes, is deemed nonexistent. Yet, as might be
recalled from chapter 2, for Levinas the relation with the Other is
preontological, a primordial relation of nonrelation that is irreducible to ontological structure. This relation is signified by the
Other's face, in proximity, exposedness and responsibility, in speaking and in addressing the other qua Other, and this anterior relation
may signify itself as silence: "The silent world is a world that
comes to us from the Other. . . . Thus silence is not a simple absence
of speech; speech lies in the depths of silence like a laughter
perfidiously held back. It is the inverse of language; the interlocutor has given a sign, but has declined every interpretation; this is the

silence that terrifies" (*TI,* 91). According to Levinas, silence is not a symptom of absence or void but rather an evocation of dependence never stated as such, yet upon which every enunciation takes place. Nor is it a frozen externality merely echoing speech, but a pure potentiality subsisting in the derivation of speech. Silence, as a modality of otherness, may find expression in the Other's face, as he remarks elsewhere: "the beginning of language is in the face. In a certain way, in its silence, it calls you" (*PM,* 169). The face does not emerge as a force limiting free action in space—or, alternatively, as a source of a louder voice—but as a destitute authority that may invoke interruption and anxiety precisely because it places a silent demand. Silence signifies the Other in his or her expectation of a word that may or may not come: "words are said, be it only by the silence kept, whose weight acknowledges this evasion of the Other" (*TI,* 195). The Other's silence is an invocation lying beneath the structure of language, which precedes and inaugurates speech.

Levinas criticizes the predominance of the Said, of logos, which consists in the circulation of messages, a property that could be compared to the circulation of merchandise in a marketplace. Such a conceptualization of discourse, which according to him characterizes the majority of philosophical discussions, reduces communication to the problem of exchange, placing it in a universal context that precedes the individual. In this respect, the speech produced by the independent speaker portrayed in liberal thought might be seen as mired in the realm of the Said, a speech that emanates from the self only to return and reify the self, an unresponse-able speech. In its radical form, one might view the liberal portrayal of free speech as a veritable demonstration of ontological-teleological discourse, a self-centric speech transpiring against the background of a faceless crowd, a complete overlapping of logos and speech—a manifestation of logocentrism itself.

By introducing the notion of the Saying, Levinas effectively reverses the implicit hierarchy of speech positing contact as the primary act of communication. The touch of otherness communicated in the Saying transcends what is said, signifying in the very act of the Other's approach. Ineffable as such, the Saying is a communication that precedes and enacts the communication of the Said: "the relationship of proximity . . . in which every transmission of messages, whatever be those messages, is already established, is the original language, a language without words or propositions, pure communication" (*LP,* 119). The Saying subsists in the Said in the form of an originary address, an address that remains, nonetheless, unsaid. Saying nothing but the eventuality of contact itself, it puts forth an appeal that interrupts self-sufficient subjectivity, "the subject resting on itself is confounded by wordless accusation" (*OB,* 127). The Saying thus establishes a discourse in which one is exposed to the Other's silence, in which one is silently called into listening. Through the silent and yielding setting of the Saying, communication becomes an ethical event of proximity.

To recapitulate, the shape of speech as sketched by the liberal argument from self–fulfillment is of a device integral to the constitution of individuality. Wrapping itself in an aegis of legitimate freedom, it proceeds to reify the stature of an independent speaking-self. However, the idea of self-constitutive speech is dependent for its integrity on an embedded obliviousness to the context of its production. Like Baron Munchausen, who reported that he extricated himself and his good horse out of a quagmire by pulling his own hair, self-centric speech comes to the surface by liberating itself from the community of listeners and potential speakers. This speech constitutes a paramount example of what Gemma Corradi Fiumara (1990) calls a reduced-by-half model of logos, a model of speech that knows how to speak but not how to listen. Speakers of such a logos lead a monadic existence where speaking is an object of continuous contestation, and in which what does not speak is necessarily beyond the scope of existence. This type of speech is circumscribed against the background of quietude, the place of the It and of the Said, the place of identity, totality, hierarchical order and authoritative monologism. It is in silence, a modality of signification ignored by the liberal conceptualization of speech, that speech finds a more fundamental context. Speech transpires in a background that may be silent but is by no means inaudible. Its reality implies a response-ability to the interlocutor even, and perhaps mostly, when she or he is silent—and still more importantly, following Stanley Fish's analysis, when she or he is *being silenced.* Silence is the place of otherness, of Thou and Saying, dialogue, responsibility and proximity of the face. Silence unfolds as the starting point of every utterance and as constitutive of speech itself. It is heard as a pure potentiality underlying all utterances, as artfully expressed by musician John Cage's "4:33," where he pays humble respect to silence, the carrier of his notes.

Beyond Freedom

The argument regarding self-fulfillment gives rise to an image of an individual that is a free and autonomous speaker who is interested primarily in realizing his or her goals. But what is the nature and shape of the social practice of speech and the relationship between potential speakers? This question is, of course, only a narrow version of one of the most fundamental issues in modern political theory: the problem of coupling private and public considerations. The challenge is, then, to devise a way that would uphold, on the one hand, the idea of a free and autonomous individual and respect the resulting rights of such an individual, and acknowledge, on the other hand, the interests and rights of the community of like individuals. Or, in terms of the current discussion, the goal would be to formulate a solution that would allow individual self-fulfillment through free speech in the company of similarly self-seeking speakers. Such mutual independency could very well be taken as constituting a launching pad for combative existence along the lines of Hobbes's "state of nature," of a war of everyone against everyone. This, in turn, would call for the establishment of a social institution to tame humans' "natural" animosity, and as such, this view provides very little insofar as ethics and the question of the social practice of speech are concerned. A much more nuanced approach, however, can be found in the concept of recognition as developed by several contemporary theorists.

A key example is Charles Taylor's (1994) analysis of the politics of recognition.[8] Taylor explores recent transformations in democratic societies, particularly with respect to current debates on multiculturalism. Within this context, the demand for recognition comes to the fore on behalf of minority or "subaltern" groups. This demand implies a link between recognition and identity, where the latter designates "a person's understanding of who they are, of their fundamental defining characteristics as human beings" (ibid., 25). Taylor contends that a major democratic challenge nowadays is the demand for equal recognition of culture, race, gender, and other group or individual orientations, a demand that has been intensified by a new understanding of *individualized* identity emerging at the end of the eighteenthcentury. The demand for equal recognition follows a particular sociopolitical perception of one's identity, whereby "there is a certain way of being human that is *my* way. I am called upon to live my life in this way, and not in imitation of anyone else's life" (ibid., 30). This relatively recent development prompts the ideal of being true to myself: "being true to myself means being true to my own originality, which is something only I can articulate and discover. In articulating it, I am also defining myself. I am realizing a potentiality that is properly my own" (ibid., 30).

Taylor further argues that in order to comprehend fully the close connection between recognition and identity it is imperative to take into account an additional issue:

> This crucial feature of human life is its fundamentally *dialogical* character. We become full human agents, capable of understanding ourselves, and hence of defining our identity, through our acquisition of rich human languages of expression. . . . People do not acquire the languages needed for self-definition on their own.

Rather, we are introduced to them through interaction with others who matter to us—what George Herbert Mead called "significant others." . . . We define our identity always in dialogue with, sometimes in struggle against, the things our significant others want to see in us. Even after we outgrow some of these others—our parents, for instance—and they disappear from our lives, the conversation with them continues within us as long as we live. (1994, 32–33)

According to Taylor, identity does not emerge in a vacuum, "monologically," in and for itself, but through relations with other human agents who contribute to the personal process (Mead's "significant others" or Bakhtin's "super-addressee"). Discovering one's identity is not an experiment carried out in isolation but through negotiation with others, partly open, partly internal, sometimes confirmatory, and at other times conflicting. In dialogue, identity finds both formation and expression, and discovers its formation through its expression. The demand for recognition appears as more than simply allowing each individual to create himself or herself. The problem of recognition, Taylor argues, is not merely a question of lack of due respect or common courtesy, but a potential wrong that can inflict serious injuries to victims of misrecognition and misrepresentation. Recognition is, therefore, more than an appropriate mode of healthy democracy; its refusal or withholding entails injustice, for the "projection of an inferior or demeaning image on another can actually distort and oppress, to the extent that the image is internalized" (1994, 36).

For Taylor, the politics of recognition rests on a claim that all manifestations of human culture have something important to say to all human beings. This, however, does not mean that all manifestations are equally important or have equal value; rather, in order to engage with what is fundamentally different there should be at least a presumption of equal worth. Worth is a "starting hypothesis with which we ought to approach the study of any other culture" (1994, 67). Such an approach to the study of what Taylor deems the "Other" cannot be based on a priori standards but would have to be open to modification and recalibration of its own standards. Its ultimate shape would be what Hans-Georg Gadamer called a "fusion of horizons": learning to move in increasingly broader horizons, within which what was formerly taken as a standard for evaluation can be situated as only one possibility by which to judge the unfamiliar. According to Taylor, this perspective might be midway between an indiscriminatory demand for equal recognition of worth, on the one hand, and solipsistic and ethnocentric standards, on the other. Thus, adopting a "working hypothesis" or presumption of equal worth does not amount to dogmatic judgment, but to a "willingness to be open to comparative cultural study of the kind that must displace our horizons in the resulting fusions" (Taylor 1994, 73).

I highlight Taylor's analysis because of its considerable sophistication in approaching free articulation. In this perspective, the demand to recognize Others' articulations does not simply follow a general rule of fairness but constitutes a process by which potential addressers and addressees may undergo a transformative exchange. In acknowledging the fundamental dialogical character of human life, Taylor's analysis reaffirms the constitutive role of speech and potential wrongs entailed by withholding certain types of expression. Hence, curtailing free expression would be synonymous with not recognizing that the Others' views have pertinence to the formation of social reality, and thereby to preventing a potential redefinition of horizons by which future expressions will be judged. As far as the issue of recognition goes, Taylor's analysis offers an apt starting point for appreciating the deeper levels involved in issues of free expression, recognition and self-fulfillment. Yet the problem lies precisely where his analysis does not and cannot go.

While acknowledging the immanence of the "Other" in dialogue, Taylor's perspective fails to appreciate the full import of the place of the Other therein. In Taylor's dialogue, the Other appears as an object of intrigue, as a specimen to be studied and evaluated, as a manifestation constituted upon its radical difference from the way an original "we" (the generic plurality from which Taylor speaks) perceives reality. The Other is consequently approached from a critical distance in order to determine the worth of what he or she has to offer to the greater community.[9] While "Other" cultures, groups and individuals are being judged for their worth, "our" (the collective homogeneity Taylor represents) position or worth is never questioned. Others would merit recognition only following a process of evaluation and, should they be found worthwhile, the resulting corollary will be in some form of reconciliation between Same and Other, in a Hegelian streak of "fusion" of horizons (compare Oliver 2000). Ironically, the Other plays only a secondary role in the story of recognition, serving as a vehicle for the enrichment of what "we" perceive as valuable, or as a sounding board for the validation of "our" truths and beliefs. The Other's intervention is a temporary break that nevertheless contributes to progressive movement from one conceptual framework to another. Instances in which the Other assumes the role of an addresser and makes "us" addressees are thus expunged in the recovery of a greater consciousness, either by synthesizing the address into collective articulation, or by refusing recognition altogether.

Viewed in this light, the argument about self-fulfillment takes up a significance that seemingly exceeds each individual's particular interests, as the ability to express oneself is tied to the much more fundamental issue of forming one's identity. And yet, by situating identity as a key issue in the discussion, Taylor effectively reaffirms the leading role given to the self in every engagement with the Other. But if identity is a way of "realizing a potentiality that is properly my own" (Taylor 1994, 30), how can the relation to the Other be anything but contestatory? And if recognition implies a progressive move to self-realization, how can the Other be anything but a supporting actor in a play that a priori sets the self at the center of the stage? While the Other may displace the horizons of judgment, his or her interjection would eventually be dissolved in the resurgence of an alternative state-of-mind. Identity understood as self-identity thus seems to be a process through which the self ultimately folds upon itself. In this sense, the politics of recognition reduces the Other to the Same, never allowing itself to be to truly interrupted by the Other's address.

The philosophy of Emmanuel Levinas, however, questions precisely what is taken for granted in Taylor's analysis as well as in traditional liberal thought: the originary freedom and autonomy of the subject. Yet his position does not amount to opposing freedom or autonomy as such: "one is not against freedom," he writes, "if one seeks for it a justification" (*TI,* 302). Levinas unfolds an alternative irreducible to the simple dichotomization between freedom and nonfreedom, one that precedes the emergence of the self as an autonomous being. In contrast to the systematic privileging of the self, Levinas veers in the direction of the Other, and as opposed to the image of a self whose spontaneous freedom is announced in the instance of its emergence, he opts for that which precedes independent freedom, namely, responsibility to and for the Other. As he writes, "To approach the Other is to put into question my freedom, my spontaneity as a living being, my emprise over the things, this freedom of a 'moving force'" (*TI,* 303). To approach the Other is therefore to unsettle the original shape of an individual who is first free and only later in relation with Others.

In opposition to a notion of original and infinite freedom operating in a finite field of action—which inevitably entails some sort of antagonism among individual agents—Levinas proposes the idea of finite freedom. A most significant point arising from Levinas's ethics is that responsibility comes before freedom. The relation to the Other, expressed in proximity, vulnerability and hence responsibility, lies at the depth of selfhood, prior to one's identity and possession of oneself. This is not merely a philosophical speculation since the ultimate attestation to the Other's immanence in the self is found in language itself, in its responsive and responsible nature, in its potential to dislocate the subject. From this perspective, speech is anything but one's property—it is, rather, a constant reminder of the transcendence of alterity through speech. The eventuality of speech may unsettle individual freedom. And yet, responsibility is not strictly opposed to freedom: it is not reducible to the distinction between freedom and nonfreedom dominating liberal thought, for this distinction already presupposes an *initial* freedom that may consequently be accomplished or compromised.

To be sure, being responsible to and for the Other does not cancel the possibility, or even the significance, of personal freedom; rather, it serves to qualify it. The notion of finite freedom does not denote socially imposed constrictions placed in order to manage individual freedoms and monitor individuals' "natural" antagonism. It evidences itself as a "positive" limitation: "The 'resistance' of the other does not do violence to me, does not act negatively; it has a positive structure: ethical" (*TI,* 197). The Other calls into question my spontaneous freedom and sovereign autonomy by speaking as a face, by interrupting self-sufficiency, by "recalling" my original responsibility. The relation to the Other is not at the outset an issue of contestation and competition transpiring in a social space where we are situated side by side. Responsibility cuts across monadic egoism and undercuts the apparent separateness of independent individuals. Freedom bears the trace of primordial responsibility, carrying within itself the mark of a subjectivity that is subjected to the Other. Responsibility is intrinsic to freedom, not as a built-in threat to its accomplishment but as conditioning its impetuosity. The introduction of responsibility into the domain of selfhood may thus provide recourse to a critical engagement with the fact that in a liberal conception of free speech, freedom, as such, is never accounted for, other than stating like Emerson that it is "man's essential nature" (1966, 5). In this sense, the untroubled complicity of speech and freedom may appear yet again as performing a Munchausen-like maneuver: being a self means being free to actualize myself through speech, and self-actualization through speech is dependent upon my initial free-dom—freedom as a tautology of itself.

An intermediate conclusion may therefore be that in traditional liberal thought, as well as in Taylor's theory of recognition, the relation to the Other moves in the range between tolerance and recognition. While entailing different schemas with which to tackle the question of free speech, perspectives along this range are nevertheless variations on a theme of "speak and let speak." On this theme, public execution of speech implies more or less independent, free and self-seeking speakers, who are first addressers and only later addressees. It follows that any dealings with other agents of speech will inevitably culminate in the social administration of oppositional forces aspiring to actualize their potential as speakers. In this way, restrictions placed to mitigate speakers' initial rivalry may themselves be a political allocation of the very right to have rights, specifically the right to individual expression. One result is that whoever or whatever unsettles such given rights is automatically perceived as a threat.

Following Levinas, I propose that the call for ethics is heard in the tangle of freedom and responsibility, where freedom is interrupted by the proximity of the Other, who may intervene with the production of self-seeking speech. It is then that otherness may be encountered most poignantly, evoking a sense of undecidability as to whether and how to assume the role of the speaker. Such undecidability furnishes the speaker with nothing except a sense of exigency that might modify prospective expressions. To be sure, this is neither to disqualify the individual right to speak, nor to curtail the ability to produce a Said—the Other's intervention is not simply a negative or oppositional hindrance on the way to self-emancipation. Rather, by situating speech on the more fundamental level of responsibility, what is revealed is that every Said is already implicated by other listeners or potential speakers, by the Other who is the other pole of every articulation. It may very well be that a phase of undecidability would be followed by an expression of a

Said. However, unlike the liberal idea of "free speech," such a Said would not be the pure Said of ontology (leaving the self only to return and reify the self), but rather a ruptured Said that maintains within itself the trace of ethical interruption. Such are the words of an exposed speaker, who renounces the aegis of "legitimate" freedom to assume the position of an addressee.

By evoking the responsibility to let speak, to listen, and to respond, one may posit freedom of speech, to paraphrase Levinas, as a difficult freedom: a freedom realized in relation to what resides outside the self. From this perspective, the emergence of speech is not merely a question of positive capacity, as the reality of speech is always and already predicated by the responsibility to and for the Other. Deeming speech first and foremost a means for self-fulfillment not only ignores its dialogical feature but, more importantly, removes it from the constitutive level of responsibility. In this respect, the reality of "free speech" may appear as leaping from the individual level to the universal level while circumventing the heteronomous tangle of freedom and responsibility. Safeguarding the possibility of responsibility to interrupt freedom goes beyond recognizing Others' right to define themselves through speech, beyond tolerating the vocalization of myriad voices. This possibility evidences itself by unsettling the idea of the self-interested speaker, an idea that depends for its cogency on the presumption of individual autonomy. What is at stake, then, is something more radical: it is the possibility of the Other to appear as a face, to challenge, to call into question, to surprise—to become an addresser. As Levinas affirms, "the trace of saying, which has never been present, obliges me; the responsibility for the other, never assumed, binds me; a command never heard is obeyed" (*OB,* 168).

For the Future of Democracy

A third argument often mentioned in relation to free speech is its role in the maintenance and furtherance of the democratic process (see, for example, Emerson 1966; Schauer 1982; Barendt 1985). Like the argument from truth, the argument from democracy is a consequentialist argument, that is, working to achieve and advance a good exceeding particular articulations. The argument from democracy is composed of two critical elements. The first is the need to make all relevant information available to the sovereign electorate so in the process of exercising their powers they could choose certain alternatives over others.[10] As Fredrick Schauer explains, "a circumscription of speech would limit the information available to those making the decisions, impair the deliberative process, and thereby directly erode the mechanism of self-government" (1982, 38). Restricting free speech, he argues, would deny access to facts by which people form their political views, reflecting on the ability to reach informative decisions, and thereby infringing on a fundamental democratic tenet of the right to vote. Second, freedom of speech is necessary for keeping leaders' power in check. Freedom of speech is a way for the people to communicate their wishes to the government and to criticize policies that might harm or do injustice to certain individuals and groups. Because government officials are essentially servants of the public, it is imperative to monitor their activities in ways ranging from political satire to organized public appeal. Thus, curtailing this right would inevitably interfere with a democratic mechanism of checks and balances aimed at preventing the government's usurpation of power.

What might be the political consequences entailed by the priority given by Levinas to initial responsibility over initial freedom? What effects might such a conceptualization of the relation to the Other have on politics in general and on the question of free speech in particular? What is its relevance to the democratic process? To address these concerns, I take as a point of departure Levinas's speculations on the concept of the third party (*le tiers*).

Levinas is indeed concerned mostly with the primacy of the face-to-face, of the ethical relation where I am confronted with the

Other in her or his singularity. Yet this preoccupation does not entail forgetfulness of, or disregard for, the society of other Others. To Levinas, the entry of the third party is not a simple addition or multiplication of the original Other, since what is pronounced with the entry of the third is a call for justice. The third, who is also the Other's Other and my Other, issues a demand that, essentially, interrupts the complacency of the relation between self and Other, a demand to be reckoned with as a face. "The third party," Levinas states, "introduces a contradiction in the saying whose signification before the other until then went in one direction" (*OB,* 157). The appearance of the third does not institute an arithmetic problem, which would posit me as one among many, side-by-side with others. Rather, this alterity calls into question precisely the unlimited responsibility to and for the Other, for now there is another Other who demands a responsible response. The third alterity is therefore not secondary but primal to ethical considerations: its appearance shatters the "naïve" relation between self and Other. It may even be said that the face of the Other already bears the trace of a general call for all Others, an appeal for the generality of justice (see Derrida 1999a, 31–35). It is here that the problems of evaluating and calculating, of priority and regulation, of comparing between incomparable alterities, and of the urgency of making a decision, are introduced. In other words, the necessity for reason itself arises as a way to address the plurality of demands.

Seen in this light, reason appears only as a means to actualize the demand for justice, as a way to facilitate decision in the face of the third (and fourth, fifth, sixth, and so on). Contrary to views grounding subjectivity upon reason (a premise shared by Milton, Mill and Lippmann), in Levinas's perspective, reason is not a cause in and of itself, as at its depth nestles an unarticulated demand for justice in the name of all Others: "The fact that the other, my neighbor, is also a third party with respect to another, who is also a neighbor, is the birth of thought, consciousness, justice and philosophy" (*OB,* 128). To resort to reason is to respond to the exigency of justice, to order among responsibilities. This reveals a radically different perspective by which to understand the role of social institutions, rules, laws and regulations—as functions that manage initial *responsibilities* rather than initial *freedoms*. The work of social institutions may be seen as producing a concrete and temporary solution to a variety of demands at any given moment. However, justice is not merely a matter of regulating human masses striving to achieve social equilibrium, not a result of some kind of distributive justice, which is already based on the preeminence of initial rights. As Drucilla Cornell expounds, "Justice understood as distributive justice always implies an already-established system of ideality in which the distribution takes place," adding that, "For Levinas, distributive justice is never a question of Justice, but only of right" (1992, 135). Justice truly worth the name is never attainable as such: deriving its justification from the face of the Other, it never overlaps existing rules and regulations but exceeds them.

Hence, justice involves a necessary lacuna, and this lacuna is precisely what makes justice just. It is the call of Others who are excluded from existing formalization that echoes in the call for justice. Justice is born from a distortion of original responsibilities— and therefore from a necessary violence exerted upon some Other(s), which is nevertheless required in order to execute a decision—yet its operation always retains its birthmark in the face of the Other. Following Cornell (1992), it may be argued that justice is aporetic: since every case is different, Other than all others, for a decision to be responsible it ought not to be guided solely by existing codes and rules, or in other words, it must be predicated by a necessary undecidability. Otherwise, a decision would be an outcome of a fixed algorithm, and the position of the one who judges could be replaced by a calculating machine.[11]

However, the call for justice is heard in the present: justice cannot be deferred indefinitely, as the demand for a responsible response does not wait for an ideal situation of perfect information. In fact, even if such a situation could be attainable, any decision would still have to make a leap of faith beyond the knowable, otherwise it would not be a decision in a deep sense of the word but an application of a preset matrix of possibilities. It thus follows that there is no moment in which one can state in the present that a decision is just. Justice exists in a perpetual state of "not yet," setting standards for itself higher than those already achieved (compare Bauman 1999). To use Derrida's words, "Justice remains *to come, it remains by coming [la justice reste à venir]*, it *has* to come [*elle a à venir*], it *is* to-come, the to-come [*elle* est *à-venir*], it deploys the very dimension of events irreducibly to come" (Derrida 2001, 256). Justice, understood as a never-ending chase after a forever-elusive goal, is therefore an impossible task; but this impossibility is precisely what constitutes its primary motivation.

This leads to some important conclusions regarding the nature of politics. Politics, as the execution of current priorities, cannot be reduced to and be justified by principles of science, knowledge or truth. Its legitimacy consists in questioning its very legitimacy, by calling the political order into the question of justice. Politics is never a done deal, but open to future demands that would call into question precisely what prevails in the present. Politics is much too important to be left to its own devices, to be denied of the interruption of ethics, as Levinas writes: "politics left to itself bears a tyranny within itself; it deforms the I and the other who have given rise to it, for it judges them according to universal rules, and thus as in absentia" (*TI,* 300). Injustice enters when politics loses sight of the face of the Other, when social organizations, with their regulations and institutions, operate independently of initial responsibilities becoming thereby autotelic mechanisms. For Levinas, then, ethics and politics do not reside in separate spheres, since one is required to execute the other; ethics and politics are not mutually excusive but tied together in a bond of mutual disruption.

Originating from the Other's call for justice, from an originary Saying, politics implies a necessary reduction of the Saying to the language of the Said, to sets of fixed laws, rules and regulations.

This reduction provides the justification and ability to do what is not possible in the ethical party of two, namely, to judge the Other, to demand that the Other respond in the name of fairness and equality, to seek and discover the truth with respect to different articulations. Furthermore, it allows one to advance his or her rights, to issue self-regarding demands, and to speak for oneself. However, this means neither a return to the liberal politics of initial rights nor the reinstitution of ontological discourse. The Said produced in reply to the call for justice is, to use Simon Critchley's (1992) term, a "justified Said." Unlike the politics of initial rights, the justified Said does not emerge from ontology: it does not actualize *what ought* following the perception of *what is*. As Critchley affirms, the justified Said is "a political discourse of reflection and interrogation, a language of decision, judgment, and critique that is informed and interrupted by the responsibility of ethical Saying" (233). The necessary thematization in the language of the Said does not betray the Saying but rather represents an attempt to traverse the passage from ethics to politics. While acknowledging the need of political rationality, Levinas's perspective points out the danger in ignoring the pre-rational relation to the Other. Political order is thus just and justified only insofar as it could be questioned by the Other.

What kind of political space could ensure that politics remain at the service of ethical difference? Following Critchley (1992), I suggest that such would be a democratic political space. And yet, here democracy denotes more than a political order whereby the people decide, vote, and, essentially, rule. It extends beyond the democracy of rights to the democracy of responsibilities, where politics is being challenged by the demand for justice. Democracy, argues Critchley, could be taken "to be an ethically grounded form of political life which is continuously being called into question by asking of its legitimacy and the legitimacy of its practices and institutions: what is justice?" (ibid., 239). Political responsibility in democracy consists of the questioning of its axioms, its boundaries, and the foundations upon which it is based—a task whose horizon extends to and is informed by the face of the Other. It is only by challenging the legitimacy of the community that a democratic community finds its legitimization. A democratic community is therefore an interrupted community, practicing "the on-going interruption of politics by ethics, of totality by infinity, of the Said by the Saying" (ibid., 240). This implies a simultaneous necessity of both concrete and abstract considerations, of rights and responsibilities, of order and "anarchism," for only the sustaining of these tensions may prevent the possibility of passing by the Other. Democracy understood as a just political order (which immediately implies a certain disorder), is marked by a persistent residue of responsibility, by an endemic incompletion, which demands that democracy be "reinvented" every time anew, once more called to justify itself. In this vein, democracy extends toward the future, to the advent of an Other yet to come.

By way of conclusion, I would like to consider the possibility of extending the conception of a just democracy to the question of free speech. To this end, I turn to the concept of the *differend* as developed by Jean François Lyotard (1988). Lyotard's work may be prefaced as an attempt to testify to and account for the ways a metanarrative finds its justification in the reduction or subjugation of competing narratives.[12] This is when one genre of discourse (consisting of legitimate and illegitimate rules for combining "language games," or what Lyotard calls "phrase-regimens") safeguards its legitimacy either by forcing other narratives to comply with its own rules or by denying their existence altogether. Lyotard calls attention to a critical point: the way one metanarrative has come to appropriate others can never find expression in the idiom of that metanarrative. It may thus appear as committing the "perfect crime": appropriating other discourses while having the capacity to deny or obliterate that very fact, an effect comparable to an earthquake that "destroys not only lives, buildings, and objects but also the instruments used to measure earthquakes directly and indirectly" (1988, 56). Lyotard calls this situation the *differend*.

"A case of differend between two parties," writes Lyotard, "takes place when the 'regulation' of the conflict that opposes them is done in the idiom of one of the parties while the wrong suffered by the other is not signified in that idiom" (1988, 9). The *differend* is a case of a conflict that cannot be phrased in either idiom (or a common one) without prejudicing, debilitating, or doing injustice to the complaining party by the very act of phrasing.[13] Hence, it is not simply a case of incommensurability, for when it takes place someone is divested of the means to express, argue and prove his or her damages and consequently suffers from a wrong (*tort*)—"a damage accompanied by the loss of the means to prove the damage"—the victim's inability to prove that he or she is a victim (1988, 5). According to this rationale, litigation can take place only when the disputing parties agree to interpret and represent their damages in ways that cause no wrongs to either side (Ophir 1997, 191). A *differend,* conversely, is a situation where one party is forced to accept the discursive rules imposed by another, thereby making its case inexpressible, a situation that inevitably puts its misfortune under erasure. This implies that the *differend,* as such, is ineffable:

> The differend is the unstable state and instant of language wherein something which must be able to be put into phrases cannot yet be. This state includes silence, which is a negative phrase, but it also calls upon phrases which are in principle possible. This state is signaled by what one ordinarily calls a feeling: "One cannot find words," etc. A lot of searching must be done to find new rules for forming and linking phrases that are able to express the differend disclosed by the feeling, unless one wants this differend to be smothered right away in a litigation and for the alarm sounded by the feeling to have been useless. What is at stake in a literature, in a philosophy, in a politics perhaps, is to bear witness to differends by finding idioms for them. (Lyotard 1988, 13)

The *differend* indicates a situation in which something that asks to be phrased suffers from the fact that it cannot be done promptly.

What is signaled thereby is a pressing "feeling," an urgency to find words, a summation to develop ways of expression that do not yet exist. The *differend,* states Lyotard, "is signaled by a silence," and that silence indicates that phrases are in abeyance, that what remains to be phrased always surpasses what can be phrased in the present (ibid., 57). It is here that Lyotard locates a crucial political obligation: to bear witness to the silence of *differends* and to develop alternative ways to express wrongs that are presently inexpressible.

I highlight the *differend* because it introduces an issue that has been excluded from the conceptualization of systems of expression in traditional liberal thought. Liberal discourse on free speech may be characterized as concerning itself with the democracy of the present, with the conditions that allow or obstruct free expression under the existing metanarrative or discourse (that is, tenets of individualism, autonomy, freedom and rights). This discourse implies that if something demands to be expressed, it can, in principle, find expression through existing avenues; alternatively, this means that what is silent is content, indifferent or simply nonexistent. Lyotard's contribution is in pointing out the fact that discursive dominance necessarily entails the omission of alternative narratives and the creation of wrongs that cannot be signified within the prevailing metanarrative. His intervention may then be seen as actualizing a critical position midway between Foucauldian analysis of disciplinary discursive practices and Levinasian concern for otherness.

Central to this position is an alternative understanding of the social role of communication. By acknowledging that at any given moment there may be someone or something that demands to be expressed but cannot (or perhaps prefers not to) do so under the existing circumstances, this position implies that language cannot be reduced to a mere instrument of communication. This realization emerges when those seeking to use language as an instrument "learn through the feeling of pain which accompanies silence (and of pleasure which accompanies the invention of a new idiom), that they are summoned by language, not to augment to their profit the quantity of information communicable through existing idioms, but to recognize that what remains to be phrased exceeds what they can presently phrase" (Lyotard 1988, 13). It may then be said that in the *differend* there is an indication (which always runs the risk of not being identified) of the gap between what *is* expressible and what *ought* to be expressed, the gap between the Said and the Saying. In the *differend,* what remains to be articulated is being enunciated through the shortcomings of the present communication possibilities.

Following Lyotard, I suggest that the conception of the *differend* may provide a different view of the social role of speech in democracy. By calling attention to the voicelessness of phrases constrained by a dominant discourse, the issue of restricting expression may indeed go far beyond concrete limitations imposed within a specific discourse (a definitive example being the quest for truth). Restriction is not only a matter of curtailing the articulation of already phrased expressions in the present, but also the a priori exclusion of articulations that cannot find expression within the dominant discourse. Such a restriction cannot be articulated within the dominant discourse without already placing at a disadvantage the one who makes the appeal. Hence the predicament accompanying democracy from ancient times: that of women and slaves in ancient Greece, and in its contemporary dress, that of the foreign worker and the refugee, the occupied and the oppressed, the insane and the criminal, the transient and the homeless, and the list goes on. As Patrick F. McKinlay expounds, the *differend* "calls attention to those events that are void of any mode of expression in our representative institutions" (1998, 499). It thus invites awareness of the unsaid, the unrepresented and the unrepresentable, and of the demand pronounced thereby to institute new modes of expression by which to replace silence.[14] The *differend* stands for the responsibility to account for and respond to—indeed to bear witness to— the social production of silence. This would involve, among other things, reconstituting the relation between potential addressers and addressees in ways that lead each to see themselves as implicated, either directly or indirectly, by the articulation of new appeals.[15]

The responsibility to respond to what is excluded from the present state of affairs introduces a formidable challenge to democracy, one of attending to *differends* and seeking ways to rectify their injury. But this challenge is not immune from the fate of any other discourse, that is, from producing new *differends*. For this reason, no consensual discourse or metanarrative can ever address all possible appeals, past, present and future. Such an engagement could only proceed by constantly questioning its own grounds, being guided solely by the commitment to embark once more on a new mission. This innate incompleteness of democracy ensures that the realm of "the political" (*la politique*) will always transcend the realm of "politics" (*le politique*), that is to say, that the ethical-political obligation will always exceed existing channels of expression. Democracy, as a political order that is based on a regular evacuation of its loci of power, may indeed maintain within itself the possibility of transformation. However, extending from Levinas to Lyotard, is a political commitment to expose politics to the horizon of alterity, to respond to *differends* by preserving a space for articulations that do not conform to restrictions imposed by dominant discourses such as those of the state, nation, class, market, tradition, and so on. To be sure, the stakes implied therein are undoubtedly high because such a commitment posits democracy as a project to be executed without any guarantees, and therefore it involves an essential risk (not unlike the risk accompanying any engagement with the Other, including that of usurpation and exploitation). A justice-oriented democracy does not deny these risks but negotiates the extent to which they could be played out. By opening itself to the unforeseeable, the unpredictable future from which a previously unheard demand may come, democracy provides political auspices not only for present participants who can speak for themselves, but also for the silent, the absent and the bygone.

*   *   *

An often cited line by Ludwig Wittgenstein is the one ending his *Tractatus Logico-Philosophicus:* "Whereof one cannot speak, thereof one must remain silent" (1960, 83). The motivation guiding this discussion may be put as a reversal of Wittgenstein's dictum: "Whereof one remains silent, thereof one must speak." My purpose in this chapter has been to problematize the concept of free speech and to call attention to what resides beyond the expressible—to that which is signaled by silence. In brief, the foregoing has proposed to consider the ethical stakes implied by preempting speech for silence, freedom for responsibility and truth for justice. The excommunication of silence from the sphere of speech entails the loss of some of its evocative modes: as a by-product of restriction and exclusion, as the background against which every articulation transpires, as a modality characterizing the receptivity of an addressee, as a speechless potentiality awaiting articulation. I have attempted to push the discussion back from freedom to speak to the responsibility to speak by pointing out the unstable origin of speech as predicated by the responsibility to listen, to let speak, and to respond to the Other's call. As a critique of the liberal notion of free speech, it does not amount to antiliberalism but may be taken in itself as a more radical version of liberalism, as exceeding liberalism, as attempting to "liberate" speech from the pursuit of truth, from individualism, from freedom and, ultimately, from itself.

Being contingent upon the context of its production, speech appears as fundamentally social, as bearing the mark of its surroundings, both when acknowledged and, more importantly, when ignored. The portrayal of speech as inherently and originally free finds its source in the liberal propensity to conceptualize speech as teleological and self-serving rather than responsive and responsible. Taking up the notion of responsible speech introduces challenges of a different kind, central to which is acquiring sensitivity to the "unexpressible" and developing new ways of expression within a democratic social space. Consequently, the role of speech in the pursuit of truth may also take a radical twist because, following Lyotard, it may be said that the "discovery" of truth is always already conditioned by the boundaries of legitimate discourses. The pursuit is therefore infinite; however, as such, it yields to the never-ending quest for justice, to the commitment to give expression to truths yet to be pronounced.

In the end, one is left with the same basic questions: Is freedom of speech worth protecting? Should certain kinds of speech be denounced or even curtailed? Should different types of speech be granted equal merit and recognition? Should the silent Other be given the right and the means to speak? Indeed, these are the same questions, but perhaps now they resonate with somewhat altered sensitivities. If there is a general guideline arising from the foregoing discussion it is merely that there can be no general doctrine by which to respond to each consideration in particular. For a decision to be responsible, it must proceed from the aporia of undecidability, from the contradiction between the generality of rules and the singularity of each case. The obligation to decide cannot be absolved by preset principles; otherwise, it would entail the foreclosure of a terrain immune to questioning and consequently excluded from the realm of decision—from "the political." Only by maintaining the irreducible complexity of decision can a social space remain open to the Other's demand.

The Messenger Is the Message

> Far from our own people, our own language, stripped of all our props, deprived of our masks (one doesn't know the fare of the streetcar, or anything else), we are completely on the surface of ourselves.
> —Albert Camus, *The Wrong Side and the Right Side*

The approach of the Other summons communication otherwise conceived. One usually learns that he or she is able to communicate most effectively when using prepaved channels of discourse: that speaking the same language, sharing the same codes and adhering to the same discursive rules guarantee an unbiased and undisturbed interaction. Common discourse assures that the proper reception and perception of a message is achieved when interacting units are equivalent and interchangeable, that easy passage is best facilitated on the basis of a common ground, and that familiarity reduces the risk of things going astray. Within such confines, one feels comfortable and secure, confident in an appearance of a harmonious state of being. But when a face that cannot, does not, or does not want to share the common idiom appears, something intelligible happens at the edge of discursive competence, which may nevertheless be resolved before long, declared a mistake, or simply ignored. This interruption conveys a message still in abeyance: an invitation that cannot be answered within existing modes of communication that seek to integrate individual fields of perception or extend one mind to the other. But precisely for this reason, one finds oneself compelled to respond and to venture beyond the familiar. It is here that one discovers that saying something matters most when it is impossible to say anything. At the end of practices one usually reckons to master, a space is opened where communication would have to proceed otherwise. The end marks a new beginning, perhaps the beginning, of communication.

The Work of Interruption

Interruptions transpire without respite. Their occurrence, however minimal or fleeting, upholds the possibility for the Other to appear, intervene and instruct. An interruption is an event that communicates through its very eventuality, and as such has no proper shape, form or structure. Although the possibility of its occurrence persists, the chances that it will be admitted as conveying an ethical message can nevertheless be reduced considerably. Interestingly, some of the most effective means of disqualifying the immanence of interruptions are found in traditional conceptions of communication. It is possible to delineate in this respect two general modalities: the one follows the Cartesian principle of extension by which communication is accomplished in a timely and accurate relaying of messages from one point to another, in the closure of the transmission-reception circuit, and in a process of encoding that is commensurate with that of decoding. The other follows a Hegelian vein of dialectics whereby different meanings, symbols and assertions compete, conflict and conflate, a transformative process through which certain options prevail while others wane, and that ultimately culminates in synthesis, agreement or reconciliation. At least in this respect, it is possible to read many traditional theories of communication not simply as perspectives to understand the exchange of ideas, symbols or meanings, but also, to a greater or lesser extent, as devices for the excommunication of interruptions.

Not only does interruption inhere in communication, it is, in fact, what constitutes the very possibility of communication. Marcel Proust once remarked that the only true voyage would be not to travel through a hundred different lands with the same pair of eyes, but to see the same land through a hundred different pairs of eyes. But embarking on a Proustian voyage into another's vision would mean interchangeability of points of view and therefore reduction of that very thing that makes another's outlook different. Thus, if accomplished, such a voyage would immediately lose its original appeal. Likewise, were the fantasy of uninterrupted interaction to miraculously materialize, its corollary would be an instant termination of communication itself. Perfect communication means noncommunication, a veritable example of a self-refuting ideal. This leads, by way of contradistinction, to viewing the possibility of communication as a paradox: the condition of its possibility as its impossibility, and instances that interrupt communication—indeed, that make it impossible—as precisely what gives rise to its possibility. Hence the immanence of failure, refusal and risk: not merely as deleterious exceptions but as intrinsic to the work of communication itself. To posit an ideal of transparent exchange is to discard interruption as a mode of communication, and communication as a mode of interruption.

Writing on interruption introduces a unique challenge. In order to be faithful to its cause, it cannot simply apply a theoretical idea to the reality of phenomena. Although conceivable theoretically, a direct approach to the study of interruption (or what could be conceived as a phenomenology of interruption) runs the risk of objectifying the thing it attempts to study, and, what is worse, of neutralizing the very manifestation it set out to study in the first place. Being in itself a form of communication, writing on interruption must therefore not resort to paradigms it already deems problematic. It requires a method that is not properly methodological—an approach that not only resists representing the object of its investigation but also avoids sketching the contours of its reflection. Thus, to be true to itself, a discourse on interruption must only gesture toward the possibilities that may arise or be involved with such an occurrence, to point out the prospects that the end of communication introduces. Bearing this problematic in mind, I have proposed the approach of dislocation. Implied therein is a double meaning and a double move: dislocating the process of communication and dislocating its ethical significance: reevaluating the status of instances in which communication seems to fail, halt, or reach an impasse, and concomitantly, pointing toward ethical possibilities opened up by such instances, an opening revealed by the work of interruption.

I initially planned for this work to study the relation to the Other in the writings of Martin Buber, Emmanuel Levinas and Mikhail Bakhtin. However, following a close reading of significant parts of their works and reflecting on potential issues for engagement, it became evident to me that remaining within the confines of theoretical-philosophical discourse would lose something essential to the intent of these texts. It seemed to me that in order to carry out their import more fully—and particularly when deciding to focus on the work of Levinas—my engagement and perspective would have to be exposed to the stakes implied by such a conceptual grounding. In other words, the nature of my intervention and the way by which it was to be communicated would have to run a certain risk. This meant, among other things, negotiating within an impossible bind of wanting to make claims as clear and compelling as possible, on the one hand, and refraining from crossing the line to unyielding formalization and thematization, on the other. The extent to which I have been successful in this task does not therefore consist only in undertaking to explicate certain complexities, but also in demonstrating these complexities through the undertaking itself. The lessons to be pointed out in my conclusion exceed what is said in

the foregoing pages. They also concern the frustration and difficulties, as well as the unexpected discoveries and surprises, that have
accompanied the writing of this work almost from its inception.
This work may then be viewed as the result of an experience whose
traces are marked, and possibly ruptured, throughout its unfolding.

Communication and Ethics, Communication as Ethics

A major consideration arising from this discussion is situating communication in the context of responsibility. Discourses and practices as varied as philosophical speculations, political thought,
social criticism, as well as clinical and scientific research (whose
combined influence has consequently percolated into popular mind
and culture) have been guided by a common understanding that
deems patent interaction to be indicative of ideals of rationality, normalcy and conviviality. Yet what appears to be a natural tendency
is, in fact, a product of a historical evolution of ideas in the course
of which the proper completion of intercourse has been promoted
to the level of a moral value. At its core is the belief that the end of
communication is what constitutes its end, and that that end upholds
the possibility of imminent reconciliation among minds, views or
aspirations. While communication may indeed bring about reconciliation, prescribing it as an end confuses one possible result with
the ultimate result. Moreover, it obfuscates the more fundamental
inkling that entering into communication is conjured up rather than
jeopardized by the irreducible difference between communicators.
The primal scene of communication is set where differences rendezvous—that is, meet, present themselves and possibly give themselves up. It involves facing that precedes interfacing, an encounter
whereby responsibility becomes complicit with response-ability.
Communication reveals itself as an ethical involvement precisely
when it transcends beyond reciprocity of exchange.

A recurrent theme throughout this work has been the ethical
stakes in evacuating communication from instances of miscommunication. A brief comparison between two fictional characters,

Jerzy Kosinski's protagonist Chauncey the gardener in *Being There* (1970) and the aforementioned Herman Melville's *Bartleby the Scrivener,* may help make the problem explicit. Kosinski's narrative tells the story of a feeble-minded gardener who rises to fame thanks to a unique talent: his ability to naively reflect people's wants and perceptions as projected onto him. Born in a mansion from which he had never stepped out, Chauncey's life had revolved around two activities: tending to the manorial garden and watching television. His forced departure from the mansion is followed by a series of fortuitous events that take him through corridors of money and power, by the end of which he becomes a media celebrity and the favorite candidate of the party in power for the vice presidency. All this transpires as he innocently recites lines about gardening and enacts scenes from years of television watching, while remaining himself ignorant of all that happens. His impact on people, which consists of a crude knack for reproducing what others want to see in him, provides comfort and confirmation, never challenging and always pacifying. Lacking internal substance, possessing gardening for a political vocabulary and having television soap operas for a past—such is the figure, in Kosinski's mordant view, most capable of sailing up the social ladder and ascending to the highest rung of American politics.

As such, Kosinski's Chauncey might be seen as constituting the opposite extreme to Melville's Bartleby: while both characters are undoubtedly eccentric, the gardener's eccentricity, unlike that of the scrivener, does not lessen (to the contrary, in fact) his social faculties. Whereas Bartleby upsets preset procedures of interaction, Chauncey is the ultimate sounding board, as he facilitates a kind of interaction in which the other party absorbs an overabundance of self-produced meanings. Bartleby, on the one hand, is a figure that surpasses all general laws of language and simple particularities of speech. Chauncey, on the other hand, both abides by and is a product of systemized communication procedures, which he literally reverberates in every utterance. While Bartleby's incompatibility ultimately brings about expulsion and demise, Chauncey's oddity allows him to glide smoothly through the system without hindrance. However, in both cases pre-established social and political orders eventually prevail, either by promoting the congruent element or by expelling the irreconcilable one. Thus, if the scrivener is an embodiment of incommunicable alterity, Chauncey is a quintessence of transmissible sameness. The ways they consequently affect their surroundings are radically different, as those who interact with Chauncey are forever spared from what Bartleby's employer faces repeatedly—dealing with an alterity that calls for a singular response precisely because it resists immediate access. The predicament of Melville's lawyer thus intimates an important lesson: that responding to the Other means surpassing readily available means and modes of interaction. It involves, indeed depends upon, venturing beyond the familiar, where responsibility is predicated by the uncertainty as to how to respond.

To consider communication in the context of responsibility entails reconsidering the relation between interacting parties. Recent theories of communication have rightly moved the emphasis from the intentions of the sender to the interpretations of the receiver. Allowing for relative independency of processes of decoding and encoding has called attention to particular practices of meaning-making while privileging the interpretive work done by the receiving end. This shift is clearly informed by a critical commitment that seeks to undermine authoritarian patterns of influence and hegemonic production of meaning, and at least in this regard, shares my concern with the rupturing of regularized procedures of communication. However, the critical point of this work differs in that it emphasizes the significance of instances of "miscommunication," of breakdown, impasse and inconsistency, rather than alternative or oppositional modes of interpretation. It thus points out the possibility that ethical messages might lie beyond the scope of existing processes of communication and perhaps even beyond the work of interpretation.

This further shift of emphasis opens up a host of issues and questions for exploration. It will suffice here to suggest only two possible lines of investigation. The first concerns the conditions under which one may become a recipient of an ethical message. While still privileging the role of the "receiver," further analysis is required in order to characterize what distinguishes the position of an addressee from that of a mere recipient, and the ways in which one could transform into the other. This question bears special significance given the abundance of images and stories of sufferings and plights, both near and far, reported regularly by the mass media. Exploring the effects of such an exposure and its impact on ethical sensitivities might help understand patterns of social indifference as well as of social involvement. In addition, it calls for a careful analysis of technological, social and political factors, and the ways they come into play both separately and simultaneously when addresses are adequately responded to (either individually or collectively) as well as when they remain unanswered.

The other line of investigation is more fundamental in nature. It concerns specifically the conditions under which one might become a carrier of an ethical message, that is, an addresser. A key question in this regard is identifying the forces, practices and apparatuses that participate in precluding individuals and groups from becoming addressers while permitting others to lay their claims. Unlike the previous line of investigation, which deals mainly with existing channels of communication, the latter entails speculating and perhaps giving voice to what is not properly in existence, or what is possibly beyond the available scope of interaction, comprehension and interpretation. It therefore implies engagement with what is, almost by definition, inexpressible within existing discursive arrangements. The task here would then be twofold: first, to chart the structure and boundaries of existing discursive configurations in order to point out omission, elimination or exclusion; next, to specify the stakes in excluding or disqualifying potential addressers, and possibly suggesting alternative avenues for expression and thereby for the production of new addresses.

Together these two parallel lines of investigation may provide a conceptual starting point for reformulating the relation between addressers and addressees and for reconstructing the ethical implications of both existing and future addresses.

The Other Community

This work invites a rethinking of the relationship between communication and community. Many have pointed out the bond between these two concepts, which goes back to their common Latin root *mun,* which is often found in words denoting association and commonality. Indeed, the triadic correlation between commonality, community and communication upholds much of the problematic I have attempted to unpack. A short episode from Tzvetan Todorov's (1984) history of the conquest of America animates some of the stakes involved herein. When approaching one of the New Continent's lands, the Spaniards shouted from the ship to the Native Americans they saw on the shore: "What is the name of this land?" The natives answered: *"Ma c'ubah than,"* "we do not understand your language." What the Spaniards heard was "Yucatan," and decided that this was the name of the province (ibid., 99). The name prevalent nowadays, so it seems, is nothing but a result of an exchange gone awry, a ship-to-shore miscommunication. While it is not clear what the Native Americans made of this peculiar event, it seems that the Spaniards were all-too-sure they had made contact. It is also safe to assume the Spaniard would have taken whatever utterance was produced in reply to their question as a valid answer. What was actually said mattered little because the answer was already implied in the question. Insofar as they were concerned, the natives not only spoke Spanish but were also waiting readily for the moment they could give their answer to one and only one question. When meeting strangeness in the flesh, the Spaniards extricated the foreign and placed it in a context furnished by their own knowledge of the world. There was no communication failure since communication was not even given the chance to fail. The superimposed commonality between the two communities had condemned communication to succeed even before it commenced. This highly condensed juncture illustrates not only a missed encounter with the Other; it also marks the moment when violence enters the picture under the cloak of innocent ignorance.

When community is invoked, it is often followed by sentiments of familiarity, belonging and security. It usually evokes an image of a social space free from strife and friction where individuals find comfort in the society of like-minded individuals. Common language, tradition, religion and rituals are presumably among the main building blocks of communities, both real and imaginary. Although such commonalities undoubtedly exist in the world, it is when they are deemed essential to human or social nature that the path to the obliteration of otherness is effectively opened. For determining what is common inevitably depends upon discarding what is different, and the more coherent the appearance of commonality, the more invasive the evacuation of difference. The stability of communal structures is troubled every time a stranger appears. Facing the Other, one is forced to step outside regular patterns of conduct and expose oneself to an alterity that has nothing in common with one's community. This encounter announces the beginning of another community, which nestles beneath routinized community—a community of difference. The Other's interruption makes evident what is oppressed and denied by communal structures: the immanency of a relation transcending similarity and like-mindedness. Rather than having or working to have something in common, this community is realized in the approach and exposure to the foreign: the outcast, the mental patient, the immigrant, the native, the enemy.

As John Durham Peters (1999) notes, many a volume has invoked the Latin *communicare* as the origin of the activity of sharing talk. The less often-cited Greek term *koinoō,* argues Peters, offers a harsher insight: like the Latin, it means to impart and to make common, but it also means to pollute, contaminate or make unclean. The duplicity of its message thus conveys something of the messiness that accompanies communication for better or worse. Communication understood as crossing the border of common and uncommon, inner and outer, self and Other, goes beyond establishing a common place for secure interaction. It implies opening the door to the Other, to the unforeseen and the unforeseeable, and hence to the risk of pollution and contamination, to incomprehension and misconstruing, to impasse and silence. "Communication," Levinas affirms, "is an adventure of a subjectivity, different from that which is dominated by the concern to recover itself, different from that of coinciding in consciousness; it will involve uncertainty" (*OB*, 120). Uncertainty and risk, then, but not merely as subsequent to striking contact with another, but rather, I repeat, as indicative of what gives rise to the possibility of striking contact— exposure, proximity, openness and vulnerability. The potential for disruptive intervention is therefore announced at the beginning— in fact, is the beginning—of every communication. Hence, not only does communication exceed the task of making things common, it effectively contains the seeds of its deconstruction, of interrupting the very construction of commonality.

Modern communication models prescribe that proper transmission and reception of messages require subtraction of interruptive noise, that purging disruptive pollutants is crucial for maintaining the coherence of a message as well as for recovering its original meaning. A community adhering to an ideal of translucent communication would therefore be one in which members not only partake in the production and consumption of messages but also subscribe to a common endeavor of reducing the interruption of noise, babble and silence. Joined by this alliance, they share a commitment to keep the inside in and the outside out. United they stand on the same side, on the side of the Same, like the Spaniards when meeting (or rather, mismeeting) the Native Americans for the first time. But if, as I contend, a deeper sense of communication lies in the Other community, in the encounter with alterity, then such vision of communal utopia is nothing short of collective myopia. Viewing communication from where it appears to be working misses something essential to its occurrence and in effect to its workability. It misses the point of contact where differences meet, a point at once internal and external to each side and irreducible to either. This singular point reveals communication as fracturing rather than working to obtain communal coherency or to construct a greater community. The Other community, in contradistinction to the community of the Same, could be described as putting the inside out and the outside in: a *u-topian* community, that is, of no-place and without place, displaced and displacing.

The singular and irreducible point of contact where commonality is challenged thus constitutes a highly condensed juncture. It marks an opening for response, for translation and approach, but also, and at the same time, an opening for refusal and defiance, resistance to incorporation. Giving this juncture its due is not merely a matter of demarcating fissures: the difference between self and Other is not exhausted in a state of disinterested separateness, but rather, as Levinas repeatedly affirms, in nonindifference, in concern and responsibility. It therefore requires restoring a point of reference that precedes and exceeds the production of commonality, a heteronomous point of contact, what Homi Bhabha (1994) calls in another context a "third space," a liminal sphere that makes the structure of communication and any meanings produced thereby an ambivalent process. This point of contact where differences meet is not merely a disjunction that divides Same and Other but, rather, a junction that brings them together as different—a disjunctive junction, a site of proximity and touch exclusive of symbiosis or merger, and as such, a veritable site of interruptions.

Witnessing

This work has attempted to outline a conceptual link between the ethical and the communicational while explicating various manifestations and modalities of this link in different texts and discourses. I would like to consider in conclusion a modality that embodies this link most concretely: the act of witnessing. As a concept, witnessing brings together many of the issues studied throughout this work. It upholds questions of distance and proximity, presence and absence, past and present, private and public, truth and justice, responsibility and response-ability—in short, some of the most fundamental questions constituting the link between ethics and communication. As a practice, witnessing calls attention to a particular historical moment, one that is implicated by two post–World War II developments: the expansion of media of mass communication and the revision of ethics after the Holocaust.

Witnessing includes two interrelated involvements: to witness and to bear witness. To witness means to be present and observe an occurrence directly; it involves firsthand knowledge of, and immediate access to, an experience exclusive to the one witnessing. To bear witness, on the other hand, implies providing an account of what happened, delivering a testimony based on that to which one has borne witness. Thus, witnessing consists in moving from the passive act of beholding to the active act of recounting, from seeing to saying (see Peters 2001).

The witness provides access to an event or experience otherwise inaccessible: summoned by the court, she or he offers knowledge about something that is beyond the reach of those who have to pass judgment; approached by the historian, the witness is asked to supply insight beyond what is already inscribed in historiographical accounts; called by a reporter, she or he is invited to describe what cannot be described by pictures and sound. The witness gives expression to something that passed but still affects, stating one's experience for the benefit of those who were not present at the time or the place of the event. Yet the witness is not merely a channel of information from one point in time and place to another. In witnessing, one testifies not only to his or her individual experiences but also to the impossibility of re-presenting these experiences, of bridging past to present and absence to presence. For if such relaying were possible, there would be neither sense nor need in what the witness has to say; put differently, if witnessing were to follow a paradigm of transmittal, it would lose what is essential, and in fact what gives rise to its eventuality—the necessary gap between witnessing and bearing witness, between the experience and the act of recounting the experience. Hence, the witness, as an addresser, also testifies to the irreducible gap between his or her address and those who are its addressees, now themselves witnesses to a witness. In this capacity, the one bearing testimony for those who lack the original experience becomes most emphatically the message—an epitome of the Levinasian formula: "the messenger is the message" (1968, 104).

Herein lies the ethical commitment taken by the witness. A paradigm case of which is Primo Levi, who having survived the Holocaust took it upon himself to tell the story of the drowned, those who had perished:

> We who were favored by fate tried, with more or less wisdom, to recount not only our fate but also that of the others, indeed of the drowned; but this was a discourse "on behalf of third parties," the story of things seen at close hand, not experienced personally. The destruction brought to an end, the job completed, was not told by anyone, just as no one ever returned to describe his own death. Even if they had paper and pen, the drowned would not have testified because their death had begun before that of their body. Weeks and months before being snuffed out, they had already lost the ability to observe, to remember, to compare and express themselves. We speak in their stead, by proxy. (1988, 84)

In bearing witness, Levi submitted to an impossible task: to speak on behalf of those who could not speak for themselves. In so doing, he admits that however compelling and eloquent his prose, it could never capture the experiences of those who had touched rock bottom. They are, in essence, the ultimate and complete witnesses of the Holocaust's atrocities, for they are the only ones who could fully attest to its extent and tell the whole story. The "true" witnesses are therefore those who cannot bear witness—the exclusive witnesses are those whose testimony will never be heard, and for whom the gap between experiencing and recounting is infinite. Levi, like others who were spared by good fortune or by other extenuating circumstances, is not a complete witness precisely because he was saved, precisely because he lived to tell the story. His survival attests to the fact that he is not, and can never be, a representative of what transpired in Nazi extermination camps and of those who perished there. He can only speak as a surrogate voice. For this reason, his testimony contains, and indeed consists in, an inextricable lacuna: at its core is something that he can never bear witness to, a deficiency that is forever silent (Agamben 1999, 34). "No one bears witness for the witness," writes Paul Celan, himself a Holocaust survivor, in his poem *Ashglory,* expressing thereby the inexpressible truth of witnessing (1971, 240). By taking upon himself the task of speaking in the name of the drowned, "on behalf of third parties," Levi witnessed the impossibility of completing this task, speaking in the name of the impossibility of bearing witness.

This incompleteness, this deficiency, prescribes the witness with the charge and responsibility to speak. The silence of the absent and the bygone compels the witness not to remain silent. As a paradigm case of a witness, Levi's writings put forth the stakes in bearing witness, most and foremost as an ethical commitment. The order that commands the witness is never heard as such, only as a trace of the irrecusable responsibility toward the Other: to express the inexpressible, to translate the untranslatable, and to respond to that which can never respond in turn. Although constituting an extreme example of witnessing, Levi's testimony captures what is essential to witnessing in general: that giving voice to the voiceless can neither expose nor put forth an underlying and coherent truth. Different witnesses would recount different stories of the same event: their individual circumstances and capabilities (memory, eloquence, motivation, and the like) would necessarily implicate the ways they would unfold their perception of what they had experienced. And even if all possible witnesses to an event could be assembled, their testimonies studied, validated and compared, such a project would still, by definition, fall short of actually being present at the event and witnessing it firsthand. What the witness has to say surpasses the Said, the thematization of an experience into words and phrases. It pronounces the inspiration of Saying, of delivering, of handing over and bearing out the Said. Thus, the gist of witnessing is not exhausted in the pursuit for truth, which is motivated by an attempt to reconstruct a comprehensive schema of what "really" happened. Transcending the Said, it is implicated by and gives expression to a general demand for justice, a demand whose origin lies in the face of the Other and whose horizon extends to the future, to justice yet to come.

Nowadays, perhaps more than at any other time, events transpiring in the remotest parts of the world are a matter of common knowledge, particularly events of violence and carnage, which are made available to audiences through various media complete with vivid depictions. As opposed to the case of witnessing represented by Primo Levi, the problem today is not so much that things are happening without people knowing, but rather that things are happening and it is almost impossible not to know. The accessibility and speed of information provided by communication technology pose some crucial questions regarding the nature of witnessing, communicational as well as ethical. Perhaps the act of witnessing itself is undergoing a transformation while stories, images and sounds of others' plights and misfortunes become increasingly ubiquitous. The excess of witnessing as seeing presents a great challenge for witnessing as saying and responding. A witness, as opposed to a mere spectator, is entrusted with an obligation following the act of seeing—the responsibility to respond. Being a witness means being implicated by what one has borne witness to in a way that singles him or her out as a messenger of an ethical message. Such is the responsibility to bear witness to the disparity between what can presently be said and what still remains to be said.

Notes

Notes to Introduction

1. The word "Other" is a translation of the French *Autrui,* designating a non-specific yet immediate person with whom the self is in relation. Thus, the Other is not simply a category of diversity (gender, race, orientation and the like) but of ethical difference. In attempting to emphasize the nonsymmetrical relation to the Other, the word "self" will appear throughout noncapitalized.

2. In its resistance to incorporation—as reduction or as dialectical transcendence of differences—*différance,* states Derrida, is a mode of self-interruption, without which there could be no responsibility (1999b, 81).

3. Engagment with Levinas's philosophy has been relatively scarce within communication thought. Among the notable exceptions are Arnett (2001, 2003), Cmiel (1996), Hyde (2001), Lipari (2004), Murray (2001, 2003a, 2003b), Silverston (1999, 2003) and Smith (1997).

4. Further discussion and elaboration on dislocation will be presented in chapter 2.

5. In *The Ethics of Deconstruction* (1992), Simon Critchley speaks of a "third wave in the reception of deconstruction," beyond its previous literary and philosophical appropriations, "one in which ethical—not to mention political—questions are uppermost" (3). While acknowledging that Derrida's work has always been highly sensitive to the ethical modalities of response and responsibility, it is when raising the question of ethics "through a rapprochement with the work of Emmanuel Levinas" that it takes up an ethical-political import (3). Thus, rather than a critique of Derrida, what is at issue is providing a Levinasian supplement, as it were, to deconstruction.

Notes to Chapter One

1. Charles Wright (1959), in his functional approach to communication, adds a fourth function—entertainment. Also compare Schramm (1973) and Thayer (1971).

2. The book was not a product of the combined work of the two. The first part, "Recent Contributions to the Mathematical Theory of Communication," was written by Weaver and presents a general (and more approachable) review of the theory. The remainder of the book, "The Mathematical Theory of Communication," written by Shannon, contains elaborate mathematical formulations of 23 theorems. One critic argues that Weaver's interpretation of Shannon's work is distorted because it is keenly attempting to apply Information Theory to general human behavior (Ritchie 1986).

3. As Peters notes, that conception also governs genetic discourse where DNA is a code containing "genetical information," neural synapses are "switchboards," and RNA proteins are "informosomes" (1988, 18).

4. Wiener states that Leibniz was "the intellectual ancestor" of his ideas (1954, 19). He was especially fascinated by Leibniz's monads, which he endeavored to interpret in informational-material terms (Heims 1977, 143). Interestingly enough, Wiener's conception of cybernetics uncannily resonates with his description of Leibnizian religious cosmology: "Leibniz . . . saw the world as a collection of beings called 'monads' whose activity consisted in the perception of one another on the basis of pre-established harmony laid down by God" (1954, 18). In that respect, Wiener's idea of cybernetics might be considered as Leibnizian cosmology, minus the role of God.

5. Russell's paradox is usually explained using the grammatical example, "I am a liar." The paradox here is clear: if I am a liar, then my acknowledgment of the truth of that statement contradicts the content of the proposition; if I am telling the truth, then the content contradicts the admission of my telling a lie. Russell argued that the nature of this paradox stems from a confusion between two levels: the first is three words that make up a statement; the second is a statement about the statement. One cannot encompass this duality at the same time, as a time element is involved in which the reader has to move through a Gestalt transformation of perception. What is implicitly suggested here is that the higher level of abstraction, or class, does not share the nature of its parts.

6. This theory also concurs with a larger antipsychiatry intellectual movement of the 1960s that was carried out by writers such R. D. Laing (1965), Thomas S. Szasz (1961) and Michel Foucault (1965).

7. This view aligns nicely with the Cartesian separation between mind and body, which still dominates communication theory, and with the extension principle (*res extensa*) designated to ether in Cartesian cosmology (compare Chang 1996).

8. Carey goes to great lengths in order to distinguish his own conception from his predecessors as far as dichotomizing the transmission and the ritual views. However, it is doubtful that the two are mutually exclusive. One convincing example is Schramm's later work, in which he effectively incorporates the two views: communication is both the exchange of information and influence, and equally the participation in a "tribal ritual" (Schramm 1973, 2–3, 18–21). See also Cooley (1983) for yet another example.

9. It may therefore be said that whereas the transmission model corresponds with Cartesian principles, the ritual view seems to correspond with Hegelian ideals of dialectics. The connection is also evident by extension to Dewey, who regarded himself, at least initially, as neo-Hegelian. See Simonson (1996).

Notes to Chapter Two

1. Serres uses the word "parasite" to denote the term "noise," which commonly appears in French translations of Information Theory texts.

2. For more on the differences and similarities between Sartre and Levinas, see Howells (1988) and Vetlesen (1995).

3. The realization that concern for the Other is embedded in language as fundamentally dialogic was also shared by Mikhail Bakhtin (1986, 1996). Like Levinas, Bakhtin was also aware of Buber's dialogical philosophy. For discussion, see Ponzio (1987, 1993, esp. chap. 5).

4. Levinas directly engaged with Buber's philosophy in two essays, see *OS* (4–40) and *PN* (17–39). Levinas often distinguishes his conceptualization from Buber's, stressing particularly that, contrary to the I-Thou relation, ethical relation is not based on symmetry, equality and reciprocity. For comparison between the two, see Lawton (1976), Tallon (1978), Bernasconi (1988) and Lipari (2004).

5. Since the face is not reducible to a theme, it may be any manifestation by which one is questioned by the Other. Thus, the face is a concept (or more precisely, a nonconcept) that may include the Other's body, expressions, reactions, address, or the like. As Levinas expounds, "I analyze the inter-human relationship as if, in proximity with the Other—beyond the image I myself make of the other man—his face, the expressive in the Other (and the whole human body is in this sense more or less face), were what *ordains* me, to serve him" (*EI,* 97).

6. "Neighbor" is the translation of the French word *prochain,* signifying the Other in proximity.

7. For an analysis on the relation between Levinas's thought and psychoanalysis, see Critchley (1999).

8. A similar realization was shared by Buber: "The importance of the spoken word, I think, is grounded in the fact that it does not want to remain with the speaker. . . . Language never existed before address; it could become monologue only after dialogue broke off or broke down" (1965, 112, 114).

9. This aspect of language is described in pragmatism as taking the role of the other, and was widely explored by thinkers such as Charles Sanders Peirce, George Herbert Mead, and was recently revived by Jürgen Habermas. For the parallels among Levinas, pragmatism in general and Habermas in particular, see Trey (1992), Hendley (1996) and Gibbs (2000). Although some parallels exist, Levinas's ethical concern is much more radical than merely taking the role of the other. The substitution he advocates involves the proximity of one-for-the-Other that cannot find expression within language. For Levinas, substitution is more than a reflective exchange—it is an obsession: "Language, contact, is the obsession of an I 'beset' by others" (*LP,* 123).

10. Rupturing, erring and inflecting are perhaps the more compelling ways chosen by scholars to describe the involvement of the Saying in the Said. See Eaglestone (1997), Taylor (1987) and Ziarek (1994), respectively.

11. This question is one of Derrida's most significant critical points regarding Levinas's ethical speculations in *Totality and Infinity.* In "Violence and Metaphysics," one of the first major texts on Levinas's thought, Derrida expresses both his appreciation of Levinas's concerns and his criticism regarding the capability of a philosophical discourse to engage in such concerns. Derrida states that, "By making the origin of language, meaning, and difference the relation to the infinitely other, Levinas is resigned to betraying his own intentions in his philosophical discourse." Levinas's exploration has therefore only one fault: "the fault of presenting itself as a philosophy" (*VM,* 151). Several scholars attribute the shift in Levinas's conceptualization from *Totality and Infinity* to *Otherwise Than Being*—specifically the shift from "ontological language" to "ethical language" and the developing the notions of the Said and the Saying—to Derrida's critique of Levinas's earlier work. In his second major text on Levinas, "At this very moment in this work here I am" (1991a), Derrida explores the ways in which Levinas moves beyond essence to develop "ethical language" in *Otherwise Than Being.* See Bernasconi (1991), Critchley (1991), and Gibbs (2000).

12. For an elaborate analysis on vision as a mode of sensitivity in Levinas's thought, see Davies (1993).

Notes to Chapter Three

1. Zealous Esperantists would contest most of these definitions, especially those referring to it as artificial and constructed, because such definitions might suggest that Esperanto is not a real, living language of communication. The number of Esperanto speakers varies and is estimated between a low of 120,000 (the number of people enrolled worldwide in various Esperanto organizations) to a high of fifteen million actual speakers (Nuessel 1988, 373). At any rate, Esperanto is far from being an occult occupation: organizations and individuals worldwide speak and practice it either as a primary or secondary language, literature is being

translated and written in Esperanto, and some schools even use it as their language of instruction.

2. The Esperanto movement was growing steadily until World War II. But the formation of international solidarity and group identity exposed Esperantists to unprecedented dangers. Adolf Hitler criticized the internationalism of Esperanto as early as 1922 and condemned it directly in *Mein Kampf* as a Jewish ploy. Esperanto was made illegal in many countries under the rule of the Third Reich, and Esperanto movements were banished in Austria, Poland, Czechoslovakia, the Netherlands, Yugoslavia and Belgium. The arrest of the Zamenhof family was especially noted by the Nazi regime—Zamenhof was regarded not only as a Polish Jew but also as the inventor of a dangerous means for Jewish world domination. Zamenhof's son and two daughters perished in concentration camps; his son's wife and her son escaped from a train and survived (Forster 1982, 220–22). In the Soviet Union, officials had initially regarded Esperanto as a positive development because it represented a form of linguistic revolution that would follow the victory of world socialism. In 1930, the Congress of the Communist Party discussed the construction of an entirely new language arising from the merger of national languages. And yet, Esperanto was not supported wholeheartedly. By 1936, some official texts, including some by Stalin, still appeared in Esperanto; however, a year later, the movement was banned and speakers were designated as anti-Soviet elements. Esperantists were suspects because of their contacts abroad, which enabled critical viewpoints to enter the USSR (202–3). The restrictions imposed by Nazism on the one hand and Communism on the other practically ended what many Esperantists considered as the movement's heyday.

3. The Universal Esperanto Association even has a flag: a green star on a white background.

4. In a similar vein, Zamenhof referred to the propagation of Esperanto in terms of "positive propaganda"; see Privat (1963, 69–75).

5. Roosevelt's initial support was soon to be changed by skepticism. In a letter to Churchill dated June 5, 1944, he writes: "I wonder what the course of history would have been if in May 1940 you had been able to offer the British people only blood, work, eye-water, and face-water, which is, as I understand, the best Basic can do with the famous words." Ogden's enterprise eventually dissipated due to bureaucratic morass, wartime shortage and personal animosities (Gordon 1988, 339–40).

6. In the novel's appendix, "The Principles of Newspeak," Orwell writes: "The purpose of Newspeak was not only to provide a medium of expression for the world-view and mental habits proper to the devotees of Ingsoc [English Socialism], but to make all other modes of thought impossible. . . . Newspeak was designed not to extend but to *diminish* the range of thought, and this purpose was indirectly assisted by cutting the choice of words to a minimum" (1949, 303–4).

7. The introduction of the Internet has added an even greater relevance to that discussion. See, for example, Fettes (1997), Kramarae (1999) and Gunkel (1999).

8. Rabbi Aryeh Kaplan's translation (1981, 30). Other translations of the verse include: "And the whole earth was of one language and of one speech" (King James Bible); "Now the whole earth had one language and few words" (New Oxford Bible); "Once upon a time the world spoke a single language and used the same words" (New England Bible). Most translations transpose the word "language" for the Hebrew *safa,* which means both language (in the general sense) and a lip (hence, a metonymy to language). The New Catholic Version, from which the citations in this text are taken, prefers the word "tongue" (again a metonymy). However, in Hebrew, the equivalent to "tongue" is *lashon,* which is both literally a tongue and language in the structural, grammatical, sense.

9. Derrida further suggests:

someone who speaks the language of Genesis could be attentive to the effect of the proper name in effacing the conceptual equivalent . . . anyone whose so-called mother tongue was the tongue of Genesis could indeed understand Babel as "confusion"; that person then effects a *confused* translation of the proper name by its common equivalent without having need for another word. It is as if there were two words there, two homonyms one of which has the value of proper name and the other that of common noun: between the two, a translation which one can evaluate quite diversely. (*TB,* 251)

Having Hebrew as my mother tongue, I find this commentary especially intriguing. I tend to agree with Derrida on the diversity-convergence of Babel in Hebrew (pronounced "Bavel"). I would add, though, that the complexity of this effect became more evident to me once I had to translate it to another language. I have tried earlier to explicate this effect by showing the differences in the translations of the first verse "And the earth was of one tongue, and of the same speech." The various attempts to render the Hebrew meaning in another language made me realize the complexity of the original. It seems that through translation the original also changes, an insight I pursue in the next section.

10. Two years before the publication of his translation, Benjamin wrote to Gershom Scholem, "To my great joy and relief I was recently able to write the preface to the Baudelaire translation." Scholem later characterized this essay as a "high point" in Benjamin's writing. In 1922, upon completing a translation of two poems by Halevi, Rosenzweig wrote in a letter to Martin Buber, "there's no getting away from it: one's time is better spent in translating ten lines than writing the longest disquisition about" (Galli 2000, 28–29, 7–8). Rosenzweig and Buber cooperated in translating the bible into German. Imbued with conviction in the importance of a faithful translation, they worked together until Rosenzweig's death in 1929. Buber eventually completed the project by himself.

11. This hypothesis is explored at length in Benjamin, "On Language as Such and the Language of Man" (1978, 314–32). I shall not elaborate further on Benjamin's philosophy of language but shall note one allusion in this essay to the role of translation within the larger scope of language: "It is necessary to found the concept of translation at the deepest level of linguistic theory, for it is much too

far-reaching and powerful to be treated in any way as an afterthought, as has happened occasionally" (ibid., 325).

12. Rosenzweig was one of Levinas's great inspirations. See Levinas's note in *TI* (28), and Gibbs (1992).

Notes to Chapter Four

1. The most recent classification in the *DSM-IV* (1994), section 299.00, reads: Autistic Disorder: (1) qualitative impairment in social interaction, (2) qualitative impairments in communication, and (3) restricted, repetitive, and stereotyped patterns of behavior, interests, and activities.

2. For more on the status of autism with respect to the nature versus nurture debate, see Hacking (2001).

3. In his later years, Kanner became more convinced that autism was inborn. In his address at the National Autism Society Meeting 1969, he declared, "Herewith I especially acquit you people as parents. I have been misquoted many times. From the very first publication to the last, I spoke of this condition in no uncertain terms as innate" (Mesibov, Adams and Schopler 2000, 624).

4. A similar reasoning was presented in Bettelheim, "Individual and Mass Behavior in Extreme Situations" (1943), which presents a study of the techniques employed in concentration camps in order to dehumanize prisoners. For an intellectual profile of Bettelheim, see Fisher (1991). Noteworthy is Giorgio Agamben's (1999b) analysis of the *Muselmann* (literally a Muslim), a name designating prisoners in concentration camps suffering from acute malnutrition and fatigue who have lost contact with the surroundings. As Agamben observes, "the *Muselmann* became the paradigm through which he [Bettelheim] conceived his study of childhood schizophrenia. . . . There is not one character trait in Bettelheim's detailed phenomenology of childhood autism described in *Empty Fortress* that does not have its dark precursor and interpretative paradigm in behavior of the *Muselmann*" (ibid., 46).

5. As though this condemnation of parents were not enough, Bettelheim later adds that prisoners at the mercy of the SS were even better off than autistic children, because the prisoners had at least known a different way of life (Dolnick 1998, 183). Leading the prestigious Orthogenic School in Chicago and enjoying wide support of professionals and therapists, Bettelheim advocated for "parentectomy"—a complete and permanent removal of the child from the parents.

6. One contemporary illustration of the dreadful cleft between a child, his parents and society was *The Who's* 1969 rock opera, *Tommy*. Tommy becomes autistic-like after seeing his father (who was presumed to be missing in World War II) shot by his mother's lover. His mother's concern is expressed in the famous lyrics: "Tommy can you hear me? / Tommy can you hear me? . . . How can he be saved?/ From the eternal grave?" (The Who 1975).

7. It is instructive to note the parallels between Bettelheim's interpretation of autism and Bateson's description of schizophrenia (1972, 194–278). Like Bettleheim, Bateson argues that the mental condition of schizophrenia is not organic but an acquired disorder associated with communication failure. Schizophrenics, according to Bateson, are incapable of classifying the right context of a message and are consequently engulfed by double-bind paradoxes. This condition is the result of growing up in an environment imbued with conflicting messages. For both Bettelheim and Bateson, the origin of extreme mental disorder is one and the same: a disturbed, cold or unresponsive mother. Thus, the persistence of symptoms indicates not only a disorder but also a possible perpetrator. Moreover, both suggest that "external" communication failures might be internalized and registered in the child's psyche as traumatic and may give rise to an "internal" breakdown. Both, I must note, were eventually proven wrong. Their theories have since undergone serious criticism; see Dolnick (1998), esp. 117–23, 169–227.

8. For a detailed review of studies, see Mesibov, Adams and Schopler (2000).

9. It is important to note that autism is currently described as a spectrum syndrome, which means that the disorder can be manifested in a variety of combinations and levels of severity. Moreover, in the latest addition of the *DSM,* autism is grouped with similar disorders like Asperger's disorder and Rett's disorder, under the heading "Pervasive Developmental Disorders."

10. A short list of precedents includes Linden (1974) and Savage-Rumbaugh, Shanker and Taylor (1998) on primates, Sebeok on zoosemiotics (1990), and Bateson on otters, octopi and dolphins (1972).

11. An interesting parallel in that respect is John C. Lilly, a psychiatrist who investigated communication with dolphins. Through dolphins, he argues, "we will see ourselves as others see us. Through dolphin communication efforts we will help ourselves" (1967, 22). His theory, which is clearly based on Shannon and Weaver's Information Theory, promises to be "useful with interspecies communication with species other than dolphins, say with elephants or with large whales, or between man and woman!" (97). Communication with dolphins is a mere segue to wider agenda as the secret of human communication might be found in nonhuman or non-communicable entities (he even ventures to speculate on communication with extraterrestrials). This fascination with the incommunicable joins Baron-Cohen with figures like Lilly and Bateson whose works invoke what might be called the "alien connection"—an uncanny theoretical link between animals, machines and mental disorder—which is believed to provide insight into ordinary processes.

12. Haraway further proposes that in post-World War II popular and scientific discourse, communication constitutes a "luminous object of attention," correlating between science and complex social behavior. Communication was located where machine, animal and human boundaries broke down. As she further explicates, it is in contemporary cognitive sciences that "Linguistics, machine

communications sciences, social theory, neurobiology, and semiology all inter-digitate and sometimes conflate" (1989, 376).

13. Recent reports describe a dramatic increase in occurrence rates since the 1990s. According to the Autism Society of America, "Autism is the most common of the Pervasive Developmental Disorders, affecting an estimated 1 in 250 births (Centers for Disease Control and Prevention, 2003)." They also estimate that autism is the fastest-growing developmental disability in America with a 10–17 percent annual growth. For more statistics, see: www.autism-society.org. Some experts claim this remarkable rise could be connected to better diagnostic skills rather than to an increase in the disorder. Another explanation might be found in what recent studies have identified as "regressive autism," which, unlike infantile autism, seems to affect children between the ages of three and seven.

14. My speculations here reverberate with some aspects of Michel Foucault's *Madness and Civilization* (1965). Indeed, the case of autism might be viewed as a small-scale example for some of the discursive practices of power/knowledge at work in demarcating the line between normal and abnormal. Moreover, as the history of madness tells the untold story of the age of reason, perhaps the story of autism provides some insight into the consciousness of an age in which communication becomes a consideration of utmost importance. My argument, however, is much closer to Jacques Derrida's critique of Foucault, which deems madness not as external to reason but as a constitutive dissention *within* reason. See Derrida (1978, 31–63).

15. The accounts presented here seem to adhere to a certain formula, according to which the critical level of communication is always at least one above the one at hand. At each level of communication, the higher or broader level is the one by which the operation transpiring on the lower is evaluated (this might be illustrated as a function of $[n+1]$, the variable being the level concerned). While problems at each level might affect others, the more apt countermeasures are usually found on higher levels. Thus, for the mental it is the interpersonal (that is, psychotherapy, conversation), for the interpersonal the group (that is, active participation, sense of community), for the group the social, national, or international, (that is, changing hostile attitudes, modifying frame of reference, reducing distorted communication). On each level, communicators are compelled to aspire to a more elevated sphere of praxis, to the betterment of existing procedures, and thereby to yield to a challenge coming beyond the immediate.

16. Derrida argues that in order to ascertain the complacent logic of a logocentric arena (communal, discursive, political), "it is thus necessary to put the outside back in its place. To keep the outside out. This is the inaugural gesture of 'logic' itself, of good 'sense' insofar as it accords with the self-identity of *that which is:* being is what it is, the outside is outside and the inside inside" (1981b, 128). But insofar as the *pharmakon,* this move also involves the incorporation of the alien element in the "inside," as a sort of vaccine: "The purity of the inside can then only be restored if the *charges are brought home* against exteriority" (ibid.,

128). This "inaugural gesture" is achieved by means of sacrificial exclusion of the Other, which allows restoring the stable arrangement of the logocentric community: "The ceremony of the *pharmakos* is thus played out in the boundary line between inside and outside which it has as its function to ceaselessly trace and retrace" (133). Inhabiting the boundary between inside and outside, *pharmakos* is both beneficial and evil, alarming and calming, never completely excluded nor included, but rather kept in as a domesticated parasite that can be ceremonially sacrificed in order to restore order.

17. Austin's (1962) theory distinguishes between a constative and performative utterance: the first being an assertion that can be taken as true or false (describing, reporting, and the like), whereas the latter involves doing something by means of speech itself ("I bet," "I wed," and so on). His analysis of speech acts also introduces the notions of illocutionary and perlocutionary acts, designating the difference between doing something *in* an utterance (pronouncing, questioning, appealing) and doing something *by* an utterance (the effect on the hearer: persuading, convincing, alarming).

18. Derrida notes Austin's conceptualization of communicative sphere wherein interlocutors participate: "This conscious presence of the speakers or receivers who participate in the effecting of a performative, their conscious and intentional presence in the totality of the operation, implies teleologically that no *remainder* escapes the present totalization" (*SEC,* 322). That no remainder can escape the entire sphere of communication is indicative to the totalizing effect at the core of an operation, which precludes the possibility of encountering an element that would question the self-containment of that field.

Notes to Chapter Five

1. A similar reasoning guides Karl Popper's (1965) explication of scientific discoveries. Theories that withstand negative criticism (falsifiability hypothesis) are closer to truth than those that cannot be falsified.

2. This exemplifies the problem of distinguishing speech from action, for in some cases speech might have just as tangible consequences as action. Yet setting a clear distinction between the two is the condition under which any legal protection of free speech can actually operate. Thus, for instance, without speech/action distinction, the American First Amendment would read "Congress shall make no law abridging freedom of action," and that would be tantamount to saying that Congress should make no laws at all. It is clear that any liberal Magna Carta advocating unrestricted action would inevitably render itself meaningless. On the other hand, this entails, at the very least, deeming speech as not as consequential as action. See Fish (1994), Heldke (1994) and Butler (1997).

3. Noteworthy is the language Lippmann uses to describe forms of improper speech. Employing such radical predicates seems to reveal a fundamental mistrust

in human nature, deeming it a priori fickle and unreliable, thus introducing the motivation in instituting laws and regulation so as to tame its natural unruliness.

4. Being both a product of the individual and constitutive of individuality, speech and expression might take up here a rather expansive meaning: not only means for social participation but also immanent features in the evolution of the self. As such, perhaps a more apposite definition of the freedom expressed in this view is the freedom to communicate: the liberty to access and receive relevant information, the right to engage in discussion and exchange ideas, the freedom to explore one's own beliefs and conscience, amounting ultimately to the freedom to think. In classical liberal thought, these liberties are directly threatened by social institutions, most specifically by the government. Viewed in this light, freedom of expression exemplifies what Isaiah Berlin coined as "negative freedom": liberty *from* interference and coercion, the desire "not to be impinged upon, to be left to oneself" (1986, 95). According to Berlin, this doctrine of liberty dominates Western liberal thought almost from its inception.

5. This is not to say that individuality is perceived as static or that the individual is conceived as a stagnated being: as noted before, the rudimentary motivation of free speech is self-improvement, development and possibly personal transformation. Thus, each single individual may change his or her opinions and beliefs. Yet this potentiality is not in opposition to the basic liberal tenet of individuality but, in fact, reaffirms its centrality. The "essence" of individuality may indeed change, but this change will always culminate in reinstating the self. The end of the exploration is reification of the self.

6. For elaboration, see Pinchevski (2001).

7. On the various communicational, linguistic and philosophical aspects of silence, see Gurevitch (1989; 1990), Ponzio (1993), Corradi Fiumara (1990) and Agamben (1991).

8. In her critical evaluation of theories of recognition, Kelly Oliver (2000) offers the following helpful description: "In general, in work that relies on a notion of recognition there is the sense that individual identity is constituted intersubjectively, that we come to recognize ourselves as subjects or active agents through the recognition of others, that a positive sense of self is dependent upon positive recognition from others while a negative sense of self is the result of negative recognition or lack of recognition from others" (ibid., 32). Versions of the theory of recognition include, among others, Honneth (1995), Fraser (1997) and Butler (1997). The notion of recognition is indeed employed by these scholars in rather divergent ways to address issues such as social relation, politics of identity, gender and sexuality. However, a common thread in these accounts deems the original nature of relation between self and Other as antagonistic. As such, the issue of recognition is approached almost at the outset in terms of struggle. For an elaborate critique of these and others, see Oliver (2000), Curtis (2001) and Bauman (2001).

9. In other versions, such as Honneth's (1995), recognition is to be conferred as a mutual act, as an act of reciprocity.

10. According to Emerson (1966), this consideration applies not only to democracies because any kind of regime requires some kind of exchange and feedback between rulers and citizens in order to maintain itself.

11. According to Cornell, the aporia of justice is the condition of justice itself or, in other words, the condition of justice is the essential deconstructibility of every law or constitution. The definitive example is the American Constitution, where all the prescriptive amendments are subjected to the exception of the Ninth Amendment: "The enumeration in the Constitution, of certain rights, shall not be construed to deny or disparage others retained by the people." The Ninth Amendment, Cornell argues, "recognizes the limit of any *description* of the conditions of justice, including those embodied in the Bill of Rights" (1992, 165). This implies that even the best constitution can never specify all the conditions for justice at the time it is written. In order to be just, it must provide recourse to what is not specified in it, to the "not yet thought" (ibid., 165). This is not to deny the practical importance of rights and regulations but to emphasize that justice is always beyond prescribed laws. For a decision to be just and responsible, it must both conserve and destroy the law so as to approach each case in its singularity. It may be said, then, that the deconstructibility of laws is precisely what upholds the possibility of justice.

12. Precursors to Lyotard's speculations are found in the *Postmodern Condition* (1984) and especially in *Just Gaming* (1985).

13. For Lyotard, a phrase is not simply a grammatical or linguistic entity but a pragmatic one. It is defined by the constellation of its instances—addresser, addressee, referent, sense—and the relations between them. Phrases are linked by "phrase-regimens" (for example, prescription, question and answer, narrative, argument), which are the building block of genres of discourse. Genres constitute the sum of legitimate and illegitimate ways to combine phrase-regimens. In so doing, certain genres are excluded at the outset, thereby giving rise to the occurrence of *differends*. Finding new idiom to replace silence (which, according to Lyotard, is also a phrase) implies problematizing the ways by which phrases are linked and reorganizing the ways phrases are formulized (status of and relation between addressers, addressees, referent and senses) and linked. For a detailed discussion, see Ophir (1997).

14. It could be said, then, that what is at issue is the radicalization of what Lloyd F. Bitzer (1968) calls "the rhetorical situation," which comprises three constituents: exigence, audience and constraints. Indeed, the urgency to give expression to *differends* follows Bitzer description of "a defect, an obstacle, something waiting to be done, a thing which is other than it should be" (ibid., 6). However, the detection of such exigence by necessity exceeds rhetorical means, perhaps even calling for the redefinition of what falls within the realm of the "rhetorical." The question of audience also takes up additional complexity, as in traditional framework of rhetoric the audience is already in a position of the addressee, while the problem disclosed above is of reconfiguring discourse in a way that would set up the very conditions of being addressed. Finally, the constraints involved in

producing articulation also exceed that of the general "rhetorical situation," beyond the constraints made up by "beliefs, attitudes, documents, facts, traditions, images, interests, motives and the like" (ibid., 8). In addition to these, the task is finding ways to express the inexpressible. See Lyotard's notes on the matter in *The Inhuman* (1991) and *Political Writings* (1993).

15. A special challenge in this respect is the contradiction between the accessibility and ubiquity of information provided by the mass media and the relative passivity of viewers and readers. Unlike Lippmann, who proposes cooperative discussion (which entails copresence of participants) as a way to involve audiences in democracy, Lyotard's perspective sets the problem in terms of transforming viewers and readers from mere consumers of information to responsible addressees; see Smith (1997). Instituting new modes of expression would therefore imply the creation of new addresses destined for new addressees who see themselves as affected by the address. For a detailed discussion with a special emphasis on the role of communication media, see Luc Boltanski (1999).

Bibliography

Ackerman, Bruce A. 1980. *Social Justice in the Liberal state*. New Haven: Yale University Press.

Adams, Douglas. 1992. *Hitchhiker's Guide to the Galaxy*. New York: Ballantine Books.

Agamben, Giorgio. 1991. *Language and Death*. Trans. K. F. Pinkus and M. Hardt. Minneapolis: University of Minnesota Press.

———. 1993. *The Coming Community*. Trans. M. Hardt. Minneapolis: University of Minnesota Press.

———. 1999a. *Potentialities*. Trans. D. Heller-Roazen. Stanford: Stanford University Press.

———. 1999b. *Remnants of Auschwitz: The Witness and the Archive*. Trans. D. Heller-Roazen. New York: Zone Books.

American Psychiatric Association. 1994. *Diagnostic and Statistical Manual of Mental Disorders (DSM-IV) Sourcebook*. Washington, D.C.: American Psychiatric Association.

Ang, Ien. 1994. "In the Realm of Uncertainty: The Global Village and Capitalist Postmodernity." In *Communication Theory Today,* edited by D. Crowley and D. Mitchell, 193–213. Oxford: Polity Press.

Ardrey, Robert. 1974. "Non-Communication: A Natural History of Human Misunderstanding." *Communication* 1, no. 2: 153–68.

Arnett, Ronald. C. 2001. "Dialogic Civility as Pragmatic Ethical Praxis: An Interpersonal Metaphor for the Public Domain." *Communication Theory* 11, no. 3: 315–38.

———. 2003. "The Responsive 'I': Levinas's Derivative Argument." *Argumentation and Advocacy* 40, no. 1: 39–50.

Artaud, Antonin. 1976. *Selected Writings*. Trans. H. Weaver. New York: Farrar, Straus and Giroux.

Austin, John Langshaw. 1962. *How to Do Things with Words?* New York: Oxford University Press.

Bakhtin, Mikhail. 1986. *Speech Genres and Other Late Essays*. Trans. V. W. McGee. Austin: University of Texas Press.

———. 1990. *Art and Answerability: Early Philosophical Papers*. Trans. V. Liapunov, ed. M. Holquist and V. Liapunov. Austin: University of Texas Press.

———. 1996. *The Dialogic Imagination*. Trans. C. Emerson and M. Holquist. Austin: University of Texas Press.

Barendt, Eric. 1985. *Freedom of Speech*. Oxford: Clarendon Press.

Baron-Cohen, Simon. 1995. *Mindblindness: An Essay on Autism and Theory of Mind*. Cambridge Mass.: The MIT Press.

Bateson, Gregory. 1972. *Steps to an Ecology of Mind*. London: Jason Aronson.

———. 1979. *Mind and Nature—A Necessary Unity*. New York: Dutton.

———. 1982. "Difference, Double Description, and the Interactive Design of Self." In *Studies in Symbolism and Cultural Communication,* edited by F. A. Hanson, 3–8. Lawrence: University of Kansas Publication in Anthropology.

Baudelaire, Charles. 1997. *Complete Poems*. Trans. W. Martin. Manchester: Carcanet.

Bauman, Zygmunt. 1989. *Modernity and the Holocaust*. Ithaca: Cornell University Press.

———. 1990. "Effacing the Face: On the Social Management of Moral Proximity." *Theory, Culture & Society* 7: 5–38.

———. 1991. *Intimation of Postmodernity*. New York: Routledge.

———. 1993. *Postmodern Ethics*. Oxford: Blackwell.

———. 1995. *Life in Fragments*. Oxford: Blackwell.

———. 1998. *Globalization: The Human Consequences*. New York: Columbia University Press.

———. 1999. "The World Inhospitable to Levinas." *Philosophy Today* 43, no. 2: 151–68.

———. 2001. *Community: Seeking Safety in an Insecure World.* Cambridge: Polity.

Benjamin, Walter. 1969. *Illuminations*. Trans. H. Zohn. New York: Schocken Books.

———. 1978. *Reflections*. Trans. E. Jephcott. New York: Schocken Books.

Bennington, Geoffrey. 1994. *Legislations: The Politics of Deconstruction.* London: Verso.

———. 2001. "Ex-Communication." *Studies in Social and Political Thought* 5: 50–55. Online journal; available at http://www.sussex.ac.uk/Units/SPT/ journal/ past/ issue5.html.

Berger, Peter L., and Thomas Luckmann. 1967. *The Social Construction of Reality*. New York: Anchor Books.

Berlin, Isaiah. 1986. "Two Concepts of Liberty." In *Social and Political Philosophy,* edited by R. M. Stewart, 92–99. Oxford: Oxford University Press.

Bernasconi, Robert. 1988. "'Failure of Communication' as a Surplus: Dialogue and Lack of Dialogue between Buber and Levinas." In *The Provocation of Levinas,* edited by R. Bernasconi and D. Wood, 100–135. London: Routledge.

———. 1991. "Skepticism in the Face of Philosophy." In *Re-reading Levinas,* edited by. R. Bernasconi and S. Critchley, 150–61. Indianapolis: Indiana University Press.

Bernays, Edward. 1936. *Propaganda*. New York: Liveright Publishing Corporation.

Bettelheim, Bruno. 1943. "Individual and Mass Behavior in Extreme Situations." *Journal of Abnormal and Social Psychology* 3: 417–52.

———. 1967. *The Empty Fortress*. New York: The Free Press.

Bhabha, Homi K. 1994. *The Location of Culture*. London: Routledge.

Blanchot, Maurice. 1993. *The Infinite Conversation*. Trans. S. Hanson. Minneapolis: University of Minnesota Press.

———. 1995. *The Writing of the Disaster*. Trans. A. Smock. Lincoln: University of Nebraska Press.

Boltanski, Luc. 1999. *Distant Suffering: Morality, Media and Politics.* Trans. G. Burchell. Cambridge: Cambridge University Press.

Bolton, W. F. 1984. *The Language of 1984: Orwell's English and Ours.* Oxford: Basil Blackwell.

Borges, Jorge Luis. 1964. *Labyrinths: Selected Stories & Other Writings,* ed. D. A. Yates and J. E. Irby. New York: A New Directions Book.

Bruns, Gerald. L. 1996. "Blanchot/Levinas (On the Conflict of Alterities)." *Research in Phenomenology* 26: 132–54.

Buber, Martin. 1955. *Between Man and Man.* Trans. R. G. Smith. Boston: Beacon Press.

———. 1965. *The Knowledge of Man.* Trans. M. Friedman and R. G. Smith. London: George Allen & Unwin.

———. 1970. *I and Thou.* Trans. W. Kaufman. New York: Charles Scribner.

Butler, Judith. 1997. *Excitable Speech: A Politics of the Performative.* New York: Routledge.

Calvino, Italo. 1974. *Invisible Cities.* Trans. W. Weaver. New York: Harcourt, Brace, Jovanovich.

Camus, Albert. 1969. *Lyrical and Critical Essays.* Trans. E. C. Kennedy. New York: Alfred Knopf.

Carey, James W. 1975. "A Cultural Approach to Communication." *Communication* 2, no. 1: 1–22.

———. 1989. *Communication as Culture: Essays on Media and Society.* Boston: Unwin Hyman.

Celan. Paul. 1971. *Speech-Grille.* Trans. J. Neugroschel. New York: E. P. Dutton.

———. 1988. *Poems of Paul Celan.* Trans. M. Hamburger. London: Anvil Press Poetry.

Chang, Briankle G. 1996. *Deconstructing Communication: Representation, Subject, and Economies of Exchange.* Minneapolis: University of Minnesota Press.

Cherry, Colin. 1978. *On Human Communication.* Cambridge, Mass.: The MIT Press.

Cmiel, Kenneth. 1996. "On Cynicism, Evil, and the Discovery of Communication in the 1940s." *Journal of Communication* 46, no. 3: 88–107.

Cohen, Richard A. 1985. Translator's introduction to *Ethics and Infinity,* 1–15. Pittsburgh: Duquesne University Press.

Cooley, Charles H. 1967. *Human Nature and the Social Order.* New York: Shocken Books. First published 1902.

———. 1983. *Social Organization: A Study of the Larger Mind.* New Jersey: Transaction Press. First published 1909.

Cornell, Drucilla. 1992. *The Philosophy of the Limit.* New York: Routledge.

Corradi Fiumara, Gemma. 1990. *The Other Side of Language: A Philosophy of Listening.* Trans. C. Lambert. New York: Routledge.

Coupland, Nikolas, Howard Giles and John M. Wiemann, eds. 1991. *"Miscommunication" and Problematic Talk.* Newbury Park, Calif.: Sage.

Craig, Robert T. 1999. "Communication Theory as a Field." *Communication Theory* 9, no. 2: 119–61.

Critchley, Simon. 1991. "'Bois'—Derrida's Final Word on Levinas. " In *Re-Reading Levinas,* edited by R. Bernasconi and S. Critchley, 162–89. Indianapolis: Indiana University Press.

———. 1992. *The Ethics of Deconstruction: Derrida & Levinas.* Oxford: Blackwell.

———. 1999. "The Original Traumatism: Levinas and Psychoanalysis." In *Questioning Ethics: Contemporary Debates in Philosophy,* edited by R. Kearney and M. Dooley, 230–42. London: Routledge.

Curtis, Neal. 2001. *Against Autonomy: Lyotard, Judgment and Action.* Aldershot: Ashgate.

Davies, Paul. 1993. "The Face and the Caress: Levinas's Ethical Alternations of Sensibility." In *Modernity and the Hegemony of Vision,* edited by D. M. Levin, 252–72. Berkeley and Los Angeles: University of California Press.

Deleuze, Gilles. 1997. *Essays Critical and Clinical.* Trans. D. W. Smith and M. A. Grecon. Minneapolis: University of Minneapolis Press.

Derrida, Jacques. 1978. *Writing and Difference.* Trans. A. Bass. Chicago: University of Chicago Press.

————. 1981a. *Dissemination*. Trans. B. Johnson. Chicago: University of Chicago Press.

————. 1981b. *Positions*. Trans. A. Bass. Chicago: University of Chicago Press.

————. 1982. *Margins of Philosophy*. Trans. A. Bass. Chicago: University of Chicago Press.

————. 1991a. "At This Very Moment in This Work Here I Am," translated by R. Berezdivin. In *Re-Reading Levinas,* edited by R. Bernasconi and S. Critchley, 11–48. Indianapolis: Indiana University Press.

————. 1991b. "Des Tours de Babel." In *A Derrida Reader*, translated by J. F. Graham, edited by P. Kamuf, 244–53. New York: Columbia University Press.

————. 1995. "Deconstruction and the Other." In *States of Mind: Dialogues with Contemporary Thinkers,* edited by R. Kearney, 156–75. New York: New York University Press.

————. 1997. *Of Grammatology*. Trans. G. Chakravoty Spivak. Baltimore: The Johns Hopkins University Press.

————. 1998. *Resistance of Psychoanalysis*. Trans. P. A. Brault and M. B. Naas. Stanford: Stanford University Press.

————. 1999a. *Adieu to Emmanuel Levinas*. Trans. P. A. Brault and M. Naas. Stanford: Stanford University Press.

————. 1999b. "Hospitality, Justice and Responsibility." In *Questioning Ethics: Contemporary Debates in Philosophy,* edited by R. Kearney and M. Dooley, 65–83. London: Routledge.

————. 2001. "The Force of Law." In *Acts of Religion,* edited by G. Anidjar, 230–98. New York: Routledge.

Dewey, John. 1966. *Democracy and Education*. New York: The Free Press. First published 1916.

————. 1954. *The Public and Its Problems*. Ohio: Swallow Press. First published 1927.

Dolnick, Edward. 1998. *Madness on the Couch*. New York: Simon & Schuster.

Eaglestone, Robert. 1997. *Ethical Criticism: Reading after Levinas*. Edinburgh: Edinburgh University Press.

Eichholz, Rudiger, and Vilma Sindona Eichholz. 1982. *Esperanto in Modern World*. Bailieboro: Esperanto Press.

Ellul, Jacques. 1970. *The Meaning of the City*. Grand Rapids: William Eerdmans.

Emerson, Thomas I. 1966. *Toward a General Theory of the First Amendment*. New York: Vintage Books.

Fettes, Mark. 1991. Europe's Babylon: Towards a Single European Language? *History of European Ideas* 13, no. 3: 201–13.

———. 1997. Interlinguistics and the Internet. *Language Problems & Language Planning* 21, no. 2: 170–76.

Fink, Howard. 1971. "Newspeak: The Epitome of Parody Techniques in *Nineteen Eighty-Four*." *Critical Survey* 5, no. 2: 155–63.

Fiske, John. 1989. *Reading the Popular*. New York: Routledge.

Fish, Stanley. 1994. *There's No Such Thing as Free Speech, and It's a Good Thing, Too*. New York: Oxford University Press.

Fisher, David James. 1991. *Cultural Theory and Psychoanalytical Tradition*. New Brunswick: Transaction Publishers.

Forster, Peter G. 1982. *The Esperanto Movement*. The Hague: Mouton Publishers.

Foucault, Michel. 1965. *Madness and Civilization*. Trans. R. Howard. New York: Random House.

Fraser, Nancy. 1997. *Justice Interrupts*. New York: Routledge.

Galli, Barbara E. 1995. *Franz Rosenzweig and Jehuda Halevi: Translating, Translations, and Translators*. Montreal: McGill-Queens University Press.

———. 2000. "Introduction: Translating Is a Mode of Holiness." In *Cultural Writing of Franz Rosenzweig*, edited and translated by B. E. Galli, 3–57. Syracuse: Syracuse University Press.

Galtung, Johans. 1989. "The Cold War as an Experience in Autism: The U.S. Government, the Governments of Western Europe, and the People." *Alternatives* 14: 169–93.

Geiger, Kent, and Robert Sokol. 1959. "Social Norms in Television-Watching." *American Journal of Sociology* 65, no. 2: 174–81.

Gibbs, Robert. 1992. *Correlations between Rosenzweig and Levinas*. Princeton: Princeton University Press.

———. 2000. *Why Ethics?* Princeton: Princeton University Press.

Glastonbury, Marion. 1997. "The Cultural Presence of Autistic Lives." *Raritan* 17, no. 1: 24–44.

Glossop, Ronald J. 1988. "Language Policy and a Just World Order." *Alternatives* 13: 395–409.

Gordon, Terrence. 1988. "Undoing Babel: C. K. Ogden's Basic English. *Et cetera* 45: 337–40.

———. 1991. "From 'The Meaning of Meaning' to Basic English." *Et cetera* 48: 165–71.

Gunkel, David, J. 1999. "Lingua ex Machina: Computer-Mediated Communication and the Tower of Babel." *Configurations* 7, no. 1: 61–89.

Gurevitch, Z. D. 1989. "Distance and Conversation." *Symbolic Interaction* 12, no. 2: 251–63.

———. 1990. "Being Other: On Otherness in the Dialogue of the Self." *Studies in Symbolic Interaction* 11: 285–307.

Habermas, Jürgen. 1984. *The Theory of Communicative Action: Reason and the Rationalization of Society.* Trans. T. McCarthy. Boston: Beacon Press.

———. 1987. *The Theory of Communicative Action: Lifeworld and System: A Critique of Functionalist Reason.* Trans. T. McCarthy. Boston: Beacon Press.

———. 1991. *Moral Consciousness and Communicative Action.* Trans. C. Lenhardt and S. Weber Nicholson. Cambridge, Mass.: The MIT Press.

Hacking, Ian. 2001. *The Social Construction of What?* Cambridge, Mass.: Harvard University Press.

Hall, Stuart. 1980. "Encoding/Decoding." In *Culture, Media, Language: Working Papers in Cultural Studies 1972–79,* edited by S. Hall, D. Hobson, A. Lowe and P. Willis, 128–38. London: Hutchison in association with the Center for Contemporary Cultural Studies, University of Birmingham.

Haraway, Donna J. 1989. *Primate Visions.* New York: Routledge.

Harben, William. 1892. "In the Year Ten Thousand." *The Arena* 6, no. 36: 743–49.

Heims, Steve P. 1977. "Bateson and the Mathematicians." *Journal of History and Behavioral Sciences* 13: 141–59.

Heldke, Lisa, M. 1994. "Do You Mind If I Speak Freely? Reconceptualizing Freedom of Speech." In *The Ethics of Liberal Democracy,* ed. R. P. Churchill, 111–27. Oxford/Providence: Berg.

Hendley, Steven. 1996. "From Communicative Action to the Face of the Other: Habermas and Levinas on the Foundation of Moral Theory." *Philosophy Today* 40, no. 4: 504–30.

Honneth, Axel. 1995. *The Struggle for Recognition: The Moral Grammar of Social Conflicts.* Trans. J. Anderson. Cambridge: Polity Press.

Hovland, Carl I. 1948. "Social Communication." *Proceedings of the American Philosophical Society* 92, no. 5: 371–75.

Hovland, Carl I., Irving L. Janis and Harold H. Kelly. 1953. *Communication and Persuasion.* New Haven: Yale University Press.

Howells, Christina. 1988. "Sartre and Levinas." In *The Provocation of Levinas,* edited by R. Bernasconi and D. Wood, 91–99. London: Routledge.

Hyde, Michael J. 2001. *The Call of Conscience: Heidegger and Levinas, Rhetoric and the Euthanasia Debate.* Columbia, S.C.: University of South Carolina Press.

Innis, Harold A. 1973. *The Bias of Communication.* Toronto: University of Toronto Press.

Kafka, Franz. 1960. *Description of a Struggle and the Great Wall of China.* Trans. W. and E. Muir and T. and J. Stern. London: Secker & Warburg.

Kanner, Leo. 1973. *Childhood Psychosis.* Washington, D.C.: Winston & Sons. First published 1943.

Kaplan, Aryeh. 1981. *The Living Torah.* New York: Maznaim.

Katz, Elihu, and Paul F. Lazarsfeld. 1955. *Personal Influence.* New York: The Free Press.

Kim, Young S. 1999. "Constructing a Global Identity: The Role of Esperanto." In *Constructing World Culture: International Nongovernmental Organizations since 1875,* edited by J. Boli and G. M. Thomas, 127–65. Stanford: Stanford University Press.

Knowlson, James. 1975. *Universal Language Schemes in England and France 1600–1800.* Toronto: University of Toronto Press.

Kosinski, Jerzy. 1970. *Being There*. New York: Harcourt Brace Jovanovich.

Kramarae, Cheris. 1999. "The Language and Nature of the Internet: The Meaning of Global." *New Media & Society* 1, no. 1: 47–53.

Krippendorff, Klaus. 1989. "The Power of Communication and the Communication of Power: Toward an Emancipatory Theory of Communication." *Communication* 12: 175–96.

———. 1996. "A Second Order of Otherness." *Systems Research* 13, no. 3: 311–28.

Kuhn, Thomas S. 1970. *The Structure of Scientific Revolutions*. Chicago: Chicago University Press.

Laing, R. D. 1965. *The Divided Self*. Baltimore: Pelican Books.

Lasswell, Harold D. 1930. *Psychopathology and Politics*. New York: The Viking Press.

———. 1935. "Collective Autism as a Consequence of Culture Contact: Notes on Religious Training and the Peyote Cult at Taos." *Zeitschrift für Sozialforschung* 4: 232–47.

———. 1946. "Describing the Contents of Communication." In *Propaganda, Communication, and Public Opinion,* edited by B. L. Smith, H. D. Lasswell and R. D. Casey, 74–94. Princeton: Princeton University Press.

———. 1948. "The Structure and Function of Communication in Society." In *The Communication of Ideas,* edited by L. Bryson, 37–51. New York: Institute for Religious and Social Studies and Harper & Brothers.

Lawton, N. Philip. 1976. "Love and Justice: Levinas' Reading of Buber." *Philosophy Today* 20, no. 1: 77–83.

Leeds-Hurwitz, Wendy. 1993. *Semiotics and Communication: Signs, Codes, Cultures*. Hillsdale: Lawrence Erlbaum.

Levi, Primo. 1988. *The Drowned and the Saved*. Trans. R. Rosenthal. New York: Summit Books.

Levin, Charles. 1989. *An Essay on the Symbolic Process*. Ph.D. diss., Faculty of Arts and Sciences, Concordia University, Montreal.

Levinas, Emmanuel. 1968. *Quatre lectures talmudiques*. Paris: Minuit.

———. 1985. *Ethics and Infinity*. Trans. R. A. Cohen. Pittsburgh: Duquesne University Press.

———. 1986. "The Trace of the Other." In *Deconstruction in Context: Literature and Philosophy*, translated by A. Lingis, edited by M. C. Taylor, 345–69. Chicago: Chicago University Press.

———. 1987. *Collected Philosophical Papers*. Trans. A. Lingis. Pittsburgh: Duquesne University Press.

———. 1988. "The Paradox of Morality: An Interview with Emmanuel Levinas." In *The Provocation of Levinas,* edited by R. Bernasconi and D. Wood, 168–80. London: Routledge.

———. 1993. *Outside the Subject*. Trans. M. B. Smith. Stanford: Stanford University Press.

———. 1995. "Ethics of the Infinite." In *States of Mind: Dialogues with Contemporary Thinkers,* edited by R. Kearney, 177–99. New York: New York University Press.

———. 1996. *Proper Names*. Trans. M. B. Smith. Stanford: Stanford University Press.

———. 1969. *Totality and Infinity*. Trans. A. Lingis. Pittsburgh: Duquesne University Press. First published 1961.

———. 1998. *Otherwise Than Being, or Beyond Essence*. Trans. A. Lingis. Pittsburgh: Duquesne University Press. First published 1974.

———. 1999. *Alterity and Transcendence*. Trans. M. B. Smith. New York: Columbia University Press. First published 1995.

Lewis, D., and R. Smith. 1980. *American Sociology and Pragmatism*. Chicago: Chicago University Press.

Lilly, John C. 1967. *The Mind of the Dolphin*. New York: Avon Books.

Linden, Eugene. 1974. *Apes, Men, and Language*. New York: Penguin.

Lingis, Alphonso. 1994. *The Community of Those Who Have Nothing in Common*. Indianapolis: Indiana University Press.

Lipari, Lisabeth. 2004. "Listening for the Other: Ethical Implications of the Buber-Levinas Encounter." *Communication Theory* 14, no. 2: 122–41.

Lippmann, Walter. 1957. *Public Opinion*. New York: The Macmillan Company. First published 1922.

———. 1962. *The Public Philosophy*. New York: Mentor Books.

Lipset, David. 1980. *Gregory Bateson: The Legacy of a Scientist*. Englewood Cliffs, N.J.: Prentice-Hall.

Long, Bernard. 1913. *The Passing of Babel.* London: The British Esperanto Association.

Lyotard, Jean-Francois. 1984. *The Postmodern Condition.* Trans. G. Bennington and B. Massumi. Minneapolis: University of Minnesota Press.

———. 1985. *Just Gaming.* Trans. W. Godzich. Minneapolis: University of Minnesota Press.

———. 1988. *The Differend: Phrases in Dispute.* Trans. G. Van Den Abbeele. Minneapolis: University of Minnesota Press.

———. 1991. *The Inhuman.* Trans. G. Bennington and R. Bowlby. Stanford: Stanford University Press.

———. 1993. *Political Writings.* Trans. B. Readings and K. Paul. Minneapolis: University of Minnesota Press.

McKinlay, Patrick F. 1998. "Postmodernism and Democracy: Learning from Lyotard and Lefort." *The Journal of Politics* 60, no. 2: 481–502.

Marcuse, Herbert. 1969. *One-Dimensional Man.* Boston: Beacon Press.

Mattelart, Armand. 1996. *The Invention of Communication.* Trans. S. Emanuel. Minneapolis: University of Minnesota Press.

Mead, George H. 1967. *Mind Self and Society.* Chicago: Chicago University Press.

Melville, Herman. 1997. *Billy Bud, Sailor and Selected Tales.* Oxford: Oxford University Press.

Melucci, Alberto. 1996. *The Playing Self.* Cambridge: Cambridge University Press.

Mesibov, Gary B., Lynn W. Adams and Eric Schopler. 2000. "Autism: A Brief History." *Psychoanalytic Inquiry* 20, no. 5: 637–47.

Mill, John Stuart. 1991. *On Liberty and Other Essays.* Oxford: Oxford University Press. First published 1859.

Mills, C. Wright. 1956. *White Collar.* New York: Oxford University Press.

Milton, John. 1882. *Areopagitica.* Oxford: Oxford University Press and Clarendon Press.

Minsky, Marvin. 1986. *The Society of Mind.* New York: Simon & Schuster.

Mortensen, David C. 1997. *Miscommunication.* Thousand Oaks, Calif.: Sage Publications.

Murray, Jeffrey W. 2001. "The Paradox of Emmanuel Levinas: Knowledge of the Absolute Other." *Communication Quarterly* 49, no. 4: 39–46.

———. 2003a. *Face to Face in Dialogue: Emmanuel Levinas and (the) Communication (of) Ethics.* Lanham, Md.: University Press of America.

———. 2003b. "The Face in Dialogue: Emmanuel Levinas and Rhetorics of Disruption and Supplication." *Southern Communication Journal* 68, no. 3: 250–66.

Natali, Joao. 1986. "Communication: A Semiotic of Misunderstanding." *Journal of Communication Inquiry* 10, no. 3: 22–31.

Newcomb, Theodore M. 1947. "Autistic Hostility and Social Reality." *Human Relations* 1, no. 1: 69–86.

Norris, Stephen E. 1976. "Being Free to Speak and Speaking Freely." In *Social Ends and Political Means,* edited by T. Honderich, 13–28. London: Routledge and Kegan Paul.

Nuessel, Frank. 1996. "The Symbolic Nature of Esperanto." *Semiotica* 109, no. 3/4: 396–85.

Ogden, C. K. 1940. *Basic English.* London: Kegan Paul.

Ogden, C. K., and I. A. Richards. 1972. *The Meaning of Meaning.* London: Routledge. First published 1923.

Oliver, Kelly. 2000. "Beyond Recognition: Witnessing Ethics." *Philosophy Today* 44, no. 1: 31–43.

Ophir, Adi. 1997. "Shifting the Ground of the Moral Domain in Lyotard's *Le Différend.*" *Constellations* 4, no. 2: 189–204.

Orwell, George. 1949. *Nineteen Eighty-Four.* New York: Harcourt Brace.

Peters, John Durham. 1986. "Institutional Sources of Intellectual Poverty in Communication Research." *Communication Research* 13, no. 4: 527–59.

———. 1988. "Information: Notes Toward a Critical History." *Journal of Communication Inquiry* 12, no. 2: 9–23.

———. 1989a. "Democracy and American Mass Communication Theory: Dewey, Lippmann, Lazarsfeld." *Communication* 11: 199–220.

———. 1989b. "Satan and Savior: Mass Communication in Progressive Thought." *Critical Studies in Mass Communication* 6 (September): 247–63.

———. 1994. "The Gaps of Which Communication Is Made." *Critical Studies in Mass Communication* 11, no. 2: 117–40.

———. 1999. *Speaking into the Air: A History of the Idea of Communication*. Chicago: University of Chicago Press.

———. 2001. "Witnessing." *Media, Culture and Society* 23, no. 6: 707–23.

Pieris, Ralph. 1952. "Ideological Momentum and Social Equilibrium." *American Journal of Sociology* 57, no. 4: 339–46.

Pinchevski, Amit. 2001. "Freedom from Speech (or the Silent Demand)." *Diacritics* 31, no. 2: 70–84.

Plaut, Alfred. 1950. "Some Psychological Undercurrents of Scientific and Medical Writing." *Scientific Monthly* 71, no. 5: 294–97.

Ponzio, Augusto. 1987. "The Relation of Otherness in Bakhtin, Blanchot, Levinas." *Semiotic Inquiry* 7, no. 1: 1–17.

———. 1993. *Signs, Dialogue and Ideology*. Trans. S. Petrilli. Amsterdam: John Benjamins .

Popper, Karl R. 1965. *Conjunctures and Refutations: The Growth of Scientific Knowledge*. London: Routledge and Kegan Paul.

Privat, Edmond. 1963. *The Life of Zamenhof*. Oakville: Esperanto Press. First published 1920.

Ramsey, Eric Ramsey. 1998. *The Long Path to Nearness: A Contribution to a Corporeal Philosophy of Communication and the Groundwork for an Ethics of Relief*. Atlantic Highlands, N.J.: Humanities Press.

Ricoeur, Paul. 1991. *From Text to Action*. Trans. K. Blamey. Evanston, Ill.: Northwestern University Press.

Richards, Ivor A. 1943. *Basic English and Its Uses*. New York: Norton.

Riesman, David. 1961. *The Lonely Crowd*. New Haven: Yale University Press.

Ritchie, David. 1986. "Shannon and Weaver: Unraveling the Paradox of Information." *Communication Research* 13, no. 2: 278–98.

Rosenzweig, Franz. 1994. *Scripture and Translation*. Trans. L. Rosenwald and E. Fox. Bloomington: Indiana University Press. First published 1926.

———. 1995. "Afterword." In *Franz Rosenzweig and Jehuda Halevi: Translating, Translations, and Translators*, translated by B. E. Galli,

169–84. Montreal: McGill-Queens University Press. First published 1924.

Rothenbuhler, Eric W. 1998. *Ritual Communication: From Everyday Conversation to Mediated Ceremony.* Thousand Oaks, Calif.: Sage Publications.

Ruesch, Jurgen, and Gregory Bateson. 1951. *Communication: The Social Matrix of Psychiatry.* New York: Norton.

Sartre, Jean-Paul. 1969. *Being and Nothingness.* Trans. H. E. Barnes. New York: Washington Square Press.

Saussure, Ferdinand de. 1983. *Course in General Linguistic.* Trans. R. Harris. London: Duckworth.

Savage-Rumbaugh, Sue, Stuart G. Shanker and Talbot J. Taylor. 1998. *Apes, Language and the Human Mind.* Oxford: Oxford University Press.

Schramm, Wilbur. 1955. "Information Theory and Mass Communication." *Journalism Quarterly* 32, no. 2: 131–46.

———. 1963. "Communication Research in the United States." In *The Science of Human Communication,* edited by W. Schramm, 1–16. New York: Basic Books.

———. 1973. *Men Messages and Media.* New York: Harper & Row.

Schauer, Fredrick. 1982. *Free Speech: A Philosophical Enquiry.* Cambridge: Cambridge University Press.

Schiller, Dan. 1996. *Theorizing Communication.* New York: Oxford University Press.

Schwartz, Barry N. 1973. "Humanism and the New Media." In *Human Connection and the New Media,* edited by B. N. Schwartz, 1–9. Englewood Cliffs, N.J.: Prentice-Hall.

Sebeok, Thomas A. 1990. *Essays on Zoosemiotics.* Toronto: University of Toronto Press.

Serres, Michel. 1982. "Platonic Dialogue." In *Hermes: Literature, Science, Philosophy,* edited by J. V. Harari and D. F. Bell, 65–70. Baltimore: The Johns Hopkins University Press.

Shannon, Claude H., and Warren Weaver. 1964. *The Mathematical Theory of Communication.* Urbana: The University of Illinois Press.

Silverstone, Roger. 1999. *Why Study the Media?* London: Sage.

———. 2003. "Proper Distance: Towards an Ethics for Cyberspace." In *Digital Media Revisited,* edited by G. Liestol, A. Morrison and T. Rasmussen, 469–91. Cambridge, Mass.: The MIT Press.

Simonson, Peter. 1996. "Dreams of Democratic Togetherness: Communication Hope from Cooley to Katz." *Critical Studies in Mass Communication* 13 (December): 324–42.

Smith, Andrew R. 1997. "Lyotard and Levinas on Otherness." In *Transgressing Discourses: Communication and the Voice of Other,* edited by M. Huspek and G. P. Radford, 329–51. Albany: State University of New York Press.

Smock, Ann. 1999. "Tongue-Tied: Blanchot, Melville, Des Forets." *MLN* 114, no. 5: 1037–61.

Steiner, George. 1975. *After Babel: Aspects of Language and Translation.* New York: Oxford University Press.

Stewart, John. 1995. *Language as Articulate Contact: Toward a Post-Semiotic Philosophy of Communication.* Albany: State University of New York Press.

Sullivan, William P. 1976. "Bartleby and Infantile Autism: A Naturalistic Explanation." *The Bulletin of the West Virginia Association of College English Teachers* 3, no. 2: 43–60.

Szasz, Thomas Stephan. 1961. *The Myth of Mental Illness.* New York: Hoeber-Harper.

Tallon, Andrew. 1978. "Intentionality, Intersubjectivity, and the Between: Buber and Levinas on Affectivity and the Dialogical Principle." *Thought* 53, no. 210: 292–309.

Taylor, Charles. 1994. "The Politics of Recognition." In *Multiculturalism,* edited by A. Gutmann, 25–73. Princeton: Princeton University Press.

Taylor, Mark C. 1987. *Altarity.* Chicago: Chicago University Press.

Thayer, Lee. 1971. *Communication and Communication Systems.* Homewood: Richard D. Irwin.

Todorov, Tzvetan. 1984. *The Conquest of America: The Question of the Other.* Trans. R. Howard. New York: Harper Torchbooks.

Trey, George A. 1992. "Communicative Ethics in the Face of Alterity: Habermas, Levinas and the Problem of Post-Conventional Universalism." *Praxis International* 11, no. 4: 412–27.

Vetlesen, Johan Arne. 1995. "Relations with Others in Sartre and Levinas: Assessing Some Implications for an Ethics of Proximity." *Constellations* 1, no. 3: 358–82.

Vincent, Howard P., ed. 1966. *Melville Annual 1965 Symposium: "Bartleby the Scrivener."* Kent, Ohio: Kent State University Press.

West, W. J., ed. 1985. *Orwell: The War Broadcasts*. London: Duckworth/BBC.

Westley, Frances R. 1982. "Merger and Separation: Autistic Symbolism in New Religious Movements." *Journal of Psychoanalytic Anthropology* 5, no. 2: 137–54.

The Who. 1975. *Tommy: Original Soundtrack Recording*. Polydor CD 841 121–2.

Whyte, William H. 1957. *The Organization Man*. Garden City, N.J.: Doubleday Anchor Books.

Wiener, Norbert. 1954. *The Human Use of Human Beings*. New York: Doubleday Anchor Books.

Williams, Raymond. 1966. *Communications*. London: Chatto & Windus.

Wittgenstein, Ludwig. 1960. *Tratatus logico-philosophicus*. Frankfurt: Verlag.

Wright, Charles. 1959. *Mass Communication: A Sociological Perspective*. New York: Random House.

Zerubavel, Eviatar. 1991. *The Fine Line*. New York: The Free Press.

Ziarek, Ewa Plonowska. 1996. *The Rhetoric of Failure*. Albany: State University of New York Press.

Ziarek, Krzysztof. 1989. "Semantics of Proximity: Language and the Other in the Philosophy of Emmanuel Levinas." *Research in Phenomenology* 19: 213–47.

———. 1994. *Inflected Language*. Albany: State University of New York Press.

Index